Cross-linguistic Mediated Communication

Linguistic Insights

Studies in Language and Communication

Edited by Maurizio Gotti,
Emeritus Professor,
University of Bergamo (Italy).

Volume 316

Rosa Rabadán / Noelia Ramón (eds.)

Cross-linguistic Mediated Communication

Hybrid Text Production English-Spanish

PETER LANG

Lausanne · Berlin · Bruxelles · Chennai · New York · Oxford

Bibliographic information published by the Deutsche Nationalbibliothek
The Deutsche Nationalbibliothek lists this publication in the Deutsche Nationalbibliografie; detailed bibliographic data is available on the Internet at http://dnb.d-nb.de.

Library of Congress Cataloging-in-Publication
A record in the CIP catalog has been requested for this book of the Library of Congress.
Library of Congress Control Number: 2025004155

This publication has been funded by the Spanish Ministry for Science and Innovation (Grant PID2020-114064RB-I00 funded by Ministerio de Ciencia e Innovación-MCIN/AEI//10.13039/501100011033)

MINISTERIO
DE CIENCIA
E INNOVACIÓN

AGENCIA
ESTATAL DE
INVESTIGACIÓN

ISSN 1424-8689
ISBN 978-3-0343-5100-3 (Print)
E-ISBN 978-3-0343-5792-0 (E-PDF)
E-ISBN 978-3-0343-5793-7 (E-PUB)
DOI 10.3726/b22833

Published by Peter Lang Group AG, Lausanne, Switzerland

info@peterlang.com - www.peterlang.com

Table of Contents

List of Figures

List of Tables

Rosa Rabadán and Noelia Ramón

Introduction: Hybrid text production across languages in the era of generative AI

Human-machine collaboration in text production has become a staple of everyday communication. In professional contexts, writing remains a secondary activity, but in today's global market, successful writing is the core of effective communication. From direct writing of specific genres to the use of translation engines, spelling and grammar checkers, predictive writing and writing templates, technology assists humans in the production of specialised texts in all domains. The presence of technology in text production is pervasive nowadays at all levels. This pervasiveness does not mean that machines can take full responsibility for the writing process yet; rather, they complement human authorship (Kaufer & Ishizaki 2024). This mutual dependency is particularly evident in cross-linguistic communication, which uses English as a *lingua franca* in professional contexts. When addressing an international audience, professionals whose L1 is not English heavily rely on machine translation (MT) engines, unaware of the genre-related and linguistic limitations of this technology.

Often, actual writing consists of a mix of MT chunks that have not been post-edited, human-produced paragraphs following the conventions of the writer's L1, and additional contributions from generative AI models via prompting. This is the environment we understand as hybrid text production: any text generation process that requires some type of input on the part of the user and then employs technology, including AI-powered techniques, to produce idiomatic, contextualised texts in a particular language.

This book presents a comprehensive exploration of how corpus-based cross-linguistic studies can contribute to the building and optimising of applications for multilingual text production. The ACTRES research group has been carrying out corpus-based contrastive research in English and Spanish for over 20 years. Initially, general language corpora, both parallel and comparable, were the basis for extensive contrast between the two languages and also between original and translated language. Results from this line of research led to the construction of a translation quality assessment prototype (PETRA 1.0).

Later on, research focused on specialised communication. Domain-specific comparable corpora in English and Spanish were compiled and annotated to develop writing support tools in a number of professional environments, including finance, technology and online marketing. This experience was then applied to promotional texts in the food and drink industry. For this purpose, the CLANES (Controlled LANguage English-Spanish) corpus was compiled and annotated in multiple layers. The aim was to obtain empirically-based expert language data on which to build aids to assist Spanish writers in producing effective texts in charge of promoting food and drink products internationally.

The contributions in this volume take the reader on a journey from building and mining linguistic information from a multilayer comparable corpus (CLANES) to describing and implementing hybrid text production in cross-linguistic communication. The stopovers include practical approaches to multilayer annotation, AI-informed data augmentation, template enhancement, interference post-editing, and the use of restricted AI models to enhance text production. Our destination is to identify new paths to optimise natural language generation (NLG) tools for users.

The first paper (Sanjurjo-González) describes the design and construction process of the English-Spanish comparable corpus CLANES, a domain-specific corpus including promotional texts of the food and drink industry. The study presents the techniques applied and the steps followed in the multilayer annotation of this corpus at four different levels: PoS, semantic, pragmatic and rhetorical annotation. The following three papers in the volume present case studies in these annotation layers.

Moreno-Pérez and López-Arroyo explore multi-word expressions (MWEs) cross-linguistically, employing two annotation levels: PoS and semantic. The authors have identified similarities and differences in the use of MWEs in English and Spanish in the specific domain of food and drink. The results are rich linguistic data that can be used to tailor and leverage NLG tools when managing these expressions optimally, both in genre-restricted templates and in larger-scale large language models (LLMs).

The exploration of the pragmatic layer in CLANES is the focus of the paper by Pérez Blanco and Izquierdo. The authors investigate the cross-linguistic realisation of two related pragmatic functions, <RECOMMEND> and <SUGGEST>, which build the persuasiveness of the promotional and instructional texts in CLANES. They have identified the multilayer metapatterns (PoS and semantic) that encode these pragmatic functions in English and Spanish. The cross-linguistic results indicate that English presents an even distribution of both <RECOMMEND> and <SUGGEST>, whereas in Spanish, <SUGGEST> is more frequent.

The level of rhetorical annotation in CLANES is addressed in detail in the paper by Pizarro Sánchez and Ortego Antón. They identify a consistent framework of rhetorical moves across various food categories, highlighting variations in their frequency and prominence. The resulting rhetorical gold standard has been employed to normalise the annotation of food and drink product descriptions in CLANES. The authors have also identified cross-linguistic differences in the rhetorical makeup of this genre in English and Spanish.

Sanz-Valdivieso and López-Arroyo embark on testing ChatGPT's ability to automatically annotate wine-tasting notes rhetorically. The study compares ChatGPT and human manual annotation. The results show that the process of synthesising and augmenting adequate datasets cannot be automated just yet, as ChatGPT struggles to identify or accurately interpret textual cues. The authors conclude that human expertise is very likely irreplaceable by machines, but quantity-wise, computer performance is strategic in making annotation easier.

If the first five chapters in this volume are concerned with ways of building, annotating and exploring an English-Spanish multilayer corpus of specialised language, the following three chapters present hybrid text production environments built using expert corpus data. Labrador and Ramón describe how the ACTRES research team has adopted a symbolic approach to design writing aids based on specialised corpus data to meet the needs of Spanish speakers when writing professional texts in English. The text generators for the food and drink industry are template-based and rely on quantitative and qualitative datasets obtained from the multilayer corpus CLANES. These templates offer the rhetorical structure and the associated language strategies for each move and step and include a retrievable bilingual glossary to assist in the writing process. These writing aids illustrate how academic research can have an impact on society.

The post-editing of MT outputs is another hybrid text production environment that can benefit from expert corpus data. Rabadán, García-Gallego and Sanjurjo-González address the post-editing of grammatical interference in food and drink specialised texts. The expert data come from contrasting original and machine-translated Spanish texts. Using statistical techniques, the study identifies a series of interference nodes and provides the acceptability band and tolerance limits for each of them. These findings are fed to an add-on (PEINT) designed to assist in the post-editing of Spanish MT outputs.

The last paper in this volume presents a third hybrid text production environment addressing how to enhance template-based text generation by means of LLMs. Sanjurjo-González, Rabadán and Ramón take advantage of the expertise and know-how derived from previous corpus-based analyses and combine them with LLMs capabilities. The goal is to overcome the limitations of the template-based approaches using AI-enhanced functionalities to expand the datasets dynamically and include a prompting feature to query information pertinent to the specific textual genre. This improves the shortcomings of symbolic text generators in terms of efficiency, accuracy, and automation in hybrid text production.

The contributions in this volume describe how rich linguistic annotation of specialised texts provides valuable data to enhance and refine hybrid text production. They also address the new challenges and opportunities raised by recent developments in AI, including data augmentation, post-editing and AI-enhanced text generation. LLMs based on the Transformers architecture have outperformed previous symbolic, statistical and deep learning approaches to text generation in terms of performance and reduction of manual effort. However, tools that rely on classic approaches still offer more control over logic and meaning, leading to more linguistically acceptable texts, particularly in specialised domains. The corpus-based findings presented in this volume demonstrate the immense value of cross-linguistic analyses and their implications for leveraging LLMs for the automatic generation of domain-specific texts. This mixed approach is replicable for other genres, domains, language pairs and directionalities.

The studies in this volume also flag undesirable consequences: machine-produced texts are less sophisticated, varied and more normalised than human-produced texts. This limitation may make sense from the industry's point of view in terms of productivity and cost-effectiveness. However, from the linguistic point of view, massive machine production over time will certainly lead to higher degrees of cross-linguistic interference and convergence (Toral 2019). Natural languages boast a large number of resources to encode meanings, but machine-produced documents do not make full use of them. Consequently, languages are simplified and impoverished. Action should be taken to address this problem, and an obvious solution would be integrating fit-for-purpose data in LLMs and MT engines to reduce 'generatese' (Do Campo Bayón & Sánchez Gijón 2024).

In this accelerated and fast-changing technological scenario, cross-linguistic research should remain the baseline for providing natural, human-like linguistic usage to be fed to AI-powered applications. ACTRES research shows that linguistic expertise in specialised domains plays a fundamental role in human control over hybrid text generation and is crucial for cross-mediated communication.

Hugo Sanjurjo-González

CLANES: A multilayer English-Spanish comparable corpus

1. Introduction

CLANES (Controlled LANguage English-Spanish) is a comparable multilayer corpus comprising six subcorpora in the food and drink industry, totalling approximately two million words. Its most relevant feature is that it comprises four annotation layers: Part-of-Speech (PoS), semantic, pragmatic, and rhetorical. The CLANES corpus has been compiled to assist in creating a domain-specific CNL prototype that allows non-expert Spanish language end-users to write their texts in English (Kuhn 2014). This paper presents the technical and linguistic features of this corpus.

To obtain the linguistic data to build this drafter CNL, researchers need a tool to create customised corpora and aggregate annotation layers at different levels (word, sentence, paragraph). Additionally, the tool must enable researchers to execute sophisticated queries on the corpus.

In the framework of the ACTRES research group ecosystem (https://actres.unileon.es/), the ACTRES Corpus Manager (ACM) tool has been constructed (Sanjurjo-González 2017, 2018) to facilitate the analysis of multilingual parallel or comparable corpora with multiple linguistic annotations. Although one of the main goals of ACM is to simplify corpus building, the CLANES corpus has some peculiarities that have led to certain modifications to the tool's usual workflow.

This chapter presents the building process of the CLANES corpus from a technological perspective, paying particular attention to the multiple layers of linguistic annotations. It further discusses the main features of ACM, emphasising its suitability for conducting various linguistic analyses. We also offer screenshots showing the tool's functionality combined with the CLANES corpus.

The paper is organised as follows: Section 2 presents previous studies on comparable and multilayer corpora; in Section 3, a number of corpus analysis software are examined, and the appropriateness of ACM is discussed; Section 4 deals with the CLANES corpus building process, along with the necessary modifications for ACM compatibility; Section 5 demonstrates how ACM and CLANES function together, and Section 6 summarises the results and outlines future improvements.

2. Related work

2.1. Comparable corpora

Following McEnery and Hardie (2012: 19) and Sanjurjo-González (2017: 9), a comparable corpus has at least two varieties of the same language or comprises texts that fulfil the same communicative function in more than one language. Comparable corpora can be classified into two main categories: general and specialised language corpora. General language corpora are compiled for research purposes and aim to represent a wide range of language varieties. These corpora provide a broad overview of language use across different contexts and genres. On the other hand, specialised language corpora consist of texts that share, at least, a language domain and similar text type. These specialised corpora offer valuable opportunities for discourse analysis, pragmatics, genre analysis, and sociolinguistics in expert fields (Maia 2003).

There are many *ad hoc* comparable corpora, as they are relatively easy to compile from a technical point of view (Otero & López 2010), contrary to parallel corpora, which require aligning. Examples of English-Spanish comparable corpora compiled by the ACTRES research group are: C-GDPE (electronic products), C-GITEC (technical reports), C-GIT (appliance instruction manuals), C-GARE (meeting minutes), C-AuRs (audit reports), C-FMR (football match reports), C-OPRES (opinion articles), C-GAC (biomedical abstracts) and C-CT (clinical trials) (see https://actres.unileon.es/wp/comparable-corpora). More recently, the EuReCo comparable corpus (Kupietz et al. 2024) is an open long-term initiative that aims at providing and using virtual and dynamically definable comparable corpora based on existing national, reference, or other large corpora.

2.2. Multilayer annotated corpora

A multilayer corpus is a corpus with several different layers of linguistic annotation. Zeldes (2019: 7) defines multilayer corpora as "annotated digital collections of textual data [...] which are collected according to certain design principles [...] and are explicitly analysed using multiple, independent annotation schemes". An essential condition is that they should "contain mutually independent forms of information, which cannot be derived from one another reliably" (Zeldes 2019: 4). As a general rule, corpora containing only simple annotations that could derive from each other in some way, for instance, lemma and PoS (part-of-speech) tags, cannot be classified as multilayer corpora.

According to Zeldes (2017), software that allows for collaborative distributed annotation across space and time has made multilayer corpora grow progressively more complex and multifactorial, going beyond tagged or even syntactically annotated treebanks to encompass multiple, simultaneous levels of analysis. The appearance of powerful corpus analysis software allowing for custom annotation corpora based on CWB (Corpus Workbench) (Evert & Hardie 2011) or ANNIS3 (Krause & Zeldes 2016) has increased the importance of multilayer corpora even more.

From a technical point of view, there are several ways to include annotations in corpora. A basic approach is simply adding a prefix (or postfix) notation in the case of word-level annotation, whereas structural annotations involve including a header before the desired structure. Figure 1 shows examples of postfix and structural annotation.

However, these approaches have been proven insufficient for complex annotations with several layers and tags on the same textual part. From a historical perspective, XML (eXtensible Markup Language) is a common technological framework for encoding machine-readable texts, and TEI (Text Encoding Initiative, http://www.tei-c.org/P5) provides a specific set of encoding rules for texts in different contexts to make it easier for linguists and researchers to include and create reusable, replicable and understandable annotations.

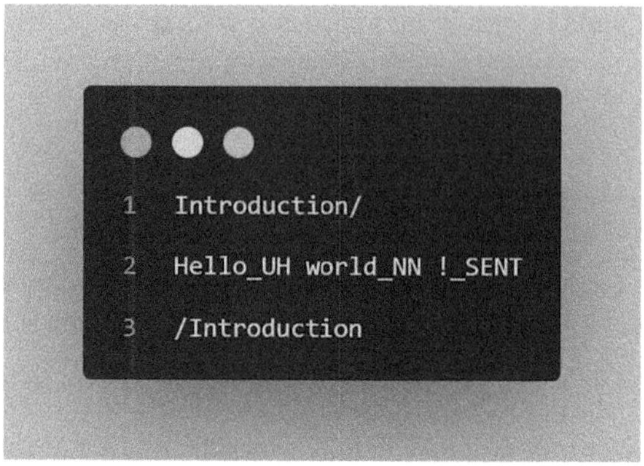

Figure 1: Example of simple postfix and structural annotation.

In addition, it should be mentioned that there is an absence of standard annotations. Even for consolidated linguistic annotations, such as grammatical tagging, this is a significant problem. Some projects have aimed at this goal, such as the Linguistic Data Consortium (University of Pennsylvania 2017), EAGLES (EAGLES 1996), and Petrov et al. (2011). The situation is even more complicated, as the same software for annotation can contain different schemes for each language. To address this issue, annotators should provide a detailed list of tags and guidelines to ensure the annotations' consistency, replicability, and clarity.

Many of the examples of multilayer corpora are related to treebank projects where the syntactic annotation is used together with other annotations such as semantics, coreference, discourse markers, and others, for instance, the Prague Dependency Treebank (Hajič et al. 2017) or the Salsa Corpus (Burchardt et al. 2006). The HCRC Map Task Corpus (Thompson et al. 1991), Switchboard Corpus (Godfrey et al. 1992), and NXT-format Switchboard Corpus (Calhoun et al. 2010) include several annotations related to spoken dialogue as well as prosodic features and discourse markers.

Other types of multilayer corpora are related to synchronic and diachronic variability of historical texts (Höder 2012) or learner corpora such as the Merlin corpus (Boyd et al. 2014) with linguistic and learning-related annotations. AnCora (Taulé et al. 2008) is a Catalan and Spanish multilayer corpus annotated with morphological, syntactic, and semantic information.

Particular attention should be given to the following multilayer corpora:

- Penn Treebank (Marcus et al. 1993) is one of the best-known multilayer corpora and includes morphosyntactic annotations, constituency structures, dependency relations, coreference annotations, semantic role labelling, discourse annotations, etc.
- Another extensively annotated corpus is the Manually Annotated Sub-corpus of the Open National Corpus (MASC) (Ide et al. 2010). It features PoS, lemmas, syntactic annotations, named entities, frame semantics, Penn Style Parsers and Head-drive Phrase Structure grammar (HPSG), discourse annotations, PropBank semantic annotation, timebanks temporal expression annotation, and coreference annotations, among others.
- The ACE 2004 Multilingual Training Corpus (Mitchell et al. 2005) is annotated for entity, coreference, relation mention, and time detection.
- The Potsdam Commentary Corpus 2.0 (Stede & Neuman 2014) is annotated with syntax trees and three layers of discourse-level information: nominal coreference, connectives and their arguments, and trees reflecting discourse structure according to Rhetorical Structure Theory.
- Finally, we can mention the GUM corpus (Zeldes 2017), one of the most widely used multilayer corpora in English, due to its data diversity and the high quality of its annotations. It includes multiple PoS tags, morphological features, morphological segmentation, lemmatisation, sentence segmentation and rough speech act annotation. Annotations also include normalised ISO date/time information, speaker and addressee details where applicable, as well as constituent and enhanced Universal Dependencies syntax. Grammatical constructions are analysed using Construction Grammar (CxG). Entity and coreference annotations, including anaphora, are present alongside entity linking. Discourse parses are captured through enhanced Rhetorical Structure Theory.

Some recent work on multilayer corpora includes AMALGUM (Gessler et al. 2020). This multilayer English web corpus includes dependency trees, non-named entity annotations, coreference resolution, and discourse trees in rhetorical structure theory. Noh et al. (2020) present a multilayer corpus featuring morphosyntactic, semantic, named entity, anaphora, coreference, and dependency parsing annotations.

The annotation levels for the CLANES corpus were determined by the final writing applications to be developed. These annotations encompass various linguistic levels, including PoS tagging and semantic labelling at the word level and pragmatic and rhetorical analysis at the structural level.

2.3. A brief survey of corpus analysis software

It should be clarified that this section focuses on programs that allow for the creation of concordances and provide a suitable set of functions for conducting corpus-based studies analysing language patterns and usage within a corpus. Annotation tools such as Brat (Stenetorp et al. 2012), EXMaRaLDA (Schmidt & Kai 2014), UAM Corpus Tool (O'Donnell 2008), and previous tools developed for ACTRES research, such as OpenTagger (Sanjurjo-González & Andaluz-Pinedo 2021) and ACTRES Move Tagger (https://actres.unileon.es/wp/rhetorical-move-tagger/) are excluded from this analysis, even though they have been undoubtedly vital for the creation of multilayer corpora in previous stages.

A corpus analysis software is any computer program that allows users to query an existing corpus and show the results, also known as concordances, on the screen. These tools usually include functionalities such as "KWIC concordancers, distribution plots, clusters and N-grams, collocates, word frequencies, and keywords" (Anthony 2013: 154).

According to McEnery and Hardie (2012), there are four generations of concordancers. The first generation consisted of simple concordancers operated on mainframes with problems of replicability as they were available only in the specific device where they were installed and showed an absence of specific functionalities related to corpus linguistics. One example of this generation is CLOC (Reed 1977).

The second generation emerged concurrently with the advent of personal computers, which improved the usability of the programs as they were no longer necessary for an expert to operate the mainframe. Hence, more independent statistical software was developed, and replicability became higher as personal computers were more widely available—for instance, MicroConcord (Scott & Johns 1993).

The third generation is characterised by incorporating proper frameworks for corpus analysis, featuring useful functionalities for linguists within the same software, primarily designed to run on personal computers. Examples of this generation include WordSmith Tools (Scott 1996) and AntConc (Anthony 2024). It is important to highlight that many of these programs continue to be updated and enhanced. They have limitations regarding the maximum size of the corpora supported as this depends on the personal computer's power and does not usually include built-in functionalities for annotation.

Concerning the fourth generation of concordancers, its main feature is the employment of the client-software architecture with a dual effect. On the one hand, it provides incredible processing power compared to personal computers and allows access to the corpus from any device with an internet connection. On the other hand, a technical specialist must install the software on a web server to be accessible to the users. They usually include built-in taggers such as multilingual PoS and incorporate more sophisticated functionalities such as parallel corpora support, one-click dictionary, etc. CQPWeb (Hardie 2012) and Sketch Engine (Kilgarriff et al. 2014) are outstanding examples of this category.

3. ACM as corpus analysis software

This section discusses the suitability of ACM as the selected corpus analysis software and compares its advantages and disadvantages to other available options.

One of the fundamental requirements of the CLANES corpus is the existence of software that facilitates its exploitation through suitable linguistic methods. As the selection of this software impacts the annotation activities and the formatting required for effectively utilising the corpus, it is essential to determine which software will be the target platform for employing the corpus.

In this instance, ACM (Sanjurjo-González 2017, 2018), a fourth-generation corpus analysis software, has been selected. The reasons for this decision can be summarised as follows: power, accessibility, comparable support features, and the possibility of incorporating an automated workflow. ACM tries to overcome technical barriers related to the corpus encoding and annotation process using a closed and unsupervised execution flow that spares the need for technical intervention. It is based on

CWB (Corpus Workbench) (Evert & Hardie 2011), a well-known toolkit for corpus processing focused on making it possible to query large text corpora (up to 2 billion words) with linguistic annotations efficiently. CWB has proven to be an excellent tool for handling large corpora with word and section annotations, as demonstrated by being the selected data model of other corpus analysis tools such as IntelliText (Wilson et al. 2010) CQPweb (Hardie 2012), as well as the backend of many websites, e.g., https://ordnet.dk/korpusdk/, https://spraakbanken.gu.se/parole/, https://corp.hum.sdu.dk/, among others. ACM also includes a user-friendly interface that allows complex queries to be made using CQP query language in the background. It also supports up to four comparable and parallel corpora incorporating an aligner. Last but not least, it includes KWIC concordances, N-grams, collocates, word frequencies, and keywords.

As an alternative, the use of ANNIS3 is considered. ANNIS3 (Krause & Zeldes 2016) is a popular web browser-based search and visualisation architecture for complex multilayer linguistic corpora with diverse types of annotation closely related to Hexatomic (Druskat et al. 2023), a cross-platform multilayer corpus annotation tool and extensible platform for the desktop. Therefore, ANNIS3 belongs to the fourth generation of corpus analysis software, although it also allows users to download and install the program locally. It provides access to a variety of corpora with multiple annotations and a user interface to make complex queries using ANNIS3 Query Language (AQL) by default. It also includes useful visualisations for annotations, such as syntax trees. Users can convert their corpora using the Pepper software, which allows for various input formats such as TreeTagger, generic XML, ConLL, etc. It provides extensive documentation; however, some technical knowledge may be required for configuring corpus and visualisations.

Although both are excellent options, the reasons for selecting ACM over ANNIS3 are the following: ACM is perhaps more linguistically oriented, offering functionalities such as keywords, collocations, and n-grams that ANNIS3 does not provide. Also, ACM has integrated the annotation tools into its workflow, so users do not need to worry about annotating the data using external tools or converting it into a format supported by other software, such as ANNIS3. A third reason is that ACM includes an interface to make comparable queries, i.e., simultaneous queries over two or more corpora, which may be helpful for some studies. Fourthly, since all the ACTRES corpora are hosted in ACM, it would need to be assessed whether their conversion to ANNIS3 is feasible without significant modifications. Finally, ACM is part of the research group's toolkit, and the potential corpus users are already familiar with its use.

4. The building of the CLANES corpus

This section comprehensively describes the CLANES corpus, including its composition and annotation layers. Detailed information regarding the computational procedures for tagging and integrating CLANES into ACM will also be presented.

4.1. Corpus description

CLANES is a Spanish-English multilayer comparable corpus. It comprises six sub-corpora containing original and prototypical texts in English and Spanish in food and drink. More concretely, it includes selected recipes, promotional texts, and technical data sheets for cheeses, wines, baked goods (biscuits, pastries, cakes, crackers, and bread), herbal teas and cured meats. Table 1 shows the composition of the corpus.

As previously mentioned, the primary objective of the CLANES corpus is to support the development of a prototype for a domain CNL processing system. This system will enable non-expert Spanish speakers to write specialised texts in English in the food and drink domain. Four annotation layers have been incorporated into the corpus - PoS, semantic, pragmatic and rhetorical - to enable linguistic data extraction from this particular text type and provide a solid knowledge base for developing the CNL drafter. These annotations allow extracting concordances to conduct linguistic analyses and support training in different experimental machine-learning models for natural language generation.

Table 1: Composition of the CLANES corpus.

Name	Number of words (English)	Number of words (Spanish)
BiTeX: Culinary recipes	307,161	275,115
C-FITECVI: Wine technical sheets and C- FIVI: Wine tasting notes	12,446	220,061
C-GDQ: Cheese descriptions	135,213	145,254
ACTEaS_Promo: Promotional texts for herbal teas	130,046	125,218
C-GEFEM: Sausages and cured meats	97,078	50,181
C-BakedGoods: Bakery and pastry descriptions	111,143	99,511
Total	905,087	915,340

4.2. Computational techniques employed in corpus building

Once the corpus has been compiled, that is, the documents for each subcorpus have been obtained following the representativeness criteria (Biber 1993), it is necessary to annotate the corpus and encode it into a compatible format. One of the advantages of ACM is that these processes are done mostly automatically without user intervention. Some minor changes had to be implemented manually to make the annotation work for the CLANES corpus.

4.2.1. Tokenisation and Part-of-Speech in CLANES

TreeTagger (Schmid 1995) is the selected system for PoS tagging because of its excellent results in English and Spanish. Other tools, such as SpaCy (Honnibal & Montani 2017), were also considered initially. However, according to the tests, TreeTagger scored better in some of the texts of the CLANES corpus. One of the consequences of using TreeTagger is that the tool uses the internal word tokenisation. TreeTagger offers a comprehensive 57-tag set for English and a 75-tag set for Spanish. A reduced version of these tagsets is used to simplify comparable queries (https://github.com/UCREL/Multilingual-USAS/blob/master/Spanish/spanish simplified-pos-tagset.txt). Moreover, this reduced version of the tagsets will also play a role in semantic annotation.

4.2.2. Semantic annotation in CLANES

The semantic annotation is based on USAS (Piao et al. 2015). This approach consists of a semantic role labelling process that searches for correspondences between lemmas and PoS tags in a semantic lexicon, returning the corresponding semantic tag. USAS is preferred over other systems, such as FrameNet or WordNet, due to its greater linguistic orientation based on the *Longman Lexicon of Contemporary English* (McArthur 1981). The USAS framework encompasses 21 discourse fields and 232 semantic categories.

The English semantic lexicon employed in CLANES has 47,607 words and has proven adequate in numerous instances, such as Potts and Baker (2012). The Spanish version has undergone numerous expansions from 5,000 original word length, such as the 1,000 most frequent words from the CORDE corpus and words related to the religious domain (Jiménez-Yáñez et al. 2018), finance domain words (Sanjurjo-González 2020) or words related to the food and drink domain (Sanjurjo-González 2021), among others, until reaching 12,541 words. As a means to overcome out-of-vocabulary issues, an NLP pipeline (Sanjurjo-González 2021) is employed to search the lexicon using different patterns based on NLP activities as well as similarity measures. Table 2 shows an example of a semantically labelled word using USAS, FrameNet, and WordNet approaches.

Table 2: Example of semantic annotation using USAS, WordNet, and FrameNet approaches.

Approach	Word	Semantic label
USAS	lemon	F1 L3 F2 O4.3 (Food; Plants; Drinks; Colour and Colour patterns)
WordNet	lemon	Yellow oval fruit with juicy acidic flesh. A strong yellow color. A small evergreen tree that originated in Asia but is widely cultivated for its fruit. A distinctive tart flavor characteristic of lemons.
FrameNet	Lemon	FOOD This frame contains words referring to items of food. Physical_object

4.2.3. Pragmatic annotation in CLANES

According to Archer et al. (2008), pragmatic annotation involves marking up corpora to highlight features such as speech acts, politeness strategies, discourse markers, and the contextual factors influencing meaning beyond the literal interpretation. The ACTRES research group identified six pragmatic labels in CLANES: State, Direct, Praise, Suggest, Recommend, and Evidence. The reasons for selecting these tags lie in their suitability and frequency of occurrence in the recipes, promotional texts and technical data sheets that compose CLANES. These tags are processed as structural annotations comprising one sentence each (Rabadán et al. 2021a).

From a technological standpoint, we initially developed several experimental pragmatic taggers using different Machine Learning and Deep Learning approaches. A dataset of 60 texts and 641 sentences was manually annotated for Spanish and another of 61 texts and 671 sentences for English. The NLTK sentence tokeniser was employed. The best performance was obtained by fine-tuning one Large Language Model (LLM) for the Spanish classification and another for the English classification. The results were promising using this strategy, with approximately 85% accuracy. The model's generalisation across languages, however, can still be improved.[1]

ACM did not include pragmatic annotation in its first stages, and this new pipeline needed integration. The query and user interfaces were modified accordingly, including new selectors for the pragmatic tags. The new ACM version updated new frequency lists, collocations features, and the results table.

The query processor Corpus WorkBench (CWB) internally handles structural annotations by marking each sentence's beginning and end with the respective tag. This feature allows searches within structural annotations, for example, all instances of the word *wine* under the <Suggest> pragmatic label. If the query does not include the pragmatic label itself, all the instances of *wine* will be displayed, including all the pragmatic contexts where it appears. Returning pragmatic annotation for individual

1 A comprehensive description of the model, along with advanced metrics for validating the results and assessing annotation agreement, will be presented in Sanjurjo-González (forthcoming a).

words was tricky as the pragmatic label was recognised only at the beginning and end of the sentence. A potential, though suboptimal, solution has been to embed the pragmatic tag within each word.

4.2.4. Rhetorical annotation in CLANES

The Rhetorical Structure Theory (RST) proposed by Mann and Thompson (1987) is a framework for analysing the organisation of texts by identifying the relationships between different parts of a discourse. RST states that texts comprise hierarchically organised units (called moves), each serving a particular communicative function within the text. Other approaches to genre studies and rhetorical structuring of specialised texts underlying the processing of the CLANES corpus are Bhatia (1993) and Swales (1990, 2004) (see Pizarro Sánchez and Ortego Antón, this volume). The ACTRES research group identified several rhetorical labels across the various subcorpora of the CLANES corpus. In the end, the following eight rhetorical tags were selected to generalise the same discourse moves across the recipes, promotional texts and technical sheets in CLANES:

- M1 ProdPres is a move that introduces a product, a cheese, a wine, a dish, etc.
- M2 ProdDescm is a section that describes the product promoted in the text.
- M3 BackInfo deals with information related to the origin and history of the product promoted.
- M4 TechInfo comprises the technical data sheets legally required for these texts.
- M5 Components lists the main ingredients of the product.
- M6 Procedure is a section that guides the reader through the elaboration and manufacturing of the product.
- M7 (Att)goal/ Result/ End-prod is a move that indicates the units, amount, weight or type of product presentation.
- M8 Product liability waiver/ disclaimer is a move that facilitates information to consumers for claiming a refund, writing a review or leaving comments about the product.

From a technological standpoint, these tags are typically processed as a structural annotation system comprising one paragraph each, a similar approach to the pragmatic layer described above. For the CLANES corpus, a sentence-based rhetorical tagger was developed instead to account for poor paragraph identification during corpus compilation. A dataset of 1,260 texts and 13,929 sentences was manually annotated for Spanish, and another composed of 1,015 texts and 13,546 sentences for English. Once more, the NLTK sentence tokeniser[2] was employed. The best result was obtained by fine-tuning an LLM for the Spanish classification and another for English, reaching approximately 90% accuracy. Applying the tagger to sentences rather than paragraphs significantly impacts the model's generalisation. However, as with the pragmatic layer, the model's generalisation can also be improved.[3] Given the importance of annotating rhetorical structure when considering sequential or contextual dependencies, a more in-depth study is required here. Algorithms such as Conditional Random Fields or Hidden Markov Models combined with LLMs could provide an effective solution.

Most of the infrastructure required to set up CLANES had initially been designed for Directors' Reports (Rabadán et al. 2021b) and was also used for similar developments in dramatic texts (Andaluz-Pinedo & Sanjurjo-González 2022) and for the corpus of Spanish translated from English (CETRI, Corpus de Español Traducido del Inglés).[4]

Finally, handling rhetorical searches with CWB was as challenging as in the pragmatic layer. The same solution, described in Section 4.2.3, was applied to return rhetorical queries.

4.2.5. The CLANES corpus data model

At the end of the annotation process, the corpus offered several structural and word-level annotations. Hardie states (2012: 389) that in CWB, "a corpus consists of a stream of tokens, where each token is assigned an integer number that represents its position in the corpus, starting at zero." Figure 2 shows an example of the internal data model of the CLANES corpus in ACM with all annotation layers.

---

2 https://www.nltk.org/api/nltk.tokenize.sent_tokenize.html

3 A comprehensive description of the model, along with advanced metrics for validating the results and assessing annotation agreement, will be presented in Sanjurjo-González (forthcoming b)

4 https://actres.unileon.es/wp/monolingual-corpora/

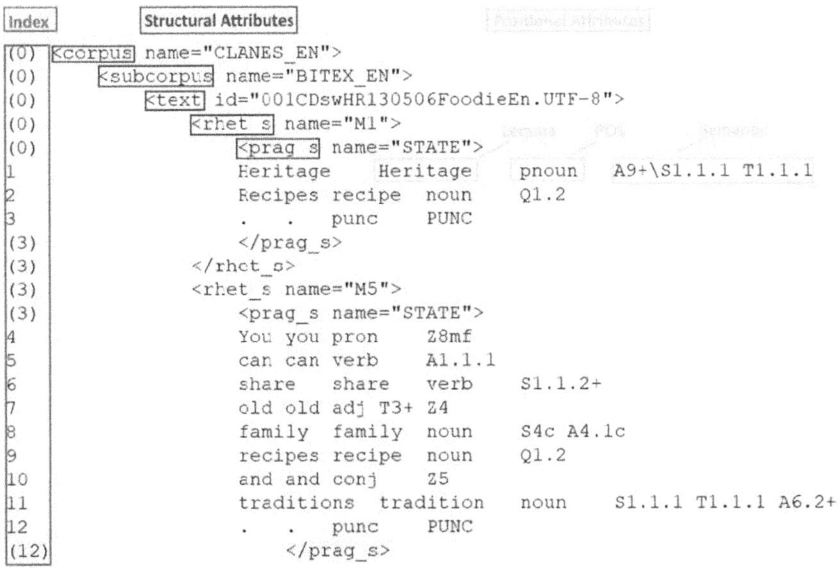

Figure 2: CLANES corpus data model in ACM.

5. Querying the CLANES corpus

This section presents several query samples in the CLANES corpus using ACM. The English CLANES subcorpus is used for the convenience of the readers. Figure 3 illustrates a simple query for the term *food*. Figure 4 shows the results of this query, highlighting the four annotation layers: the rhetorical and pragmatic layers appear in the left-hand side columns, the PoS tagging in blue, and the semantic tagging in green. Users have the option to turn these annotations on or off as needed.

Figure 5 shows a more complex query: words with the semantic tag of "General actions, making, etc." ending in -ing, appearing in the pragmatic tag "Direct" and belonging to the rhetorical move M2 ProdDescm.

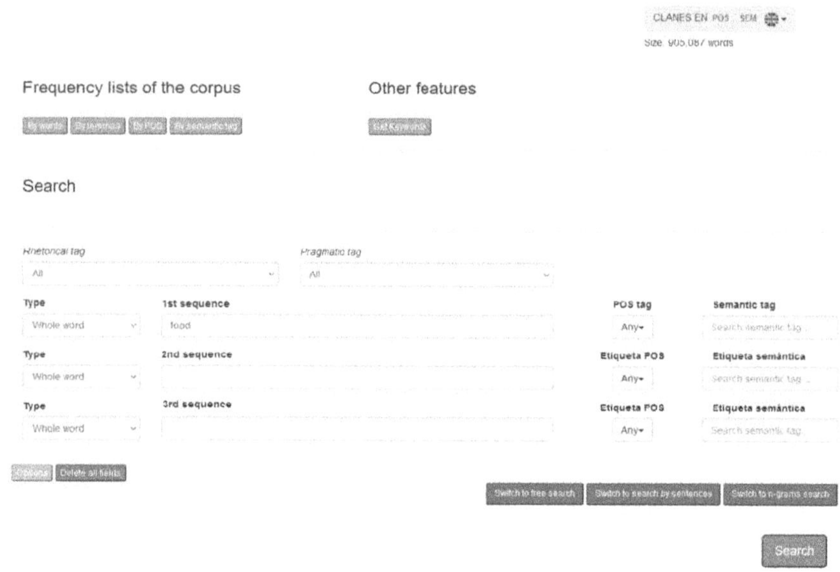

Figure 3: Example of query of CLANES corpus in ACM.

Figure 4: Results highlighting the different types of annotation.

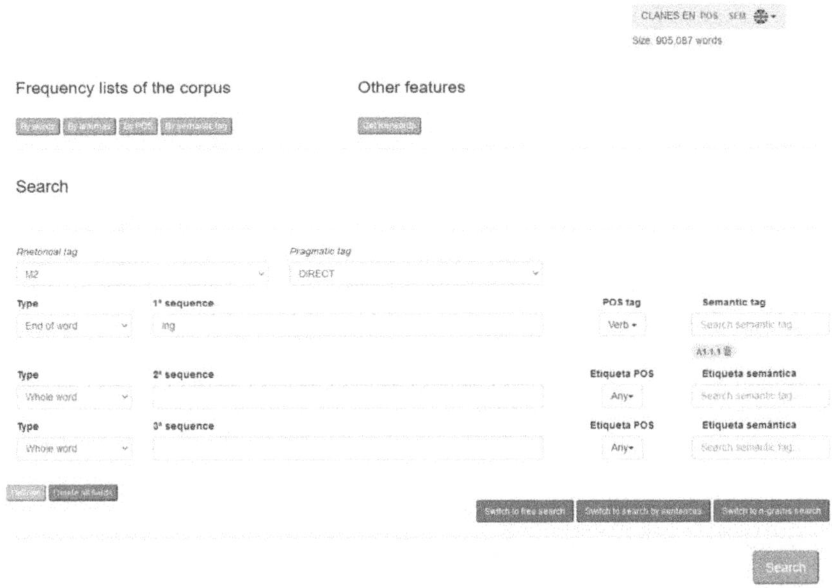

Figure 5: Example of a multilayer query of CLANES corpus in ACM.

Figure 6 shows the results of this complex query.

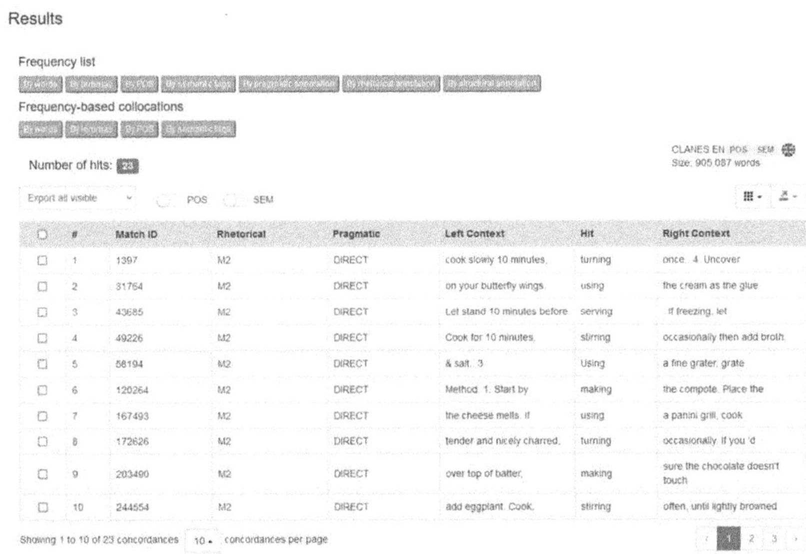

	#	Match ID	Rhetorical	Pragmatic	Left Context	Hit	Right Context
☐	1	1397	M2	DIRECT	cook slowly 10 minutes,	turning	once. 4. Uncover
☐	2	31764	M2	DIRECT	on your butterfly wings.	using	the cream as the glue
☐	3	43685	M2	DIRECT	Let stand 10 minutes before	serving	. If freezing, let
☐	4	49226	M2	DIRECT	Cook for 10 minutes,	stirring	occasionally then add broth
☐	5	58194	M2	DIRECT	& salt. 3	Using	a fine grater, grate
☐	6	120264	M2	DIRECT	Method. 1. Start by	making	the compote. Place the
☐	7	167493	M2	DIRECT	the cheese melts. If	using	a panini grill, cook
☐	8	172626	M2	DIRECT	tender and nicely charred,	turning	occasionally. If you 'd
☐	9	203490	M2	DIRECT	over top of batter,	making	sure the chocolate doesn't touch
☐	10	244554	M2	DIRECT	add eggplant. Cook,	stirring	often, until lightly browned

Showing 1 to 10 of 23 concordances 10 concordances per page

Figure 6: Results of the multilayer query.

Finally, Figure 7 offers a comparable query, i.e., two simultaneous queries in two subcorpora (herbal teas and wine), shown in a single screenshot. The KWIC for this query is the word *enhance*.

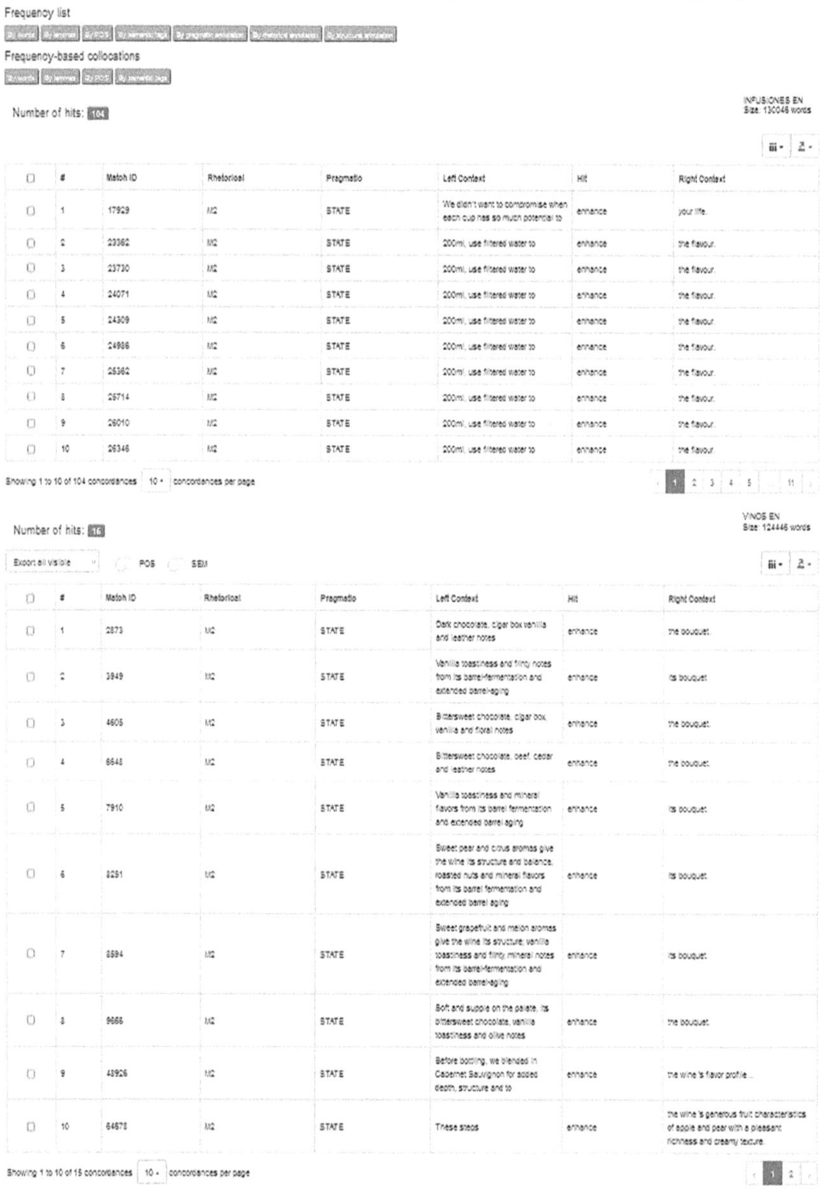

Figure 7: Example of comparable query of CLANES corpus in ACM.

6. Conclusions and further work

CLANES is an English-Spanish comparable multilayer corpus comprising around two million words across both languages. It contains four linguistic annotation layers: PoS, semantic, pragmatic, and rhetorical. This chapter has offered a comprehensive overview of the corpus construction from a technical perspective. It justifies the selection of each technological tool employed while also emphasising the innovative aspects of the corpus and the tools used in its development.

Concerning the tools for analysing comparable multilayer corpora from a linguistic perspective, ACM has been chosen due to its automation of annotations within its internal pipeline and stronger linguistic orientation. Two novel tools have been developed: two unsupervised rhetorical and pragmatic taggers, which, although experimental, provide a solid foundation for future studies. We have explained how to incorporate the CLANES corpus into ACM, focusing on the taggers used and the final data model. We have also outlined the various modifications and adjustments required for ACM software to process the corpus. Several illustrative cases have been presented, showing sample queries performed on the corpus using ACM.

Regarding ongoing and future work, improving the performance of the experimental pragmatic and rhetorical taggers is essential, as some generalisation issues remain. The complete pipeline is not entirely efficient yet, as it is slow if all the annotations are searched for simultaneously. Further work must focus on automatic paragraph detection and improving structural taggers by incorporating sequential and contextual dependency information.

Leticia Moreno-Pérez and Belén López-Arroyo

Semantic processing and description of multiword expressions in CLANES

1. Introduction

Multiword Expressions (MWEs), also known as phraseological units, are specific language constructs found within specialised domains that exhibit a certain degree of lexical fixation based on semantic relationships rather than syntax and are frequently used in texts within their respective domains (Becerro 2020). The study of MWEs has attracted much attention from researchers to date, mainly due to its importance in language use (Jackendoff 1997; Mel'cuk 1998; Sinclair 2000; Gray & Biber 2015, among others) and the difficulties it poses for linguists in terms of conceptualisation, classification, and scope (Granger & Paquot 2008; Gray & Biber 2015, among others). The evolution of linguistic research into technological fields, specifically in Natural Language Generation (NLG), has led to new challenges currently being addressed, along with others that will emerge as more sophisticated tools are developed.

This chapter describes the process followed by the ACTRES Research Group to handle MWEs and leverage NLG tools in the food and drink industry. This goal will be reached in different interwoven stages: we will explain the methods followed to extract, tag, and standardise the MWE-related data retrieved from the CLANES corpus, a multilayer English-Spanish comparable corpus of the food and drink domain with more than 1.8 million words (Sanjurjo-González, in this volume); the data obtained in this stage will allow us to provide a specific definition of what an MWE is in this restricted field; then, we will describe and classify the units in this domain according to their composition and semantics, focusing on recurring patterns between the different subgenres of the corpus (promotional texts for wine, cheese, tea, dried meats, biscuits, as well as recipes), and the differences between the two languages under study. Finally, we will reflect on how the data obtained through this methodology could help improve the performance of NLG tools, such as controlled natural languages (CNLs) and large language models (LLMs).

2. Approaches to the management of MWEs

The study of MWEs in language for specific purposes (LSP) goes beyond traditional linguistic analysis to consider the specific language needs and communication requirements of professionals in various disciplines. By focusing on word combinations, which cluster together in predictable ways (López-Arroyo & Moreno-Pérez 2019: 34), researchers in LSPs aim to facilitate effective communication, knowledge transfer, and language learning within specialised domains.

The exploration of MWEs extends to various disciplines, including lexicography, computer science, translation studies, and language learning. Scholars have delved into the equivalence of MWEs in different languages, their role in scientific texts, and their impact on foreign language learning and teaching (Nikolenko & Shapovalova 2021; Meunier & Granger 2009; Hassan & Menacere 2019). The study of phraseology has practical implications in translation, enhancing linguistic competence, and facilitating communication by ensuring accurate identification, interpretation and translation of MWEs (Azarova et al. 2020; Savelyeva et al. 2019).

MWEs encompass different highly heterogeneous units such as compounds, collocations, idiomatic expressions, and phrasal verbs. These constructions are frequent in LSP, and their study and classification have been the object of analysis from different approaches and perspectives. Different typologies for the study of MWEs have been developed depending on the approach, varying from lexicography to Natural Language Processing (NLP). Most of the categorisations give prominence to one or more of the following features: "internal structure, extent, degree of semantic (non) compositionality, degree of syntactic flexibility and collocability and discourse function" (Granger & Paquot 2008: 35).

In this sense, two primary categorisations can be distinguished: the conventional or linguistic approach and the frequency-based or statistical approach, each providing distinct methodologies and perspectives. The linguistic approach focuses on the structural and semantic analysis of Phraseological Units (PUs), providing insights into their significance and usage patterns in LSP (Cowie 1998; Glässer 1994, 1998; Roberts 1998, among others). This traditional method delves into the unique characteristics of MWEs, highlighting their role in professional communication and LSP use (Walker 2011). One of this approach's concerns is finding linguistic criteria capable of differentiating among various types of MWEs.

On the other hand, the statistical approach (Sinclair 1987; Nesselhauf 2004, among others) involves analysing the occurrence and distribution of MWEs in texts through quantitative methods. By utilising computational tools, such as collocation analysis, n-gram modelling, association measures, and statistical measures, the statistical approach offers a systematic way to explore the prevalence and significance of MWEs in specialised language contexts. The statistical approach does not aim to distinguish between different linguistic categories and subcategories of MWEs but to set clear boundaries for phraseological units.

Despite the apparent irreconcilability of both approaches, they can mutually benefit from each other, given the strengths inherent in the opposing paradigms. In this sense, linguistic approaches do not take full advantage of automated corpus-driven methodologies for extraction and analysis. Conversely, statistical approaches appear to underestimate the gain from fine-grained linguistic analyses inherent in the traditional approach (Granger & Paquot 2008: 41). Taking the previous argument into account, some scholars started claiming the development of functional approaches combining both as the most appropriate way to classify MWEs.

Based on function, two main typologies are worth mentioning: Biel's (2014) and Granger and Paquot's (2008). Biel (2014) suggested a typology tailored for legal contexts; Moreno-Pérez and López-Arroyo (2023) have shown its applicability in other specialised domains, such as food and drinks. Biel argues that phraseology is based on "fixed recurrent patterns at the textual, grammatical, and collocational level" (Biel 2014: 177) and makes a functional classification containing five different categories at the macrostructural and microstructural levels. Her classification of MWEs includes the following (Biel 2014: 178–181):

1. “text-organising patterns”, which are repetitive structures sometimes prescribed in drafting guidelines, such as *on the nose, on the palate,* or *ingredients*;
2. “grammatical patterns” or genre-specific recurrent grammatical structures, e.g. verbless sentences, i.e., *delicate aromas and flavours of butter and pure olive fruit* or the passive voice like *the entry is honeyed with*;
3. “term-forming patterns”, described as “collocates of a generic term” that add a higher degree of specificity like *zippy acidity* or *tertiary aromas*;
4. “term-embedding collocations”, which are verb-based structures that denote what one can typically do with (or to) the object denoted by the base noun like *aged in wood* and
5. “lexical collocations” or routine formulae, which are not constructed around terms and are identified through recurrence, for instance, *with hints of* or *in the aftertaste.*

On the other hand, Granger and Paquot (2008) integrate the linguistic and statistical approaches and propose the classification included in Figure 8.

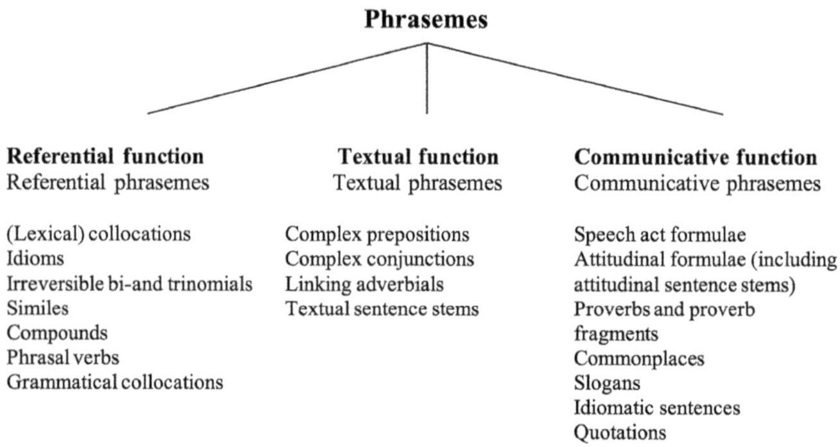

Figure 8: The phraseological spectrum (Granger & Paquot 2008: 42).

According to their classification, referential phrasemes convey a content message, referring to "objects, phenomena or real-life facts" (2008: 42); in this sense, examples in CLANES are *to linger on the finish* or *to coat the mouth*; textual phrasemes are used to structure and organise the content which is similar to "text-organising patterns" in Biel's classification, i.e., *on the nose* and communicative phrasemes express feelings or beliefs.

The next step Granger and Paquot develop is a definition of each of the MWEs included in their typology (2008: 43–44) and based on definitions provided previously by Cowie (1998), Benson et al. (1986) or Burger et al. (2007). In contrast to the traditional approach, this functional approach is more inductive, moving from the top-down method, which relies on linguistic criteria, into a bottom-up corpus-driven approach to identify lexical co-occurrences (Granger & Paquot 2008: 43–44). It considers units that had traditionally been excluded from phraseology, as it understands language as "essentially made up of strings of co-selected words that constitute single choices" (Granger & Paquot 2008: 29). As usual in the statistical approach, these authors consider all combinations instead of identifying MWEs through semantic criteria, they take into consideration all recurring or co-occurring strings containing two or more elements, they give prominence to the connection between lexis and grammar and emphasise stylistics and rhetoric (Granger & Paquot 2008).

Even though both functional classifications present some common grounds, Biel's typology does not have clear boundaries between the macro and microstructural levels, making her classification of the expressions fuzzy. In addition, Granger and Paquot focused on the linguistic analysis of MWEs and proposed a classification based on the types of units obtained depending on the extraction method used. In this categorisation, MWEs are understood as "recurrent continuous sequences of two or more words" (Granger & Paquot 2008: 38), and the MWEs resulting from this method of extraction are divided into the distributional categories shown in Figure 9:

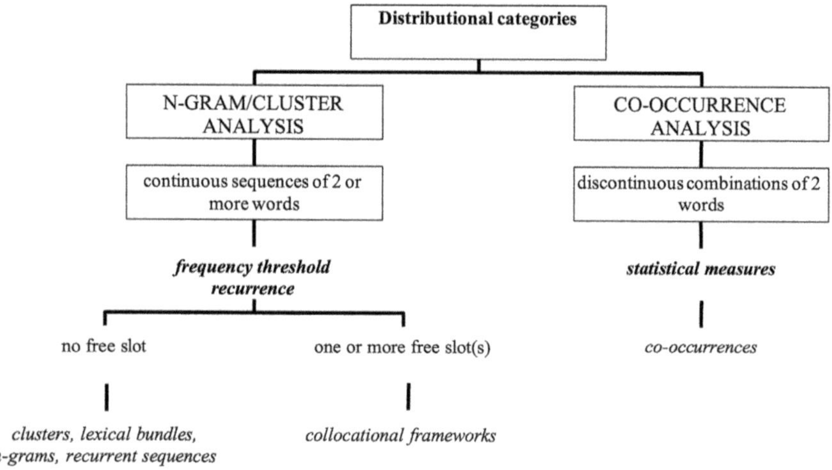

Figure 9: Distributional categories (Granger & Paquot 2008: 39).

This specific typology is especially important for our purposes since the statistical approach is the basis for analysis in the ACTRES research group. This study will follow Granger and Paquot (2008) for the analysis and definition of MWEs in the domain of food and drink (Section 3).

3. Method: processing MWEs in CLANES

The method described in this chapter results from the need to manage linguistic information at all levels - and more specifically, the MWEs - of the CLANES corpus. (For a detailed corpus description, see Sanjurjo-González, in this volume). This corpus aims to serve as the basis for fine-tuning a bilingual text production environment in the food and drink domain. This section will first describe the process followed for extracting the most common MWEs in the corpus and later describe the tagging process; this information will help us define MWEs in the domain of food and drink.

3.1. MWE Extraction

The most relevant MWEs in the particular field of food and drink promotional texts were extracted from the corpus using a tailor-made browser developed by the research group, the ACTRES Corpus Manager (ACM) (Sanjurjo-González 2017). This browser is a multi-purpose tool that allows for corpus search and comparison between two subcorpora by using keywords or by selecting the different moves, steps, or substeps in the rhetorical structure of the genre involved. Also, the tool can retrieve and export statistical data, such as frequency lists, word numbers, and the percentage of texts that contain the element being searched for.

The extraction of the prototypical MWEs from the CLANES corpus was carried out by obtaining common co-occurring patterns from the key terms in the genre, which had been retrieved through wordlists of the most frequent lexical items in the corpus. Keyword retrieval is based on the statistical measure chi-square test. Co-occurring pattern results are based on frequency, so an *ad hoc* screening had to be carried out: those expressions that were too broad or not specific to the food and drink domain were discarded manually. The frequency threshold used to find the MWEs in the corpus coincides with the one by Biber et al. (2007): 40 times per million words. As MWEs were extracted by subcorpus, the corresponding threshold for each was calculated; an average number of 5 occurrences was set for the six subcorpora. No word limit was set for the sequences, and, as the texts in the corpus are relatively short, most MWEs appear only once per text: this ensures that MWEs are representative and not used for individual stylistic reasons (e.g., the specific terminology of a winery).

The resulting list of representative MWEs allowed researchers to picture the usual patterns on each subcorpus to systematise them and train an algorithm for more accurate and extensive detection in the whole corpus or in future extended versions; this train-test split procedure is a common practice adopted in machine learning for algorithm performance validation (James et al. 2013). A detailed description of the MWEs obtained will be provided in Section 4 below.

3.2. MWE Tagging

MWEs from the CLANES corpus are tagged for Part-of-Speech (PoS) and semantic function, mirroring the process followed with simple terms in the corpus. PoS tagging was carried out using TreeTagger (Schmid 1995), while semantic tagging was based on USAS (UCREL Semantic Analysis System, Rayson et al. 2004[1]) developed at the University of Lancaster, which contains 21 major discourse fields and 232 labels. This tagging process was carried out manually, as USAS was developed for the general language and required some adjustments to be used in the food and drink domain.

The PoS tagging of MWEs was straightforward: each MWE contained the TreeTagger tags of each component, separated by a plus sign (+) for practical reasons, as shown in Table 3.

Table 3: Examples of MWE PoS tagging.

	MWE	**PoS TAGGING**
English	*sweet and savory*	JJ+CONJ+JJ
	Protected Designation of Origin	JJ+N+PREP+N
Spanish	*sugerencias de presentación* (serving suggestions)	N+PREP+N
	amarillo pajizo (straw yellow)	N+JJ

On the other hand, semantic tagging was far more complex and required the development of a specific method: it stemmed from the methodology used for simplex terms. It was refined to provide advanced NLP and AI-based systems with as much information as possible to make them more accurate and efficient in both automation and production processes. A double-layer tagging was carried out to reach this goal: MWEs were tagged as single units of meaning after individually tagging each component. The reason behind this decision was that to decode the semantic information assigned to each MWE, the individual tags for each component were required to complete the information contained in the unified tag.

Unified MWE tags follow the same pattern: after tagging each component of the MWE separately, each MWE as a unit is assigned the tag corresponding to food (F1) or drink (F2) – the two main categories in

1 The USAS semantic tagset can be found at: https://ucrel.lancs.ac.uk/usas/USASSemanticTagset.pdf

the domain – plus the tag corresponding to the headword of each MWE, to have a more specific description at first sight. Both are linked by an underscore, as shown in Table 4.

Table 4: Semantic tagging of the MWE 'pea fibre'.

pea fibre	**F1_O1**	**Food_ Substances and materials generally**
pea	F1_L3	Food_Plants
fibre	O1	Substances and materials generally

During this process, some decisions had to be made to ensure systematic tagging, especially in the case of the individual tags for each component, as the unified tag derives from them. The most relevant decisions concerned the standardisation of tags and consistency validation.

As for the standardisation of tags, tag similarity, low specificity and extrapolability were key issues. The USAS Semantic Tagset is very broad and was created for general language; therefore, some tags required a refinement of limits when applied to the lexicon of the food and drink domain in CLANES. It was necessary to set specific criteria for distinguishing the tags that could come into conflict and avoid meaning overlaps, defining the cases in which each tag should be used. For example, the tags 'Z2 - Geographical names' and 'M7 - Places', which might be considered as related, were defined in the USAS Semantic Tagset in a way that did not completely match the idiosyncrasy of the domain of the CLANES corpus: Z2 covers "nouns that distinguish/identify a specific place (e.g. the name of a road, a city, a country, a continent, etc.)" (Archer et al. 2002: 35), such as *Aberdeen, acropolis, castle* or *station*, while M7 is specific for "terms depicting geographical/conceptual spaces" (Archer et al. 2002: 18), such as *countries, district* or *kingdom*. To make the tags more accurate for the context, their limits were refined: a distinction was made between places with a proper name or derived from them, such as Worcestershire in *Worcestershire sauce* or *francesa* in '[food] *a la francesa*' (French-style [food]), which were assigned the tag Z2, versus places without a proper name, such as *cottage* in *cottage cheese*, which was assigned the tag M7.

Regarding low specificity, in the CLANES corpus, most elements correspond literally to the tag categories 'F1 – food' (*fruit, chicken, cheese*, etc.) or 'F2 – drink' (*milk, water, liquor*, etc.), no matter how different they are from each other. Specification was required in such cases, so more distinctive tags were added to those terms (e.g. *lemon* was tagged not only as 'F1' but as 'F1_L3 – Food_Plant' to make it more precise). Special attention was paid to terms which denominate a class or type of the headword, as in the case of *green tea*; as *green* is a class of the headword *tea*, distinctive from other types of the same drink, this component was specified by adding the tag 'A6.3 – Variety', so that in this case *green* is not only colour but also indicates variety (O4.3_A6.3 – Color_Variety)

As opposed to low specificity tags, other tags were highly specific, and generalisation helped facilitate the extrapolability of tags that apply to all the subcorpora in CLANES. Generalisation would help with algorithm training without any relevant loss of meaning. An example is the tag 'O1 - Substances and materials generally', which was finally used in all cases instead of using the specific subtags for solid (O1.1), liquid (O1.2), or gas (O1.3), as this information was found not to interfere with the distinction of, for example, *yeast* from *starch* in the context of CLANES. Since specificity was ensured by double tagging (unified MWE + individual components), this simplification was feasible and desirable in these instances.

Another set of decisions that had to be taken involved consistency validation: subdomain and language consistency. As the different subdomains are related, terms often appear in more than one subcorpus (e.g., *trace* as in *milk or egg traces* applies both to biscuits and cured meats). Since tagging was carried out manually, it was necessary to check that all the terms appearing more than once on the list of MWEs had been assigned the same tag (e.g., *traces* were consistently tagged as 'N5 – quantities'). It was also checked that equivalent components or MWEs were assigned the same tag in English and Spanish. For example, the equivalent of the term *oak* in the field of wine also appeared in the list of prototypical MWEs in Spanish (*roble*); it was checked that the tag assigned to each language was the same, in this case, 'L3_T3 – Plants_Time: Old, new and young; age', as it refers to the ageing of wine.

3.3. Definition of MWEs in the food and drink domain

The procedure followed to extract the MWEs in our corpus coincides with the n-gram/cluster analysis proposed by Granger and Paquot (2008), as mentioned in the previous section. The MWEs resulting from this method of extraction are divided into two categories: 1) continuous sequences called n-grams, such as *on the other hand*, and 2) continuous sequences which contain one or more free slots, called collocational frameworks, such as "a + ? + of". A list with examples of MWEs extracted from the CLANES corpus following this classification is offered in Table 5:

Table 5: Some MWEs from the corpus classified according to Granger and Paquot (2008).

	Multiword Expressions	
	English	**Spanish**
N-grams	*certification trademark* *sweet and savory* *witch hazel*	*sugerencia de presentación* (serving suggestions) *morro de cerdo* (pork's snout) *punto de nieve* (stiff peaks)
Collocational frameworks	*a __ (pinch/squeeze) of (flour/lime)* *___ (extra/medium) mature cheese* *partially hydrogenated ___ (vegetable/cottonseed) oil*	*___(entrada/ataque) en boca* (mouth attack) *con sabor a ___ (leche/miel)* (honey/milk flavoured) *extracto de ___ (pimentón/romero)* (paprika/rosemary extract)

According to the results obtained in the analysis of the CLANES corpus, MWEs in the genre of promotional texts for the food and drink industry could be defined as recurring strings of more than two continuous elements, whether these elements are stable or variable, which convey a specialised and specific description within the food and drink domain.

4. Results

The list of the most representative MWEs provided the usual patterns found in the CLANES corpus, which will be used in systematisation and algorithm training. Two elements will be analysed explicitly for this purpose: the composition of MWEs regarding PoS and the semantic components that characterise MWEs in the domain. Only the unified tag of the MWE will be analysed, as the tags of the individual components were used to create the unified tag accurately.

4.1. Length and PoS Structures of MWEs

This section will show the patterns found in the number of components that comprise the MWEs in CLANES (length) and the patterns in the grammatical elements forming the MWEs (PoS structures). Regarding length, we can observe in Table 6 that MWEs in Spanish range from two to six components, while in English, they range from two to five.

Table 6: Number of components.

Number of components		
	Spanish	**English**
2	27.2%	29.3%
3	38.3%	43.1%
4	22.2%	22.4%
5	11.1%	5.2%
6	1.2%	–

In both languages, the most common length for MWEs is three components, closely followed by two, then four, to finish with five and six. We can conclude that there is not much difference between the two languages in the corpus. However, Spanish tends to focus more on longer units, reflecting a common typological feature in this language.

Table 7: Prototypical PoS structures.

Spanish		**English**	
N+PREP+N	22.45%	ADJ+N	32.77%
N+ADJ	7.83%	N+N	30.92%
PREP+N	5.22%	ADJ+N+N	6.25%

Spanish		English	
N+PAST PART	3.92%	VB+N	4.61%
N+PREP+N+ADJ	3.66%	ADJ+ADJ+N	2.63%
PREP+N+ADJ	3.66%	N+PREP+N	2.30%
PREP+ART+N	3.13%	Other structures	20.52%
N+N	2.61%		
Other structures	47.52%		

Concerning PoS, Table 7 shows eight structures in Spanish and six structures in English that are statistically relevant in frequency. There is a significant difference between the popularity of the most usual structures and the rest: in Spanish, one structure stands out from the rest (N+PREP+N), while in English, we can find two (ADJ+N; N+N). Therefore, there seems to be a slight variation in grammatical categories when forming MWEs in both languages. The preferred structure in Spanish is the sixth most common in English, and even though some other structures are common to both languages, the frequency of use differs. In conclusion, there are typological differences in how MWEs are formed in the two languages, and the patterns found match the usual characteristics of specialised terminology in other fields.

In summary, according to CLANES corpus data, prototypical MWEs in food and drink promotional texts usually range from two to four elements and typically contain nouns, prepositions and adjectives.

4.2. Semantic units of MWEs

The individual tags for the components of MWEs will be briefly explained first, as they provide interesting data on the general semantics of the domain. A total of 123 semantic tags have been used in Spanish and 95 in English, which, in general terms, correspond to the following general categories in USAS (see Section 3.2), which are shared in both languages:

- A: general actions, change, classification, evaluation
- B: anatomy and health
- F: food, drinks
- I: business

- L: living creatures, plants
- M: movement, places
- N: quantities, measurement
- O: substances, objects, physical attributes (colour, shape, texture, temperature, etc.)
- T: time, age
- W: weather
- X: sensory (taste, smell, etc.)
- Z: names, grammatical words

It is worth mentioning that the relationship between language and food, known as *semiofoodscape* (Järlehed & Moriarty 2018), can be defined as the lens through which semiotic landscapes pertaining to food can be analysed. It comprises types of *foodstuffs* (like wine, cheese, coffee, beer, chocolate, dried meats and others), spaces (the places they are made, stored, sold, and consumed), actors (producers, regulators, distributors, marketers, connoisseurs, and consumers), practices (drinking, branding, differentiation, localisation, standardisation, regulation), norms (extrinsic, such as laws, and intrinsic, rules and expectations), inscriptional genres (product labels, tasting notes, expert reviews), and semiotic resources (names, linguistic code, script, orthography, typography, colour, material, images) (Järlehed & Moriarty 2018). Analysing the subfields in CLANES offers interdisciplinary insights that enrich our understanding of food studies, linguistics, cultural studies, and marketing. Each product offers unique semiotic elements, yet overarching patterns and themes emerge when viewed collectively. This holistic approach allows researchers to identify commonalities and differences, enhancing the depth and breadth of the analysis. It also enables the identification of broader trends and innovations in using semiotic resources across different food categories.

Semiofoodscapes "vary depending on the pragmatic components involved; according to the type of product, the actors and the inscriptional genres, they may share some language features, particularly their subjectivity in the description and evaluation (López-Arroyo & Sanz-Valdivieso 2024: 84). In this sense, at the semantic level, the CLANES analysed data show a variety of references which match the two main objectives of these genres: product description and product elaboration but also display some intra and interlinguistic differences, among the subfields to describe each particular product. Table 8 shows coincidences and differences in both languages.

Table 8: Unified tags per language.

Spanish & English	Spanish Only	English Only
F1 – food F1_A6.3 – food_variety F1_B1 – food_anatomy F1_I2 – food_business F1_L2 – food_ living cr. F1_L3 – food_plants F1_N5 – food_quantities F1_O1 – food_substances F1_O1.2 – food_liquid F1_O2 – food_objects F1_O4.3 – food_color F1_O4.4 – food_shape F1_Z6 – food_negative F2 – drinks F2_A6.3 – drinks_variety F2_L3 – drinks_plants F2_N5 – drinks_quantities F2_O1 – drinks_subst. F2_O4.3 – drinks_color	F1_A1.1.1 – food_action F1_A2.1 – food_modify F1_A5.1 – food_evaluation F1_B2 – food_health F1_I2.2 – food_selling F1_M2 – food_transport F1_M7 – food_places F1_O1.1 – food_solid F1_O4.1 – food_appear. F1_O4.5 – food_texture F1_O4.6 – food_temp. F1_Q2.2 – food_speech acts F1_S2 – food_people F1_T2 – food_begin/end F1_T3 – food_age F1_X3.1 – food_taste F2_O2 – drinks_objects F2_O4.5 – drinks_texture F2_X3.1 – drinks_taste F2_X3.5 – drinks_smell	F2_A2.1 – drinks_modify F2_B1 – drinks_anatomy F2_B2 – drinks_health F2_B3 – drinks_medicine F2_L2 – drinks_living cr. F2_T1 – drinks_time
TOTAL: 19	TOTAL: 20	TOTAL: 6

Regarding the unified tags of the MWEs, 39 different tags were assigned to the Spanish MWEs and 25 tags to the English MWEs. The semantics of MWEs is more varied in Spanish than in English. It seems that Spanish MWEs are used to describe a broader spectrum of characteristics. More specifically, MWEs in both languages describe food and drink varieties, ingredients and physical attributes. In general terms, the Spanish MWEs paint a more technically detailed and precise picture using more expert terminology. In contrast, English MWEs use more approachable language focused on the general reader's sensory experience and enjoyment. Both languages provide a vivid, positive impression designed to make the products appealing. Ishizaki and López-Arroyo (forthcoming) state that Spanish food description texts are written with an expert audience in mind, whereas North American texts seem to be written with the general public in mind, which is less interested in a detailed description of sensory properties and perhaps more interested in the credibility of the brand.

We will now present more detailed explanations of the similarities and differences between English and Spanish. Both use a lot of description, especially visual, smell and taste, to depict the products' colour and appearance and to convey their aromas and flavours to provide readers with a sensory impression, as in the following examples: *Our 2008 Zinfandel boats […] while displaying a delicate clear rim surrounding beautifully clear garnet color with a touch of blue; Suave de sabor y agradable al paladar, con un delicado aroma*, (Soft texture and pleasant on the palate, with a delicate aroma).

Both languages employ positive emotions, relations and values to convey an appealing impression; words like *elegant*, *delightful*, and *harmonious* in English and *sedoso* (silky) and *elegante* (elegant) are common in the MWEs analysed. English and Spanish often compare the product described to familiar flavours and provide specific details to help readers understand the products better, as shown in the following examples: *it has a sweetness like caramel candy* or *sabor dulce como la nata fresca* (sweet taste like fresh cream).

In both languages, we often find narrative elements telling a brief story of experiencing the product from appearance to aroma to mouthfeel and finish. This narrative takes the reader on a guided sensory journey, as in *The blue veins running through the white body immediately suggest intensity. As you bring it closer, the aroma is sharp, almost like the ocean air on a windy day*, or, in Spanish, *Al cortarlo, el cuchillo atraviesa su textura blanda y cremosa. En el primer bocado, el queso se derrite, liberando un sabor suave y dulce, como la leche recién ordeñada. El final es ligero, dejando una sensación aterciopelada en la boca, como un susurro de mantequilla.* (When cut, the knife cuts through its soft, creamy texture. In the first bite, the cheese melts, releasing a smooth, sweet flavour, like freshly milked milk. The finish is light, leaving a velvety sensation in the mouth, like a whisper of butter).

Among the main differences between English and Spanish in the semantics of the MWEs is the Spanish use of adjectives like *potente* (powerful), *intenso* (intense), and *profundo* (deep) to leave an impression of a product with compelling, impactful characteristics compared to the English descriptions. Also, the Spanish MWEs have more visual descriptors focused on tiny details like glycerin legs, reflections, crust colours, colour gradations, and others. These descriptors help to provide an extremely precise visual image compared to the more general visual strokes in the English MWEs.

The Spanish MWEs use more specialised terms related to product making, like *lías* (lees) in the wine industry. This signals a higher knowledge of the making process on the part of the readers, in contrast with the English MWEs, which seem to be aimed at a less knowledgeable audience. The English example *aged on its sediment* avoids the technical term *lees*. In contrast, the Spanish example assumes the reader's familiarity with this particular term: *removiendo las lías cada dos semanas para proporcionar al vino su textura cremosa* (stirring the lees every two weeks to give the wine its creamy texture).

The English MWEs present more evidence about the making process to draw conclusions about why the product has certain qualities. The Spanish MWEs focus more on just describing the result without explaining the reasoning, as can be observed in *aged in French oak barrels, this Chardonnay displays a buttery texture and notes of vanilla, which are a direct result of malolactic fermentation* and *Su cuerpo es robusto, con taninos suaves y bien integrados* (It is full-bodied, with soft, well-integrated tannins).

Another difference is that the English MWEs display more facilitating or encouraging language to make the products seem approachable and easy to enjoy. In contrast, the Spanish MWEs focus exclusively on describing the products without overtly encouraging the reader: *Crisp and zesty, this Sauvignon Blanc is a breeze to enjoy, perfect for a summer day or a casual get-together with friends* and *un vino fresco y cítrico, con una acidez viva y aromas a manzana verde* (A fresh, citrusy wine with lively acidity and green apple aromas).

Further research is necessary to verify the reasons behind these findings. Is English less thorough in describing food and Spanish in describing drinks because of genre expectations? Are these descriptions more often encoded using simplex terms instead of MWEs in both languages? Questions such as these cannot be answered at this stage.

Contrasting subcorpora in both languages, we can observe that the differences found in individual tags are translatable to unified tags. In Spanish, no unified tags appear in all the six subcorpora. Table 9 illustrates two tags that appear in five subcorpora: F1_A6.3 (food_variety) and F1_L3 (food_plants), and five tags in four subcorpora: F1_L2 (food_living creatures), F1_N5 (food_quantities), F1_O1 (food_substances), F1_O1.2 (food_liquid) and F2_A6.3 (drink_variety).

Table 9: Examples of repeated unified tags in Spanish.

Tag	**Example (Spanish)**
F1_A6.3	*azúcar moreno* (brown sugar)
F1_L3	*frutos silvestres* (berries)
F1_L2	*carne de cerdo* (pork meat)
F1_N5	*trazas de leche* (traces of milk)
F1_O1	*prensa quesera* (cheese press)
F1_O1.2	*aceite de oliva* (olive oil)
F2_A6.3	*vino tinto* (red wine)

We can observe in Table 9 that the most repeated tags correspond to the description of food, which coincides with the findings explained above. The remaining unified tags in Spanish, especially the numerous tags used to describe physical and sensorial attributes (e.g. *con sabor ahumado* (with a smokey flavour), vary depending on the subcorpora; as explained above, this is not unexpected, as the products being described in the different subcorpora are quite unalike.

The same results regarding MWE repetition in the six subcorpora were obtained in English. In general terms, repetition is lower since the most repeated unified tag is F2_A6.3 (drink_variety), which appears in only four subcorpora. The fact that this is the most repeated tag supports the previous finding that MWEs are more common in English when describing drinks. The other most repeated tags are present in only three subcorpora and match those more repeated in Spanish, as shown in Table 10: F1_A6.3 y F1_L3 and F1_O1.2.

Table 10: Examples of repeated unified tags in English.

Tag	**Example (English)**
F2_A6.3	*fortified wine*
F1_A6.3	*rice flour*
F1_L3	*bell pepper*
F1_O1.2	*soy bean oil*

As for the remaining tags, they also vary depending on the subcorpora, but it is noteworthy that there are significantly fewer MWEs in English for the description of physical and sensorial attributes, also in line with previous findings.

Considering all this, we have not found a prototypical semantic pattern in any of the two languages. What can be confirmed is that food and drink MWEs in both languages are mostly compositional, i.e., their global meaning comes from the sum of its individual parts, e.g. *cocoa butter, dried fruit*; a few exceptions were found in the corpus, e.g. *butcher's broom* (a type of herb used for infusions). Being compositional leads to literal interpretability and semantic transparency. The concrete and tangible nature of food and drinks maintains a direct link between the individual components and the overall meaning.

From this analysis, we can deduce that the nature of the content and the linguistic tendencies in each language influence the repetition and distribution of tags. The Spanish subcorpora emphasise food descriptions more, resulting in a more frequent use of specific MWEs. In contrast, the English subcorpora favour MWEs for describing drinks and show fewer tags referring to physical and sensorial attributes. These findings reflect how each language handles descriptions and categorisations in the analysed texts.

5. Data applications

One of the challenges emerging from the evolution of linguistic research into technological fields is the readjustment of MWE processing so that NLP and AI-based systems can manage these expressions optimally, both as input and output. Scholars in the computational linguistics field agree that the heterogeneous nature of MWEs entails highly relevant difficulties for "successful (computational) linguistic treatment" (Villavicencio et al. 2005: 2). According to Moreno-Pérez (forthcoming), some of the main obstacles posed by MWEs stem from the fact that they are "culturally and linguistically bound, present variation, are closely related to context and creativity, and that their limits are not canonically defined"; these characteristics make it difficult for language-processing systems to recognise and delimit MWEs, to correctly predict relationships with other elements in the sentence, solve ambiguity, and detect context, among other issues.

MWEs pose problems for algorithm training in NLP. The usual techniques for word representation, such as word embedding and tagging each word separately, involve a loss of meaning if the components of the MWE are not linked at some point in the process. This linking process doubles the work necessary for an accurate result to the point that the complex nature of these relationships has had experts trying to find an effective solution to this undeniable "pain in the neck" (Sag et al. 2002) for decades.

The methodology presented in this chapter for processing MWEs can help tailor and leverage NLG tools, whether they are more restricted (CNLs) or larger-scale neural language models (LLMs). The following sections analyse the data applications to the NLG tools mentioned above.

5.1. Data application in CNLs

"A controlled natural language is a constructed language that is based on a certain natural language, being more restrictive concerning lexicon, syntax, and/or semantics, while preserving most of its natural properties." (Kuhn 2014: 123). Controlled languages are the result of a process in which real language interactions are analysed in order to understand how the language works, followed by the implementation of some grammatical and lexical restrictions "in order to reduce both ambiguity and complexity of full natural languages" (Schwitter 2010: 1113); the final step is to reproduce this language through computer engineering.

Constructing a CNL is complex and has historically dealt with issues directly related to MWEs. One of the most relevant tasks, whose handling is essential for the success of a CNL, is entity recognition, "the task of determining individual occurrences of MWEs in running text" (Baldwin & Kim 2010: 280). Entity recognition "becomes a problem in cases where it is complicated to differentiate a MWE from the literal usage of a given word combination [...]; also, it can be complicated to set the boundaries of syntactically-flexible MWEs when written as discontinuous sequences" (Moreno-Pérez, forthcoming).

The extraction and tagging methodology proposed in section 4 can also be helpful for algorithm training in the entity recognition phase of the construction of a CNL. Research has suggested that a hybrid combination of statistical methods (based on lexical co-occurrence and frequency) and rule-based methods (based on representative PoS patterns) is the most effective solution to date (Moreno-Pérez, forthcoming). In CLANES, co-occurring patterns were extracted to establish the prototypical MWEs in the corpus. In addition, the resulting patterns were tagged, obtaining a list of the representative PoS patterns in the two languages under study. This information could serve to train the algorithm to recognise MWEs automatically.

5.2. Data application in LLMs

"A large language model is the language model with massive parameters that undergoes pretraining tasks (e.g., masked language modeling and autoregressive prediction) to understand and process human language, by modeling the contextualised text semantics and probabilities from large amounts of text data." (Yao et al. 2024: 1). LLMs have revolutionised the NLG scenario, consolidating as the most advanced tools that understand and generate human language. This revolution stems from the fact that they "they don't require any labeled data or pre-programmed rules; instead, they learn from patterns observed in existing text datasets [...] without requiring manual setup or programming" (Gokul 2023: 1).

LLMs are formed by different components, commonly an encoder to process input data, a decoder to generate language, attention mechanisms to provide context, a tokeniser that separates texts into manageable units, a text-to-speech module to make language sound more natural, and a dialogue manager that helps with the logical flow of the conversation (Gokul 2023). As LLMs evolve, developers have encountered different challenges related to the training and functioning of the model, some of which could be improved by a more refined management of MWEs. The findings presented in this chapter could help upgrade performance and data quality management in two specific situations, as illustrated in sections 5.2.1 and 5.2.2.

5.2.1. Pre-tokenization

The ongoing development in LLMs made models more complex; paradoxically, the need has arisen for solutions that make models more effective and simpler. Even though larger size entails greater precision of LLMs, it also involves higher production, maintenance, and fine-tuning costs (Gee et al. 2022). As a result, some of these models are economically unviable in real terms, so finding a way to make LLMs more efficient, smaller, cheaper and sustainable is necessary. Recently, the focus has been on finding a more effective tokenisation of texts, dividing the text into smaller segments that the model can comprehend and analyse successfully by reducing the size and the processing speed of LLMs without losing quality (Gee et al. 2022).

In this scenario, MWEs play a key role. In order to develop a more efficient architecture, some researchers consider MWEs as a way to "lighten" tokenisation by "representing frequent multiword expressions as single tokens [...] thus allowing for major speedups via early sequence truncation" (Gee et al. 2023: 612). The pre-tokenisation process of MWEs requires a previous compilation of the most common MWEs in the field, which has proven to increase efficiency (Otani et al. 2020; Gee et al. 2023). This customisation of tokens is particularly relevant in LLMs of specialised domains, which stem from general vocabulary but contain specific terminology to name the field's concepts. These terms are most commonly MWEs (Sag et al. 2002).

The methodology used by the ACTRES group is based on extracting the most representative MWEs in the field and assigning each MWE an individual tag as a single unit, turning them into single tokens. This methodology could also be replicated for other specialised domains.

5.2.2. Finetuning

"Fine-tuning involves adjusting the weights of an already existing pre-trained model to enhance its performance on specific types of problems" (Murtuza 2024: 2). Even though current LLMs can learn from unlabeled data, research has confirmed that it is very complicated to guarantee that the output obtained aligns with what is wanted from the model when using unannotated information (Zhang et al. 2023). In this context, fine-tuning is necessary to produce more precise results if labelled data is used, specifically in specialised domains (see Sanjurjo-González et al., this volume).

The resulting annotated dataset provides in-depth details on the extracted MWEs. These data could be used to improve the output of LLMs when generating texts for the food and drink domain. Ensuring the quality and relevance of the training data is crucial for model performance; the high-quality data obtained could contribute to avoiding inaccurate MWE generation.

6. Conclusions

This chapter addresses the necessity to make phraseology and computational linguistics meet in the specialised field of food and drinks promotional texts: the final objective was to obtain relevant data to improve the performance of NLG tools in this domain, which could be extrapolated to other fields.

We have provided context to help understand the characteristics of typical MWEs in the domain of food and drink. MWEs in CLANES tend to be strings of two to four continuous stable or variable elements that convey a specialised specific description in the food and drink domain. These MWEs usually contain nouns, prepositions, and/or adjectives that match the standard practice in other specialised domains. MWEs in food and drink texts aim at making the products appealing to readers: Spanish MWEs tend to be more detailed and precise, addressed to a more knowledgeable audience, whereas English MWEs try to make products more approachable to the general public. MWE prototypical patterns common to both languages were not found. As for meaning relations between the constituents of the MWEs, it was observed that MWEs are primarily transparent, as their meaning results from compositionality, i.e., the sum of the meanings of their constituents.

Annotating MWEs for PoS and semantics allowed researchers to extract the most relevant MWEs in the CLANES corpus. Considering the current issues in the development of NLG tools, the procedure followed in this chapter and the data obtained could be helpful for the leveraging process of both CNLs and LLMs. The information obtained could be used to train the algorithm in CNLs to recognise MWEs automatically. The resulting data constitute high-quality, relevant information that could also help with the pre-tokenisation process and the fine-tuning process of LLMs to enhance model performance.

Even though the discipline of NLG is evolving at a vertiginous pace and new problems will emerge, we consider that the methodology presented in this chapter is replicable in other domains and genres, as it can be adapted and expanded to meet future needs.

María Pérez Blanco and Marlén Izquierdo

Contrasting pragmatic functions in CLANES: <RECOMMEND> and <SUGGEST>

1. Introduction

Within the relatively new sub-field of corpus pragmatics, pragmatics and corpus linguistics are still trying to find the best way to benefit from each other. On the one hand, corpus linguistics has enabled a qualitative shift in pragmatics research, deviating from a long-lasting dominance of philosophical approaches to introducing an empirical methodology that accounts for real use of authentic language data in context (O'Keeffe et al. 2011). On the other hand, pragmatics would represent an upper layer of language description that is partly elusive to corpus description. While some endeavours have already been able to store, annotate, and browse pragmatic phenomena, these are rather limited in scope and also in replicability, especially when it comes to the automatic annotation of pragmatics. Early empirical approaches to pragmatics relied on elicited data that somehow recreated real contexts of interaction. This might explain that most corpus-based pragmatic research to date deals with spoken data (Deutschmann 2003; Kohnen 2008; Milà-Garcia 2018; Weisser 2018, 2020), where textual evidence is enriched with metadata that accounts for extralinguistic information. Little, however, has been done on pragmatic interpretation of written corpus data (see Section 3), as is our intention in this case study.

Among the pragmatic phenomena widely analysed from a corpus approach are discourse markers (Aijmer & Simon-Vanderbergen 2006; Stenström 2006, Downing 2006, to name a few) and speech acts (Deutschmann 2003; Kohnen 2008; Milà-Garcia 2018; Weisser 2018,

2020). This case study adds to existing research on the latter aspect, as we are intent on characterising the discourse of the food-and-drink specific domain by identifying the illocutionary acts that the writer invokes to achieve persuasion. "A weakness associated with using corpora for speech act research lies in the difficulties in automatically retrieving all the linguistic manifestations of a particular speech act, or identifying an appropriate 'lexical hook' (…) for extracting quantitative manifestation" (Vaughan & Clancy 2013: 21). A way of mitigating this limitation is by using a domain-specific corpus like CLANES, as "specific domains of discourse involve the use of language in pragmatically-specialised ways" (O'Keeffe et al. 2011: 115). Moreover, CLANES is annotated for part-of-speech, semantics, and rhetoric information. As a tool, thus, CLANES provides the researcher with metalinguistic data that might help us bridge the boundaries between semantics and pragmatics.

The aim of this case study is both descriptive and applied. First, this case study argues in favour of the use of written data in corpus pragmatic research. In particular, we will look into the linguistic realisation of two related pragmatic functions, namely <RECOMMEND> and <SUGGEST>,[1] that build the persuasiveness of the promotional and instructional texts that CLANES is composed of. Second, the study explores in what way pragmatic annotation can be developed on the basis of regular patterning of combined levels of language description (PoS, semantics, rhetoric), or, in other words, multi-layered metapatterns in co-text.

Our research questions are:

1) What is the linguistic realisation of the functions under examination like in English and Spanish? Is there much variation in the realisation per function and/or across functions and languages?
2) What co-textual information motivates the interpretation of an utterance as <RECOMMEND> and/or <SUGGEST>?
3) How can we translate the collocational patterns (form) into pragmatic metapatterns (function) to automatise annotation?

1 The act of <DIRECT>is closely related to <RECOMMEND> and <SUGGEST>. However, in this chapter we deal with the latter two alone to add to CLANES-based research in general and to corpus pragmatics in particular. We might mention <DIRECT> occasionally when describing our data or discussing our findings.

All in all this case study will prove how corpora "can make important contributions to speech act theory" (Rühlemann 2010: 298) and how pragmatic interpretation of corpus data is a (tentative) first step towards the development of pragmatic annotation schemes, which may help produce datasets to be used in the optimisation or enhancement of text.

2. CLANES: a domain-specific corpus for pragmatics research

As described in Sanjurjo-González (this volume), CLANES is mainly composed of culinary recipes and online food descriptions, which represent various foods and drinks (cheese, dried meats, cookies, wine and herbal tea). The rhetorical description of the corpus (see Pizarro Sánchez & Ortego Antón, this volume) reveals a macrostructure common to both CLANES genres, where a number of moves serve two main communicative purposes, namely, to inform and to persuade. In short, CLANES greatly features informational-persuasive discourse (Biber & Zhang 2018). While some moves seem to favour one function over the other, it is not possible to keep them well apart, for there may be overlaps. Let us consider the utterance "These classic shortbread cookies contain only the organic ingredients and are baked to perfection", originally found in MOVE 2. An overall interpretation of the intended meaning of the utterance would be 'informative'. However, the presence of the word "perfection", evaluative in nature, together with the descriptor "organic", socially in demand, add on to the content by presenting it in a positive way. All together would contribute to the persuasiveness of the utterance in particular and the text it is taken from in general.

Previous research based on the CLANES corpus (Pérez Blanco & Izquierdo 2022; Izquierdo & Pérez Blanco 2023; Pizarro Sánchez & Pérez Ruiz 2024; Labrador & Ramón 2024) has brought to light that persuasion is sought for in various ways and in different moves, making CLANES feel more persuasive than (merely) informative. Persuasion involves "linguistic choices that aim at changing or affecting the behaviour of others or strengthening the existing beliefs and behaviours of those who already agree" (Virtanen & Halmari 2005: 5). In this regard, the CLANES genres aim to persuade the reader to buy, prepare or eat a food and/or a drink in a specific way, this being the perlocutionary effect of our texts. The question is, what are the illocutionary acts that lead to it? Rabadán, Ramón and Sanjurjo-González (2021) identified seven major pragmatic functions of the food-and-drink genres within CLANES: <STATE>, <DIRECT>, <SUGGEST>, <RECOMMEND>, <PRAISE>, <EVIDENCE> and <RELATE TO READER>. <STATE> and <EVIDENCE> focus primarily on information, while the remaining five foreground persuasion. As already mentioned, we are interested in looking into the acts of <RECOMMEND> and <SUGGEST>. These acts, together with <DIRECT>, are conceived of as a cline of persuasive strength in the writer's intention to prompt the reader to do something, be it in the context of buying, preparing or eating food and in the context of drinking. We will therefore analyse our written data in the light of the Speech Act Theory (SAT), whereby utterances perform actions.

3. Corpus Pragmatics and Speech Acts

One of the areas that has received a great deal of attention in the corpus pragmatics literature is speech acts, which have been, nevertheless, undertaken almost exclusively on spoken data. Searle's SAT (1969) proposes five major types of illocutionary speech acts:

- Assertives or representatives commit the speaker to the truth of the proposition, for example 'asserting'.
- Expressives express a psychological state such as 'apologising'.
- Commissives commit the speaker to some future course of action, as when 'promising', among other possibilities.
- Directives are attempts by the speaker to get the addressee to do something.
- Declarations effect an immediate change in the institutional state of affairs, as in marrying.

Directives are related to Sinclair and Coulthard's interactive speech acts 'informative' and 'directive' (1975), in turn bound up with the two main communicative purposes of our corpus. CLANES <RECOMMEND> and <SUGGEST>,[2] also <DIRECT>, would belong to this type of act as they impose an expected reaction on the reader. While such an act has been acknowledged as face-threatening (Brown & Levinson 1987), these three directives are actually non-impositive in the sense that they benefit the reader/customer (Haverkate 1984). In this regard, CLANES-based research has attested the usage of positive politeness strategies to put the reader first and mitigate the threat posed by the act (Izquierdo & Pérez Blanco 2023). Rabadán, Ramón and Sanjurjo-González (2021) define <DIRECT> as an "action to be carried out to fulfil a goal" (p. 214), in other words, to instruct - as opposed to order. <RECOMMEND> "indicates the best course of action (to do something) among those available" (p. 215) while <SUGGEST> "offers alternatives to carry out the task that may be or may not be put into practice" (p. 216). Other scholars (Searle 1969; Jiang 2006; Martínez-Flor 2010) have also acknowledged that suggestions and recommendations may be observed as two different actions, although the former might be considered as a parent category: "the speech act of suggestions is construed as encompassing what we know as advice, proposals, suggestions and recommendations" (Martínez-Flor 2010: 259). In our study, we keep them apart; we understand <RECOMMEND> as conveying normativity and <SUGGEST>, by contrast, optionality.

Corpus pragmatics research has dealt with a number of speech acts, such as, apologies (Deutschmann 2003; Lutzky & Kehoe 2017), compliments (Jucker & Taavitsainen 2014), and agreement and disagreement (Milá-Garcia 2018), among others. Nasser (2022) looks at various speech acts (asserting, describing, suggesting, thanking, praising, among others) in her pragmatic analysis of online reviews; we praise the fact that it is a pragmatic interpretation of digital written discourse. Similarly, Huang's study (2018) does not deal with one speech act in particular, but delves into all the co-textual variables that should be considered to annotate a

2 Aware as we are that the term 'speech' refers to the act of speaking, not really that of writing, we will use the term 'illocutionary act' instead, to avoid confusion. Having said that, however, we defend that the Speech Act Theory is applicable to a pragmatic interpretation of written data when such data is language used for the purpose of *driving* the reader to do something.

"performance unit" (p. 320), hence resulting in a multimodal corpus of speech acts.

Regarding studies about the two illocutionary acts under examination, i.e., <RECOMMEND> and <SUGGEST>, several have approached the broad typology of directive acts as a whole, without really focusing on a particular sub-act that seeks to provoke an action on the addressee, that is, orders, commands, requests, invitations, advice, suggestions and so on. Flöck and Geluykens (2015) investigate directives in three different datasets comparing spontaneous and elicited discourse. The authentic data is taken from the spoken component of the ICE but also written data from a small corpus of business letters. Their study proves the influence of the type of genre and the conditions of use in the linguistic choices users make, accounting for a great deal of variation from sub-act to sub-act. Also Garcia McAllister (2015) analyses different data from the spoken component of the TOEFL 2000 Spoken and Written Academic Language Corpus (e.g. conversations, business interactions and university lectures). The author concludes that the role of each situational context is key in predicting the characteristic type(s) of directive acts. Kohnen (2008) also examines directives in the genre of church sermons from a diachronic perspective in order to come up with an inventory of genre-specific forms. Other investigations have focused exclusively on one or two illocutionary acts.

Cristobalena's (2016) contrastive analysis of instruction in English and Spanish is a good example of a domain-specific corpus-based analysis of the pragmatic function <DIRECT>, out of the scope of this chapter. Although much less researched (Pollock & Blaker 2021), <RECOMMEND> has been the object of analysis in Placencia (2012) and Glide (2016), both from an English-Spanish cross-linguistic perspective. In addition, both studies refer to recommendations under the umbrella term of 'advice', and analyse computer-mediated discourse. By far, the illocutionary act that has received greater attention is <SUGGEST>. Among the first to use naturally-occurring data are Bardovi-Harling and Harford (1993), in their analysis of suggestions produced by L2 English-speaking postgraduates during authentic academic advising sessions in an American university. The study revealed an increase in the learners' production of suggestions during their stay abroad, although they did not manage to correct non-native uses of mitigators and aggravators when suggesting. Martínez-Flor's taxonomy (2005) of strategies for the linguistic realisations of <SUGGEST>

has meant a significant contribution to the literature. This author proposes three main strategies: direct, conventionalised forms and indirect, which we have slightly adapted to classify our data (see Section 4.3). Adolphs' (2008) work on suggestions is of interest to us in that it also looks at distributional and collocational patterns to establish "functional profiles" (p. 10). We will also try to explain the difference in function between <RECOMMEND> and <SUGGEST> utterances on the basis of metalinguistic information in sequence (see Section 6). Al-Aadeli's work (2013) on suggestion and advice in theatre plays is one of the few pragmatic studies on written data, although he analyses theatre discourse, which is planned to mirror spoken discourse and is, therefore, prefabricated orality (Baños & Chaume 2009). Al-Aadeli echoes Searle's understanding of <ADVISE> as "telling you what is best for you", which equals our definition of <RECOMMEND>. In his formal and functional contrast, Al-Aadeli observed that advice-giving relies on Martínez-Flor's direct formal strategies, while suggestions are conveyed through indirect conventionalised strategies.

To the best of our knowledge, no empirical analysis has been done to contrast the formal realisation and pragmatic implications of suggestions versus recommendations, particularly on a domain-specific written corpus, which is the niche of our investigation.

4. Case study

4.1. Method

In this case study we use pragmatics as a model to interpret written data which clearly performs an action for the purpose of persuading the reader. Our unit of analysis is the illocutionary act, which we first have to identify in our corpus. While traditional corpus linguistics research takes a form-to-function approach by exploring the lexico-grammatical realisation of speech acts based on the well-established taxonomy mentioned above, more recent attempts (such as, Weisser 2018, 2020 or Milà-Garcia 2018) advocate for a function-to-form orientation that would allow researchers to come up with a finer-grained speech-act taxonomy (such as DART taxonomy, Weisser 2018). Both methods have their flaws. The insurmountable weakness of the first one is the obvious "lack of correspondence between speech acts and linguistic forms" (Milà-Garcia 2018: 265); as for the latter, going from function to form requires careful close reading and painfully time-consuming manual annotation in spite of some attempts at (semi) automatic speech act annotation in the last years (Weisser 2018, 2020). Such investigations deal with small, domain-specific spoken corpora which allow a deep analysis that takes into account the contextual details that larger corpora cannot provide. Admittedly, CLANES is too large (over 1.8 million words) for a manual pragmatic analysis. However, it is annotated at different levels of metalinguistic description, which has been highly beneficial to narrow down a potentially relevant sample, that is, a set of utterances that perform the illocutionary acts under examination. To isolate such a sample from CLANES, we followed Ädel and Reppen (2008: 2–3), who put forward four approaches to form-to-function corpus analysis: frequency-based listing, one-to-one searching, sampling, and sifting. We have adopted these strategies to identify the prototypical linguistic manifestations of the illocutionary acts <RECOMMEND> and <SUGGEST> in CLANES:

1) First, we have taken a bottom-up approach looking at the frequencies of forms in our corpus (frequency-based listings) to work from there to their typical patterns and pragmatic meanings.
2) Verbal forms have been used as search items, or Illocutionary Force Indicating Devices (IFIDs) in pragmatic terms (Deutschmann 2003; Lutzky & Kehoe 2017), to sample possible instances of the illocutionary acts under examination. The fact that CLANES is PoS-tagged has allowed a one-to-one search of all verbal forms under examination.
3) It has been necessary to sift through an initial population of the frequent verbal forms that potentially indicated pragmatic functions to eliminate instances which do not realise any of the illocutionary acts we are interested in, i.e. <RECOMMEND> and <SUGGEST>.

All in all, our analysis follows an eclectic methodology by, first, going from form to function (corpus-based approach) and, second, aligning with horizontal reading (Aijmer & Rühlemann 2015), i.e., doing a manual analysis. Such a stage "of manual microanalysis to separate unwanted hits from examples" of patterns with a specific pragmatic function (Lutzky & Kehoe 2017: 54) is required to compensate for a search based on forms which cannot detect (non-conventional) indirect illocutionary acts. In this way, data relevant for the study has emerged in a corpus-driven fashion (Tognini-Bonelli 2001).

4.2. Selection of the data

An existing debate in the framework of the SAT theory discusses whether "lexico-grammar or speech act verbs should be taken into account as guides to illocutionary forces, or whether the classification of speech acts should be based solely on pragmatic criteria, such as felicity conditions" (O'Keeffe et al. 2011: 92). We have benefited from both points of view in our analysis. First, we have taken into account the situational context (preparatory felicity condition), that is, the instruction and promotion of foods and drinks. On the assumption that linguistic features of a register tend to reflect the situational context (felicity condition) and the intended meaning (communicative function), we deemed appropriate to start from verb forms. Initially we considered among our anchoring elements not only performative verbs but also domain-related action verbs which are, in co-text, indicative of the intended illocution.

Data was taken from CLANES using the ACTRES Corpus Manager (ACM) tool (Sanjurjo-González 2018). Given that the English and Spanish verbal systems differ morphologically, each language set had to be browsed differently. To ensure qualitative representativeness of the initial population and ultimate sample, we benefited from Ramón and Rabadán's (2024) observation that English texts display a higher frequency of base-form verbs, while the first-person plural form and the infinitive are salient in the Spanish dataset. Accordingly, we searched for our input verbal forms using the PoS tagging functionality ACM is equipped with. To extract the English data we first used a wordlist provided by ACM with the most frequent lemmas in the corpus. After discarding part-of-speech categories other than verbs, we ended up with a list of 148 verb forms. To extract Spanish verbs that would be the node of an illocutionary act of <RECOMMEND> or <SUGGEST>, we browsed ACM for all first-person plural forms. To do this, we combined searching possibilities by choosing <Any Verb> in the PoS Menu and specifying the end of the verb as *"-amos", "-emos", and "-imos"*, one at a time, on ACM, building a list of 404 lemmas.

The population retrieved per language was far too large for the manual analysis. Therefore, for the purposes of this study, we limited our analysis to two co-texts where the IFIDs are modal and performative verbs, whose pragmatic role has been widely attested (Depraetere 2017; Cappelle et al. 2019). Thus, this study on <RECOMMEND> and <SUGGEST> contributes to previous research on CLANES-specific verbal forms where the English imperative and Spanish first-person plural forms are typical of <DIRECT> (Ramón & Rabadán 2024). Table 11 summarises the actual IFIDs and number of occurrences analysed.

Table 11: IFIDs for <RECOMMEND> and <SUGGEST>.

ENGLISH IFIDs		**SPANISH IFIDs**[3]	
Modals	**784**	**Modal periphrases**	**890**
Can/Could	371	*Poder + inf*	653
Should	336	*Deber + inf*	159
May/Might	62	*Tener que + inf*	78
Must	7		
Have to	5		
Need to	3		
Performatives	**108**	**Performatives**	**183**
Recommend	78	*Recomendar*	136
Suggest	27	*Aconsejar*	37
Urge	3	*Proponer*	7
		Sugerir	3
TOTAL	**892**	**TOTAL**	**1,073**

Our approach has moved from general frequency counts to investigating items in context, as in many previous studies of corpus pragmatics (Vaughan & Clancy 2013). The analysis has been daunting and time-consuming but an adequate pragmatic interpretation "can only be

3 Translation of the Spanish IFIDs: *poder*= 'can', *deber*= 'must', *tener que*= 'have to', *recomendar*= 'recommend', *aconsejar*= 'advise', *proponer*= 'propose', and sugerir= 'suggest'.

achieved by a close reading of corpus material and subsequent annotation" (O'Keeffe et al. 2011: 92).

4.3. Description of the data

Before describing the realisation of each illocutionary act under examination, we must report on a few concordances whose pragmatic force is hooked neither to a modal nor to a performative. While analysing the language datasets, a few concordances caught our attention as potentially indicating constructions of <RECOMMEND> and <SUGGEST>. Upon closer examination of such concordances, we found some regular lexico-grammatical patterns that prompt the pragmatic interpretation. By analogy, we will refer to this corpus-driven data as illocutionary force indicating constructions (IFICs), which we have classified into four main semantic categories. These, in turn, encompass a variety of <RECOMMEND> and <SUGGEST> linguistic realisation strategies. Table 12 summarises our proposal and indicates total occurrence rates.

Table 12: Corpus-driven IFICs for <RECOMMEND> and <SUGGEST>.

IFICs categories	**ENGLISH**		**SPANISH**[4]	
Evaluative construction	**The best thing is to** wrap your cheese… **It is a perfect (snack) to** have…	70	Esta mezcla **puede ser muy deliciosa al tomarse como** té frío. **Es mejor que** pongamos (SBJ) garbanzos o… **Siempre viene bien** cuando queremos un menú…	48
Sensory-cognitive construction	**Why not** try adding a little honey?	79	**¿Puedes resistirte a probar? Tenemos el orgullo de ofrecer** este té Matcha	24

(*Continued*)

4 Glosses of the Spanish IFICs in bold: *puede ser muy deliciosa al tomarse como* (can be very delicious if taken as), *Es mejor que* (it is better that), *Siempre viene bien* (it always works), ¿Puedes resistirte a probar? (Can you really resist to try it?), *Tenemos el orgullo de ofrecer* (We are proud to offer), *nos gusta cocinarlo* (we like to cook it), alternativa… para (alternative for (moments)).

Table 12: (*Continued*)

IFICs categories	**ENGLISH**		**SPANISH**[4]	
Volitional construction	**You will want to** reserve them until the end …	63	Cuando tenemos un buen pescado **nos gusta cocinarlo** solo…	18
Lexical cue	–	–	Una **alternativa** diferente **para** momentos especiales…	32
TOTAL		212		122

As its name indicates, evaluative constructions feature an evaluative resource, be it an adjective, adverb, even a verb, a comparative/superlative form, or an intensifier, amongst others. Volitional constructions anticipate, to certain extent, what the reader should want, even need, to achieve a pursued effect, which usually relates to the best course of action for a successful cooking. Most importantly, the majority of these constructions contain 'will', overtly conveying 'volition'. The sensory-cognitive IFICs are so called because they either appeal to the senses or to a logical reason in the reader to take the recommendation, on the assumption that it will do good to them. Finally, the fourth category revolves around a lexical cue, usually a noun that points at an opportunity or advantage not to be missed. All these resources are always embedded in a lexical bundle that, as a whole, seems to <RECOMMEND> and/or <SUGGEST>.

All concordances examined, whether they were retrieved in a corpus-based fashion or driven by the data, amount up to a sample of 1,104 English concordances and 1,195 in Spanish (see Table 13).

Table 13: English-Spanish sample of analysed concordances.

	ENGLISH	**SPANISH**
IFIDs	892	1,073
IFICs	212	122
Total	1,104	1,195

5. Results

5.1. <Recommend> in English

As many as 579 concordances have been coded as <RECOMMEND> in the English dataset. The IFIDs that have prompted the pragmatic interpretation are various modal verbs in 370 occurrences (63.9%) and various performative verbs in 81 cases (14%). In addition, we have considered 128 data-driven constructions (22.1%) or IFICs that result from the combination of various lexical and grammatical items. Figure 10 illustrates the distribution of each device:

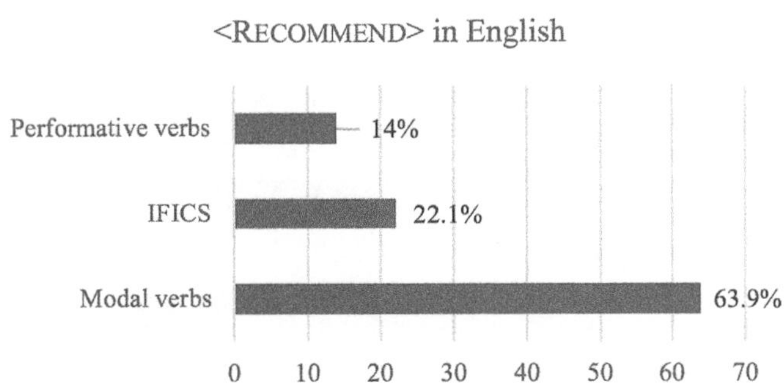

Figure 10: Distribution of <RECOMMEND> indicating devices in English.

5.1.1. Modals

Having a modal verb of necessity as the lexical hook of English <RECOMMEND> is a frequent linguistic realisation. 90% of the concordances identified rely on 'should', as in example 1:

(1) *You **should** always read the product label before consuming.*

Much less frequent are 'must', 'need to' and 'have to', which canonically express <DIRECT>. In some of the few cases identified, the negative polarity of the verbal phrase is key to the interpretation as <RECOMMEND> (see example 2).

(2) *Brown chicken on both sides. (You **don't need to cook** the chicken completely because it will finish cooking in the oven).*

In addition, (2) shows a regular pattern in which the recommendation occurs right after a <DIRECT>, so it is some elaboration on the former to specify the best way of getting a good result. As illustrated in the example, such a recommendation is often found between parentheses, or as part of a relative clause.

5.1.2. Lexicogrammatical IFICs

A total of 212 English concordance lines display a lexicogrammatical IFIC, 128 of which do <RECOMMEND>. Figure 11 shows the semantic categories of the constructions indicating this pragmatic function in English.

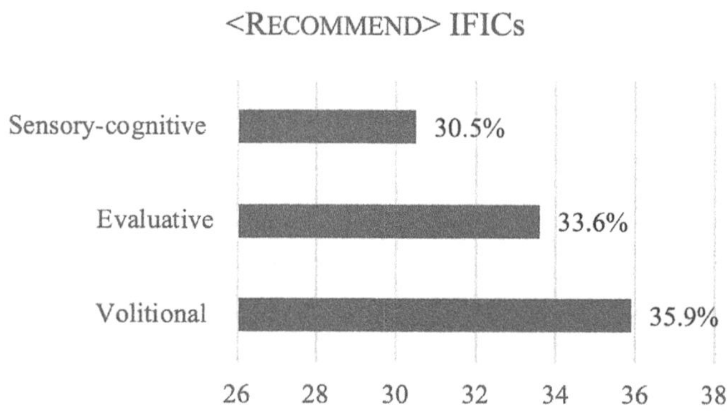

Figure 11: Distribution of the semantic categories of the constructions indicating <RECOMMEND> in English.

Their distribution is rather even in the sample, with the most frequent category being volitional with 46 instances (35.9%), closely followed by 43 evaluative bundles (33.6%) and 39 sensory-cognitive constructions (30.5%).

(3) *The important part about steaming the squash is that* ***you want to*** *steam for as little time as possible.*

(4) *...would pair it with many beers, but a pale ale* ***would work best****.*

(5) *...but* ***I would serve it*** *with a vanilla or rum raisin frozen yoghourt.*

In (3), the overt address to the reader is key to make them willing to do an action, while foregrounding the importance of doing it as indicated.

Example (4) compares two ways of having a meal, while the second is clearly stated as the best, hence recommended, one. In example (5) the writer's self-mention together with habitual 'would' confer authority and trust to the recommendation, as if the right model to follow. No instances of lexical cue for <RECOMMEND> occur in the English dataset.

5.1.3. Performatives

The performative verbs present in our English dataset are *recommend* (78 instances), and *urge* (3 instances). This IFID seems rather marginal in our text types. The majority of cases appear in an active-voice co-text with a first-person subject, either in the plural or in the singular. The former is slightly more frequent, but there is an even distribution.

(6) *Once opened,* ***we recommend*** *wrapping your cheese in grease-proof paper.*

Only 'recommend' is preceded by a modal verb (18 cases), 'would' being almost exclusive of such a pattern:

(7) *To drink, we'****d recommend*** *a large lager or pilsner...*

5.2. <RECOMMEND> in Spanish

The number of occurrences coded as <RECOMMEND> in Spanish amounts up to 472, distributed into 252 modal periphrases (53.4%), 180 occurrences of a performative verb (38.1%), and 40 IFICs (8.5%), as shown in Figure 12:

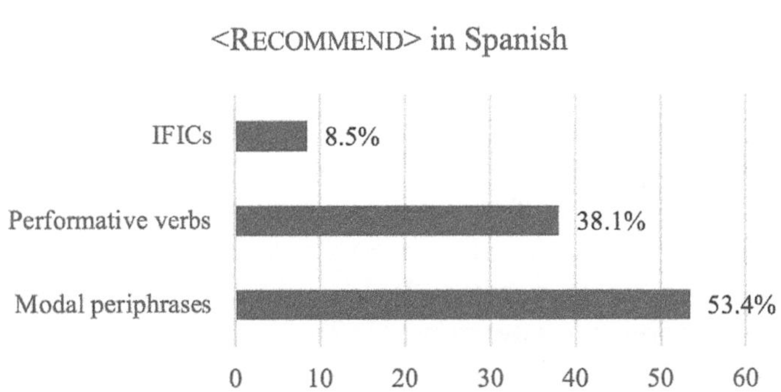

Figure 12: Distribution of <RECOMMEND> indicating devices in Spanish.

5.2.1. Modal periphrases

Regarding the Spanish instances of <RECOMMEND>, over half of the occurrences (252, representing 53.4%) are realised by one of the following modal periphrases, *deber+inf*, *tener que+inf*, or *poder+inf*. The first two would be functional equivalents to English 'must' and 'have to' which were observed to express recommendations in English. In Spanish, *poder*, by contrast, equals *can* and *could* in English which have not been observed to <RECOMMEND> in our data (see Section 4.3.3.). *Deber+inf* is, by far, the most frequent modal periphrasis (158 occurrences, 62.7 %) meaning <RECOMMEND>. The main verb usually describes how to best store or consume a product or meal as in example (8):

(8) *El lomo embuchado* ***debe consumirse*** *crudo cortado en finas rodajas.*
(The stuffed loin must be eaten raw and in thin slices)

This pattern is common to modal periphrasis *tener que+inf*, of which there are 72 occurrences (28.6%).

(9) *Lo vertemos sobre la cazuela (**tiene que** estar bien caliente).*
(We pour it into the casserole (**it must be** very hot))

As seen in English, recommendations are frequently provided as extra information, in a parenthetical, related to a clear instruction or <DIRECT>, which is predominantly conveyed in Spanish by means of a first-person plural form in the present tense (Ramón García & Rabadán 2024).

5.2.2. Performatives

Other direct strategies of the illocutionary act <RECOMMEND> are performative verbs (180 occurrences represent 38.1%). Thus, the verb *recomendar* (recommend) is found in CLANES both in impersonal constructions *se recomienda* (it is recommended that) (74) as in example (10), as well as in the first-person plural present *recomendamos* (we recommend) (62). We have also found a few examples of performative *se aconseja* (it is advised that) (32), *(des)aconsejamos* (5) (we (do not) advise) and *proponemos* (we propose) (7).

(10) ***Se recomienda servirlo*** *ligeramente fresco.*
(We recommend to serve it slightly chilled.)

As is the case with other <RECOMMEND> pragmatic hooks, the overall meaning of the utterance as to how to take, make or serve a meal seems to be the *raison d'être* of the recommendation in our CLANES texts.

5.2.3. Lexicogrammatical IFICs

In only 8.5% of the instances in Spanish CLANES <RECOMMEND> is conveyed in a more indirect way by means of a lexicogrammatical IFIC (40n) prompting this pragmatic meaning.

(11) ***Cuantas más*** *verduras* ***echemos, más bueno*** *estará el puchero.*
(**The more** vegetables **we add, the tastier** it will be)

(12) *Lo dejamos cocer (...) pero no mucho porque* ***no queremos quedarnos sin salsa.***
(We leave it simmer (…) but not much because **we do not want to run out of gravy**)

(13) *…así ya se puede comer, no obstante* ***yo lo suelo hacer con*** *un huevo escalfado.*
(…as it is, it can be eaten, but **I usually cook it with** a poached egg)

(14) *Este té es uno de los* ***recomendados*** *para terminar el día…*
(This tea is one of the **recommended** ones to end the day…)

There are 26 evaluative constructions as in example (11), where the emphatic frame *cuanto más X más Y* (the more X the more Y) sounds convincing and even praising. There are 9 occurrences where the recommendation lies on a volitional verb. It is interesting that, as in example (12), the verb is often in the first-person plural form, whereby the writer implies that the recommendation would benefit both writer and reader alike, hence building rapport, and therefore persuasion. All three sensory-cognitive constructions rely on a periphrasis with *soler* (13) in Spanish ('be accustomed to' or more frequently 'usually + verb' in English), which implies the usual action that the writer, here the voice of expertise on cooking, prefers. Finally, there are two examples where a lexical cue prompts the interpretation (14), usually presented as *the* action to carry out.

5.3. <SUGGEST> in English

We found a total of 525 occurrences meaning <SUGGEST> in the English dataset. As shown in Figure 13, the most frequent IFID is a modal verb

(78.9%), then a lexicogrammar IFIC (16%), and finally the performative verb *suggest*, of which there are few occurrences (5.1%).

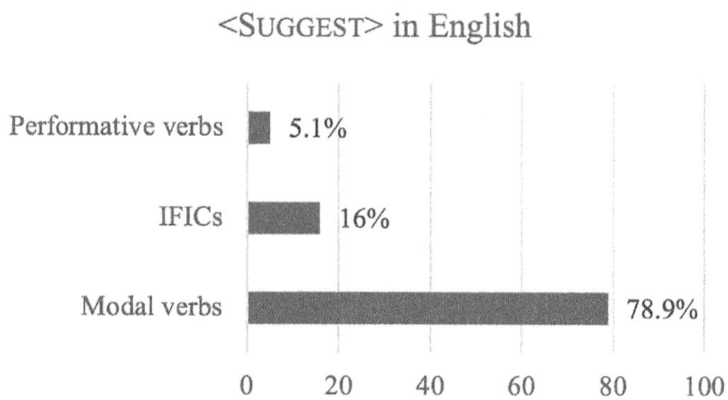

Figure 13: Distribution of <SUGGEST> indicating devices in English.

5.3.1. Modals

414 occurrences of <SUGGEST> revolve around a modal verb. Although six different modals realise such a function, there is one outstandingly preferred modal, namely *can* (82.4%), as in example (15), drastically more frequent than *may* (10.6%), shown by example (16) or *could* (5.3%) in (17).

(15) *It is also very versatile and* ***can be used*** *in hot or cold recipes.*

(16) *If desired, a splash of the pasta water* ***may be added*** *to the sauce to thin it slightly.*

(17) *Note that* ***you could also pour*** *the stock into the pan with the rice.*

Regarding form, the presence of 'you' addressing the reader is observed in slightly more than half of the data. The other half, by contrast, takes a passive voice.

A marginal 1.5% of <SUGGEST> relies on *should*, *must*, or *have to*, whose suggestive connotation depends on the semantics of the verb and/ or the rhetorical context the utterance is taken from, as in (18).

(18) *If you've never grated butter before, you* ***must try*** *it.*

The verb does not encode a cooking-related action that is usually done as part of a culinary process. Rather, it appears as an invitation to taste something for the sake of indulgement and delight.

5.3.2. Lexicogrammatical IFICs

Among the 84 IFICs identified, nearly half of them belong to the sensory-cognitive category (40 n= 47.6%) as in (19). There are also 27 evaluative constructions (32.2%) as in (20) and some (17n=20.2%) volitional ones as in (21). We have not identified any lexical cue in the English dataset for <SUGGEST> either.

(19) ***Why not try*** *adding a little honey?*

(20) *If you've never tried green tea,* ***this is a great way to*** *start.*

(21) ***You will want to*** *savor it alone or enjoy it with chicken.*

5.3.3. Performatives

As few as 32 occurrences of *suggest* were retrieved from CLANES. Yet, only 27 were considered valid for our analysis, as in example (22).

(22) *We therefore* ***suggest*** *that you boil several cans at the same time.*

Regarding the other five, it was observed that their aim is not to persuade but to report that something is the case (informative function).

5.4. <SUGGEST> in Spanish

We have identified a total of 723 occurrences meaning <SUGGEST> in the Spanish dataset. The distribution is shown in Figure 14: a verb conveying modality is by far the most frequent IFID (88.2%), followed by a lexicogrammatical IFIC (7.6%). Finally, the use of the performative verb *sugerir* (suggest) is extremely rare in CLANES (0.4%).

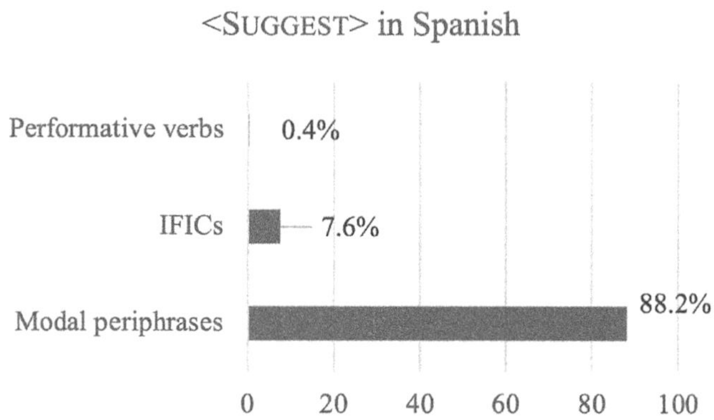

Figure 14: Distribution of <SUGGEST> indicating devices in Spanish.

5.4.1. Modal periphrases

In a large number of occurrences in Spanish (n=638) <SUGGEST> is conveyed by a modal periphrasis. *Poder+inf* is unquestionably the modal periphrasis this illocutionary act relies on, with a 98.9% share of all the sample.

(23) ***Se puede acompañar*** *de miel o de membrillo.*
(It can be served with honey or quince jelly.)

Example (23) is a prototypical one where the suggestion is conveyed through a *se*-passive in the present tense. This type of suggestions provide the reader with a range of options, or an alternative, or a novel way of preparing, serving or taking a food and/or drink. Linguistic and typographical devices signalling optionality such as *también* (too), *o bien* (either … or; or even), *o* (or), parentheses, among others, are frequently found in the co-text as in the example above.

5.4.2. Lexicogrammatical IFICs

82 <SUGGEST> occurrences belong with the so-called data-driven IFICs. The most frequent categories are lexical cues (30n= 36.6%), as *opción* (option) in example (34), and evaluative constructions (22n = 26.8%) like *ideal para* (ideal for) in (25). Cognitive-sensory IFICs are also fairly frequent (21n= 25.6%), usually through a cognitive verb like *creo que* (I think that) in (26) while the volitional category, shown in (27), is the least frequent (9n=11%).

(24) ***Otra opción*** *si no tenemos crema de vinagre balsámico* ***es*** *emulsionar la vinagreta…*
(**Another option** if we do not have balsamic vinegar cream is to emulsify the dressing by adding a teaspoon of honey)

(25) *…**ideal para** servir como tapa **o** elaborar infinidad de recetas.*
(…**ideal to take as** a tapa **or** cook an infinite number of recipes)

(26) ***Creo que puede ser una forma de*** *tomar una rica infusión que te ayude a bajar el ritmo…*
(**I think that it can be a way of** taking a tasty infusion that will help you slow down the rythm…)

(27) *…empezaremos a saltear a fuego fuerte,* ***buscamos que*** *queden al dente.*
(…we will start to stir fry over low heat, **we seek that** they stay al dente)

In addition, we have classified within these constructions, 11 instances that could be a performative verb. We are referring to examples like (28) and (29):

(28) *…**tenemos el placer de ofrecer** este té Matcha denominado Supreme.*
(…**we have the pleasure to offer** you this Matcha tea, known as Supreme)

(29) *…**te traemos** una receta donde podrás aprovechar al máximo las frutas que lo componen.*
(**We bring you** a recipe where you will enjoy to the full the fruits that make it)

However, neither did we consider them in the one-to-one searching stage nor do we find it easy to argue for their performative force out of context. Embedded in their sequence, these verbs are accompanied by stronger pragmatic lexical cues or fit in the sensory-cognitive category. In this regard, such verb forms arguably verge on the expressive, rather than the directive. Our interpretation is that they are inclined to the promotion by appealing to emotions.

5.4.3. Performatives

Performative verb *sugerir* (suggest) is extremely rare in CLANES. Only 3 instances were found, all of them conjugated in the first person singular. Two of the instances occur in the rhetorical context of a promotional move, whereas the other example provides a serving suggestion (example 30).

(30) *Servicio: 6–8 ºC Aunque resulta excelente en cualquier momento,* ***te sugiero que*** *lo disfrutes con (...) el maridaje es perfecto*
(Serving: 6–8 ºC Although it is excellent at any time, **I suggest you enjoy** it with (...) the pairing is perfect)

The results of this descriptive stage answer our first research question. In short, we have identified a list of illocutionary force indicating markers, whether a device such as a modal (or modal periphrases in Spanish) or performative, already acknowledged in the literature, or a wider set of constructions, driven by our data. Both languages share these markers, except for the data-driven lexical cue. The illocutionary acts under examination also share these markers, but metalinguistic information regarding the PoS and the semantics of the marker -or of surrounding collocates- account for the different interpretation of the pragmatic force. Differences and similarities of use, from a quantitative but mainly qualitative point of view are discussed in the following section.

6. Discussion

Table 14 juxtaposes the linguistic realisation strategies per illocutionary act in the two working languages, including the raw numbers and the percentages in each case:

Table 14: Juxtaposition of linguistic realisation per illocutionary act in English and Spanish.

<RECOMMEND>				**Illocutionary Force Indicating Marker**	<SUGGEST>			
ENGLISH		**SPANISH**			**ENGLISH**		**SPANISH**	
370	63.9	252	53.4	IFID Modal	414	78.9	638	88.2
81	14	180	38.1	IFID Performative	27	5.1	3	0.4
43	7.4	26	5.5	IFIC Evaluative	27	5.1	22	3.1
46	7.9	9	1.9	IFIC Volitional	17	3.3	9	1.2
39	6.8	3	0.7	IFIC Sensory-Cognitive	40	7.6	21	2.9
–		2	0.4	IFIC Lexical Cue	–		30	4.2
579	%	**472**	%		**525**	%	**723**	%

Figure 15 shows this contrasting distribution more graphically:

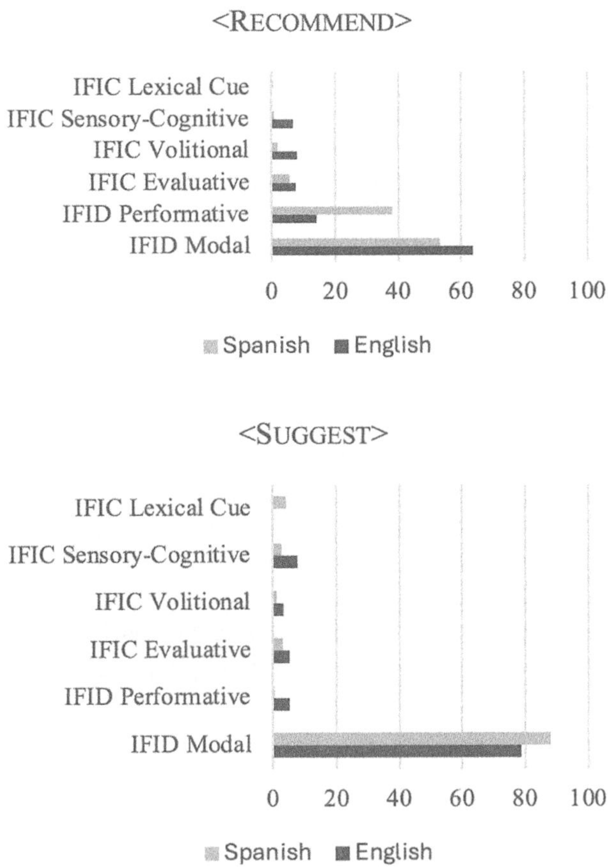

Figure 15: Juxtaposition of illocutionary indicating devices per function and per language.

Adapting to recommendations Martínez-Flor's taxonomy of suggestions (2010), performatives would belong to direct strategies of linguistic realisation, English modals and their equivalent modal periphrases in Spanish match conventionalised forms, and IFICs are indirect strategies of realisation.

From a quantitative point of view, Table 14 points at a clear cross-linguistic difference in the type of illocutionary act preferred; while the

English dataset displays a slightly bigger proportion of <RECOMMEND>, Spanish favours <SUGGEST>. Not only is there a cross-linguistic difference, but also intralinguistic, especially in Spanish. The distribution of IFID verb and the rest of illocutionary force indicating markers in Spanish <RECOMMEND> is rather balanced, even when a modal periphrasis or a performative verb are clearly more frequent. If we compare this marker distribution to what happens in <SUGGEST>, we observe that this force is outstandingly indicated by a modal verb. The other markers are substantially less common. Spanish performative verbs play a drastically different role, with the <RECOMMEND> verbs being the second most preferred marker and *suggest* being the very least. By contrast, the data-driven IFICs are twice as prominent in Spanish <SUGGEST> than when <RECOMMEND> is meant.

Notwithstanding similarities and differences in the marker preferred or the frequency of use of one marker over the other, distinguishing one illocutionary act from the other needs to be explained in qualitative terms. As part of a continuum, the boundaries between <RECOMMEND> and <SUGGEST> are indeed fuzzy or difficult to pin down. However, by looking at the collocational configuration of one and the other, we identify sequences that account for a differing pragmatic interpretation. In particular, the semantics of the actual type of marker or surrounding items has been observed to be key in distinguishing <SUGGEST> from <RECOMMEND>.

6.1. Modal-indicated[5] <RECOMMEND> and <SUGGEST> in contrast

English and Spanish recommendations mainly rely on a modal verb with a meaning of necessity, such as *should, must, have to*, and the Spanish periphrases *deber+inf*, and *tener que+inf*, whereas the possibility modals *can, may, could*, and the periphrasis *poder + inf* feature in <SUGGEST>. This observation aligns with most grammar rules and

5 While there is a closed set of modal verbs in English, Spanish does not have such a verb class. Instead, it resorts to some periphrases where a normal verb combines with an infinitive to convey modality (Rabadán 2006). Given their functional equivalence, we may here use the term 'modal' in the two languages, yet the reader is warned that the verbal systems differ, as briefly explained.

dictionary meanings. However, "modal verbs are notoriously ambiguous (…) and can be used in utterances with often specific pragmatic effects" (Cappelle et al. 2019: 220). Indeed, some instances have been found where modal *must* performs the function <SUGGEST>, while *podemos* (we can) is used in context prompting <RECOMMEND>. Although few, such examples foreground the role of context in interpreting a modal verb. In the case of example (18) above, the combination of *must* with the verb *try* communicates the possibility of doing something for the first time, on the conviction that the reader will enjoy it, rather than instructing a specific procedural action or imposing a need on the reader (as in *Do not eat raw, must be cooked*). In addition, in case that the suggestion was not followed, this would be harmless for the reader. So, the dictionary meaning of *must* is weakened in this context of use.

Let us now consider the use of *poder*, in (31):

(31) *Para mayor seguridad* ***podemos hacer*** *el vacío a los botes hirviéndolos.*
(To be on the safe side, we can vacuum the jars by boiling them)

In this utterance, the co-textual purposeful prepositional phrase *para mayor seguridad* bestows upon the epistemic verb greater strength, which moves it one step up in the directive continuum.

Another interesting observation across acts relates to the presence of a conditional clause in the co-text of the modal verb. In a few instances of *may*, we have observed that a phrase like *if desired* in (32) stresses the dictionary meaning of the modal, in this case possibility, motivating the <SUGGEST> coding of the concordance. It has been observed that most if-clauses boosting <SUGGEST> contain an emotional or attitudinal verb (Biber et al. 1999). Similarly, if the clause bears necessity content in the co-text of a necessity modal like *should* in (33), the meaning <RECOMMEND> has been coded. While the co-textual item is, grammatically speaking, the same, the semantics entailed has been key to the pragmatic interpretation.

(32) ***May*** *be fully baked ahead* ***if desired.***

(33) *You'll also find the manufacturer's details on there and* ***should drop*** *them* ***a line if you need further*** *information.*

Therefore, we could argue that the differing pragmatic force of modal-led <RECOMMEND> and <SUGGEST> is explained in terms of the pragmatic strengthening and weakening effect and in terms of modality strength (Depraetere 2017). In the contexts analysed, the modal verbs, while embedded in a directive context, indicate differing degrees of necessity, this being more pressing in <RECOMMEND> (33) than in <SUGGEST> (18). If the former implies the best course of action, missing it would entail greater risk than in the case of the latter, which leaves it to the reader to do as suggested or not.

One last remark is that possibility modals are more frequent than necessity modals, which has already been observed to be common of so-called unidirectional genres (Koester 2010). The modal behaviour described is common to both language datasets.

6.2. <RECOMMEND> and <SUGGEST> performative verbs

As markers of illocutionary force, CLANES performative verbs have been unequivocally ascribed to <RECOMMEND> or <SUGGEST> based on their lexical meaning. On the one hand, it may be worth highlighting a cross-linguistic difference, whereby Spanish relies on performatives more than English for the indication of <RECOMMEND>, given that expected *suggest* is virtually non-existent in our data. Furthermore, among the <RECOMMEND> performatives, concordances of 5 different types were found, 2 in English and 3 in Spanish, with *recommend* being the only performative common across languages, and unsurprisingly the most recurrent. On the other hand, in contrast to a performative verb, the Spanish dataset hints at a preference for the data-driven indicating constructions meaning <SUGGEST>, whose occurrence rate is lower for the interpretation of <RECOMMEND>.

6.3. <RECOMMEND> and <SUGGEST> IFICs in contrast

A closer examination of what we have called IFICs has revealed a wide variety of lexicogrammatical constructions for both <RECOMMEND> and <SUGGEST>, which adds on to ongoing discussions about indirect illocutionary acts. On a cross-linguistic note (see Table 14), both English and Spanish show a similar overall frequency of IFICs that realise the illocutionary act <SUGGEST> (English: 84; Spanish: 82), whereas for <RECOMMEND> the number of IFICs in English (128) is more than three times larger than the number of IFICs in Spanish (40). What we find more interesting, though, are the differences in the distribution of the four semantic categories of IFICs per each illocutionary act across languages. In the case of English <RECOMMEND>, the distribution of IFICs is quite balanced. More importantly, volitional constructions notably outnumber those in Spanish where the majority of IFICs are classified as evaluative constructions. It could be said that by addressing readers' wants or needs overtly, the recommendation is worded in such a way that it feels as if it cannot -nor want to- be missed, without being any kind of imposition or instruction (34). This, in turn, builds rapport with the reader, strengthening persuasion. In Spanish, in contrast, the recommendation is conveyed in a more impersonal way by highlighting the positive outcome of the recommended course of action (35).

(34) *If your berries are too tart,* ***you will want to*** *increase the sugar.* (volitional)

(35) ***Mejor si*** *esta operación la realizamos con algo de antelación.* (evaluative)
(**Better if** we do this operation a bit in advance)

Regarding <SUGGEST>, English favours sensory-cognitive constructions (36) which again address readers openly in instances of dialogic interaction typical of persuasive promotional discourse (Izquierdo & Peréz Blanco 2023). In turn, Spanish <SUGGEST> is mainly expressed by constructions revolving around a lexical cue in declarative sentences that present alternatives in a more informative than emotion-laden utterance (37).

(36) ***Shall we*** *get together and* ***have*** *one?*

(37) ***Otra opción*** *si no tenemos crema de vinagre balsámico es emulsionar la vinagreta añadiendo una cucharadita de miel.*
(**Another option** if we do not have balsamic vinegar cream is to emulsify the dressing by adding a teaspoon of honey)

More importantly, regardless of the quantitative differences in the distribution of the four types of IFICs across illocutionary acts and languages, the constructions found raise awareness of how fuzzy the boundaries between the illocutionary acts of <RECOMMEND> and <SUGGEST> may become. Only by looking closely at the collocational patterns of use is it possible to pinpoint co-textual elements that foreground one function over the other.

For instance, evaluative IFICs are largely found conveying <RECOMMEND> but also, in a smaller number of cases, they perform the illocutionary act <SUGGEST>. If the presence of a positive evaluative item is common to both functions, then, what is different? We have observed that <RECOMMEND> usually takes a superlative form (38) or an intensifying device (39) in normative-like utterances that are felt as convincing and giving readers no room for choice or disagreement.

(38) *Maris Pipers are **the best** potatoes to use for chips as they're consistently better throughout the year.*

(39) ***Es muy importante que** el caldo esté muy caliente cuando lo añadamos a la paella.*
(It is very important that the stock is very hot when we add it to the paella)

On the other hand, the interpretation <SUGGEST> is prompted by linguistic devices, such as downtoners, as in examples (40) and (41) below, or clauses targeting a particular audience or having a specific purpose(s). These constructions are read as a good way of doing something among other possible alternatives, but not necessarily the best or only one.

(40) *If looking to pair this cheese (...), a light Somerset cider would **work well**.*

(41) *Es una receta que puede **venir bien** para los postres de Navidad.*
(It is a recipe **that might work** for Christmas desserts)

<SUGGEST> volitional constructions are distinguished from volitional <RECOMMEND> because they co-occur with phrases encoding options as in (42) or as part of a conditional clause that contains a verb of intention or volition (43).

(42) ***You will want to** enjoy this Chardonnay alone or enjoy it with chicken, pasta with cream sauces, richer seafood or other...*

(43) *...añadimos las rebanadas (**si queremos**, yo esta vez no le he puesto).*
(...we add the toasts (**if we want**, this time I have not added any)

Finally, sensory-cognitive constructions are easier to identify as <RECOMMEND> or <SUGGEST> since their formal realisation differs considerably. On the one hand, sensory-cognitive <SUGGEST> looks like invitations or offers to taste or try a product, drink or meal. In general terms, the verb semantics does not denote a cooking action but a sensorial experience. The formal realisation may take shape as a rhetorical question (see (19) above) or as an imperative as in *Give this simple dish a try*. This kind of suggestions are found in rhetorical moves in CLANES with a more promotional than instructive function (see Pizarro Sánchez and Ortego Antón, this volume). On the other hand, sensory-cognitive <RECOMMEND> has been identified in instances of *I would* where the writer, as a source or authority and expertise, gives tips on how to cook or serve a meal as in (5), and even offers readers cautious advice through expressions like *make sure to…* or *be sure to…* which seem to be half-way between a recommendation and an instruction.

We propose that all the observations above answer research question 2, enquiring about the co-textual information that motivates the interpretation of an utterance as <RECOMMEND> and/or <SUGGEST>. Yet, when doing pragmatic analysis, we learn that "the relationship between linguistic form and function is characterised by ambiguity and unpredictability and it is the unfolding of dynamic contextual elements that facilitates the correct understanding of the function a particular form fulfils" (Rühlemann & Clancy 2018: 244). This unpredictability hinders automatisation and, therefore, retrievability of pragmatic units for corpus analysis.

6.4. *Pragmatic annotation: chance or challenge?*

At first glance, corpus pragmatic annotation is a *challenge* if we take into account that "*meaning*, as a defining feature of what pragmatics is concerned with, is not seen as a stable counterpart of linguistic form. Rather it is dynamically generated in the process of using language"[6] (Verschueren 1999: 10). However, in analysing naturally-occurring discourses, the surrounding co-text often points to the intended meaning of an utterance, so if we are able to pin down recurrent patterns in as wide a context as possible, we at least have a *chance* to attempt pragmatic annotation. Rühlemann (2010) asserts that "corpus evidence (….) suggests a view of speech act expressions which emphasises the role less of inferences but more of collocational patterning" (p. 297). In this regard, we have benefited from the multi-layered tagging CLANES is equipped with to look for regular combinations of the various tags that, as a unit, do as evidence of meaning (as if inferential cues). In other words, the

6 Italics in the author's original words.

illocutionary indicating marker or node of the utterance together with metalinguistic information of its surrounding co-text may be translated into a functional tag for pragmatic annotation.

Drawing on part of speech tagging and semantic annotation based on USAS (UCREL Semantic Analysis System, Rayson et al. 2004), Rabadán et al. (2021) identified some typical patterns for <RECOMMEND> and <SUGGEST>. Capitalising on their findings, our aim has been to continue to build up expert linguistic knowledge, by considering other function-related metapatterns, especially focusing on those constructions prone to ambiguity that pose a greater challenge for automatisation.

Metalinguistic patterns that code <RECOMMEND> usually include as a recurrent distinctive feature an evaluative adjective semantically tagged as A5.1+ Evaluation: good/bad; O4.2 Judgement of appearance; X3.1+ Sensory: taste, or X3.5 Sensory: smell or a superlative form as in example (44) which reads as follows:

(44) Maris NP NULL_2 Pipers NP F1_L3 are VBP O2 **the DT NULL_2 best JJS X3.1_X3.5_O4.3_I1 potatoes NNS F1_L3 to TO T1.1 use VB A1.1.1_A1.5 for IN NULL_2 chips** NNS F1 as IN F2_L3_B3 they PP F2_O1.2_B3 ’re VBP NULL_2 consistently RB NULL_2 better JJR X3.1_X3.5_O4.3_I1 throughout IN A3+ the DT NULL_2 year NN T1.

Additional <RECOMMEND> patterns found in CLANES feature adverbs of degree, that is intensifiers or boosters (A13.3), sometimes followed by an adjective of importance semantically tagged as A11.1+

(45) **Es VSfin A3+_L1_Z5_X2.4 muy ADV A13.3 importante ADJ A11.1+ que** CQUE Z5_Z8 el ART Z5 caldo NC F2 esté VEfin A3+_M8 muy ADV A13.3 caliente ADJ O4.6+ cuando CSUBX Z5_T1.1 lo PPC Z8m añadamos VLfin A2.1_A1.8+ a PREP Z5 la ART Z5 paella NC S6_A7+
(It is very important that the stock is very hot when we add it to the paella)

In (45) above, the it-clause (*Es muy importante que…*) frames the recommended course of action.

We have also found patterns where <RECOMMEND> can be retrieved from the meaning of obligation and necessity semantically tagged in USAS as S6+:

(46) …and CC L3_O1.1 **should MD S6+** drop VB M2 them PP A9+ a DT NULL_2 line NN A1.1.1 **if IN O4.3_O1 you PP I2.2_A1.1.1 need VBP S6+** further JJR B1_O1.1_F1 information

In (46), the meaning of necessity is conveyed both by the modal and the verb ‘need’ preceded by a condition marker. The automatic pragmatic labelling as <RECOMMEND> of examples (44) to (46) could be less problematic as the function seems to match one or various metalinguistic components or strings key in conveying one given pragmatic meaning. The same can be said for metapatterns identified for <SUGGEST> which usually revolve around a modal indicating possibility either in a passive construction or active-voice with a ‘you’ subject (47). The verb needs to be semantically tagged as A1.1.1 General actions or A2.1 Affect: Modify, change.

(47) **May MD A7+ be VB O2 baked** VBN A2.1_O4.6_F1 ahead RB O4.6-, ,PUNC **if IN O4.3_O1 desired VBN O4.6**

However, things may become fuzzier. Such is the case of example (48) featuring positive evaluation (*well*, A5.1) but in a <SUGGEST> utterance.

(48) ...**if IN O4.3_O1 looking VBG T1.3 to TO T1.1 pair VB S3.1_F1_A4.1** this DT A2.1_A6.3 cheese NN F1 **with IN NULL_2 any DT NULL_2 drinks NNS** A1.1.1_A9+_F2 then RB NULL_2 a DT NULL_2 light JJ O4.3_O4.1 Somerset NP NULL_2 cider NN F2 **would MD A7+ work VB I3.1well RB A5.1+**. SENT PUNC

Close reading and manual annotation as done in this chapter favour the suggestive interpretation given the preceding context (looking for options for cheese and drinks pairing). But the string is so long that it would be unfeasible to ascertain a valid and replicable metapattern that translates all the slots into an automatic pragmatic tag. Yet, we believe that the modal meaning of *would* (MD A7+) has a downtoning effect of the positive evaluation, then, facilitating the interpretation of <SUGGEST>. In contrast, in example (49) the superlative *work best* in the co-text of a contrast is used to recommend one pairing in particular.

(49) ...would MD A1.1.1_F1 pair VB S3.1_F1_A4.1 it PP N5 with IN NULL_2 many JJ NULL_2 beers NNS F2, , PUNC but CC I2.2_A1.1.1 a DT NULL_2 pale JJ O4.3_X3.1 ale NN F2 would A7+ **work VB I3.1 best RBS A13.2_A5.1+++**

Another example of <SUGGEST> in a challenging context is illustrated by example (50). The volitional construction *you will want to* has been identified in our study as conveying <RECOMMEND> but the list of options in the unfolding discourse lead clearly to the interpretation of <SUGGEST>. Here the metalinguistic pattern translates as:

(50) **You PP Z8 will MD T1.1.3. want X7+ to** TO T1.1 savor VB E2 this DT A2.1_ A6.3 Chardonnay NP NULL_2 alone RB A1.1.1 A10 **or** CC Z5 enjoy VB A1.1.1 E2+ it PP N5 **with** IN Z5 chicken NN F1 L2 F4, , PUNC pasta NN F1 **with** IN Z5 cream NN F1 O1.2 O4.3 sauces NNS F1, , PUNC richer JJR X3 O4 A5.1 seafood NN F1 **or CC** Z5 **2 other** JJ A6.1-

In such a string we find the verbs of liking *savor* and *enjoy* (E2) taking as a complement a noun phrase or a prepositional phrase where the head noun is semantically tagged as food. The disjunctive coordination *or*, the adjective *other* (tagged as A6.1 Comparing) and commas (,PUNC) signpost the alternatives given. All together in combination make up one more replicable metapattern of <SUGGEST> worth considering in automatisation attempts.

All in all, the analysis above demonstrates the way in which we can translate the collocational patterns (form) into pragmatic metapatterns (function) to automatise annotation. In other words, the response to research question 3 is that all this language expert knowledge could be translated into a pragmatic annotation scheme to test automatic annotation. This task, however, falls within the realm of computational engineering (see Sanjurjo-González, this volume; and Sanjurjo-González et al., this volume).

7. Conclusion

This chapter has interpreted CLANES data from a pragmatic perspective, to identify regular collocational patterns that prompt <RECOMMEND> and <SUGGEST>, which are representative illocutionary forces within the context of promotional discourse, instantiated as online food descriptions and culinary recipes. All the concordances retrieved have been manually analysed to annotate their pragmatic force. In this way, the case study proves that written data is suitable for corpus pragmatics, and that, aware of the communicative purpose of the text type, the co-textual information around the key word or illocutionary indicating marker in context is a valid cue for pragmatic inference. In fact, the semantics of an item in the utterance, or its grammatical category, might make a difference in pragmatic interpretation and explain why a given utterance does <RECOMMEND> instead of <SUGGEST> or the other way round, as shown by many of the examples given. The study has taken a double contrastive perspective: across languages and across illocutionary acts or pragmatic functions.

On a cross-linguistic note, the interpretation of the data points at an even distribution of both illocutionary acts in English, while in Spanish, a larger number of utterances perform <SUGGEST>. On a cross-functional note, <RECOMMEND> shows a greater array of manifestations than <SUGGEST>. Overlapping these two dimensions of contrast, a conventionalised strategy of realisation is key in both English and Spanish <SUGGEST>; however, this strategy governs the realisation of <SUGGEST> almost single-handedly. There are also conventionalised strategies of realisation in English and in Spanish <RECOMMEND>, but the larger difference between the languages is that Spanish <RECOMMEND> seems to prefer a direct strategy, while English <RECOMMEND> seems to prefer indirect strategies. Our study has demonstrated that linguistic choices may be due to both idiomatic patterning and writer/reader meaning at the same time.

One limitation of this case study is that it does not report on rhetorical realisation. However, we believe that the functional move an utterance appears in is meaning-making or, in other words, may account for a different pragmatic interpretation of formally similar patterns. Future investigations should improve this study by operationalizing the rhetorical level of language description in the multi-patterns 44–50. Future avenues of research are many, both descriptive and applied, and with this study we have taken a first step into both.

Isabel Pizarro Sánchez and María Teresa Ortego Antón

Unpacking the rhetorical structure of online food and drink descriptions

1. Introduction

Genre knowledge plays an essential role in producing texts that meet the conventions and expectations of specific discourse communities. This knowledge involves understanding the genre's rhetorical structure, i.e., how its moves are organised according to their purpose (Bhatia 1993; Swales 1990, 2004), and a sound command of its main linguistic features (Biber et al. 2007). It is particularly relevant in the agri-food sector, where product descriptions' quality can influence marketing activities' success and, consequently, export performance. Therefore, it is crucial to understand and use rhetorical structures effectively when writing and translating in the context of international trade and digital marketing. Writers and translators should have a contrastive knowledge of the source and target rhetorical structures, as they need to adapt them to the expectations and preferences of the target audience by producing a text that fulfils the communicative purpose in the target linguistic and cultural context (Hatim & Mason 1990). As Bhatia (2004) argues, genre-based approaches can improve the effectiveness of intercultural communication, especially in promotional genres, and the genre under study—online food and drink descriptions—falls into this category, according to Bhatia's (1993) definition.

The agri-food sector significantly impacts the gross domestic product (GDP) and export revenues of different countries. For instance, the Spanish agri-food industry accounts for approximately 11% of the country's GDP and generates more than €70 billion in annual exports (MAPA

2024). Similarly, countries such as Mexico, Argentina, and Chile have increased their agri-food exports, where this sector now contributes between 8% and 15% to their respective GDPs, as reported by the World Bank (2024). Given that English is the *lingua franca* in international business contexts (Nickerson 2005), and therefore in international trade, the ability to write persuasive product descriptions in English has become a key factor in the success of agri-food exports, as these texts facilitate communication between producers and international buyers.

Online descriptions, the core element of e-catalogues and digital marketing platforms, are a distinct genre characterised by a specific rhetorical structure and a dual function: describing the product characteristics and persuading potential buyers to purchase. This dual purpose is reflected in the structure of the text, which can be analysed in terms of moves and steps as proposed by Swales (1990) and developed by scholars such as Bhatia (1993) and Biber et al. (2007), among others. Moves, in this context, are functional units that contribute to the main communicative purpose of the genre. Each move may consist of several steps, which are smaller rhetorical units that work together to achieve the function of the move and genre (Biber et al. 2007).

Considering the significant economic contribution of the agri-food sector and the necessity for effective communication in international trade, this study examines the rhetorical structure of English and Spanish online food and drink descriptions for a range of products, including herbal teas, wine, olive oil, cheese, dried meats, and baked products. This research aims to analyse the CLANES corpus (Controlled LANguage English Spanish), an English-Spanish comparable corpus of texts covering these products (see Sanjurjo-González, this volume), in order to a) compare the rhetorical structure across various products in each language, building on previous research, to determine if there are significant differences related to product type, and quantify the frequency and distribution of specific rhetorical moves across different product categories and languages, b) establish a common rhetorical structure for food and drink promotional texts in each language, c) describe how the moves and steps of the rhetorical structure shape the overall communicative purpose of the text, and, finally d) contribute to the development of a methodology for rhetorical annotation.

Specifically, we hypothesise that while English and Spanish online food and drink descriptions share some common rhetorical patterns, reflecting both descriptive and persuasive functions, there may also be differences in cultural expectations, market norms, or linguistic conventions. By identifying the effective rhetorical strategies used in both languages, we offer practical linguistic data that can be applied to pre-AI writing tool applications (see Labrador & Ramón, this volume) and genre-specific writing GPTs to assist in creating these texts (see Sanjurjo-González et al., this volume). Thus, this research contributes to genre analysis by providing detailed linguistic data on the rhetorical structure of agri-food genres through move analysis, developing a methodology for rhetorical annotation.

2. Move analysis and rhetorical annotation in academic and professional genres

2.1. Move analysis and rhetorical annotation

Corpus annotation is essential for subsequent analysis, providing the framework for extracting and interpreting patterns from the annotated data. Developing rigorous annotation methodologies that adhere to the field standards is imperative for all corpus annotation projects (Leech 1997). Several levels of annotation can be found, corresponding to different linguistic categories. These include part-of-speech (PoS), phonetic, prosodic, syntactic, semantic, discoursal, and pragmatic annotation (see Sanjurjo-González, this volume). While extensive research has been conducted on various types of corpus annotations, the specific application of rhetorical tagging based on Swales' (1990, 2004) and Bhatia's (1993) move analysis framework remains an ongoing interest and development in corpus linguistics. This study aims to contribute to this growing body of research by developing a gold standard for rhetorical tagging tailored for food and drink descriptions.

Although numerous corpus linguistic tools are available for automating syntactic and lexical annotation, options for rhetorical annotation are more limited and less frequently used, primarily because they have been designed for specific genres or fields. Notable examples are AntMover (Anthony & Lashkia 2003: 192), which is "optimised for only a small number of text types in science and engineering related fields," namely research article abstracts in computer science, and the Research Writing Tutor (RWT), which "identifies the rhetorical structure of research articles (RA) in terms of communicative moves and functional steps" (Cotos & Pendar 2016:93). Both tools use supervised learning techniques based on a given set of previously annotated data as input and achieve average accuracies ranging from 68% (AntMover) to 73% (RWT). Nevertheless, introducing and implementing large language models (LLMs) in linguistic research, specifically in corpus annotation, is redefining corpus research methodology, changing corpora annotation and analysis. In this regard, it is worth noting the findings of a recent study by Kim and Lu (2024), which explores the potential of applying artificial intelligence (AI) to automate rhetorical annotation. The study found that fine-tuned AI models, specifically ChatGPT, are more accurate than other automated genre analysis tools, including AntMover and Research Writing Tutor (see Sanz-Valdivieso & López-Arroyo, this volume).

Move analysis has predominantly focused on the English language and has been more extensively explored in academic genres than professional ones. Most research refers to distinct sections of RAs (Posteguillo 1999; Samraj 2002; Kanoksilapatham 2005; Basturkmen 2012; Tseng 2018; Jin et al. 2020), abstracts (Lorés 2004; Pho 2008; Blake 2021), university lectures (Thompson 1994), lab reports (Parkinson 2017), grant proposals (Connor & Upton 2004; Cotos 2019), etc. It has also been applied to various genres in professional contexts, including direct mail letters in business discourse (Upton & Connor 2001; Upton 2002), journalistic reported versions of research articles (Nwogu 1991), Directors' reports (Rabadán et al. 2021b), and technical brochures (Ramón & Labrador 2015), among others. However, its application in these professional areas remains limited.

Similarly, much of the focus in contrastive move analysis has also been on academic genres such as RAs, abstracts, and theses. These analyses often involve comparisons between English and other languages, reflecting the dominance of English as the primary language of academic communication. Examples of these are Chinese-English RAs introductions (Loi & Evans 2010), English-Spanish PhD thesis introductions (Soler-Monreal et al. 2011), English-Montenegrin university lecture introductions (Živković 2022), English-Brazilian Portuguese book reviews (Junqueira 2013), and English-Spanish food science abstracts

(Del Saz Rubio 2019). Professional genres have also been studied from a contrastive approach, covering a range of topics such as English-Italian sales promotion letters (Vergaro 2004) and corporate social responsibility reports (Bondi 2016), English-Spanish instruction manuals for household appliances (Cristobalena 2015), web forms (Jiménez-Crespo 2010), and advertisements of electronic products (Labrador et al. 2014), to name but a few.

Among these professional genres, those related to food advertising are of particular interest due to the prominence of the food industry as a major advertiser across all sectors. In 2022, global expenditure on food and drink advertising worldwide was projected to reach US$1.62 billion, representing a significant proportion of the advertising market (Statista 2023). In this field, food product descriptions, such as those found in online catalogues, are an interesting genre, as they share covert and overt marketing features. It is, therefore, particularly important for the food industry to understand the rhetorical structure of this genre, as well as the contrastive differences between English and Spanish. This cross-linguistic knowledge may affect how genres are adapted to the different linguistic and cultural markets.

Most of the previously mentioned studies are based on small corpora due to the labour-intensive nature of applying top-down analytical approaches, including move analysis, to large corpora (Upton & Cohen 2009). Consequently, the application of rhetorical move analysis has often been constrained by the need for manual annotation, a time-consuming process that restricts its applicability to smaller corpora. Despite the recognised utility of rhetorical annotation, its applicability continues to be constrained by corpus size in current research, as noted by Casal and Kessler (2023). Although there have been significant advances in linguistic tools and computing over the past 15 years, the process of rhetorical tagging has continued to require manual identification and electronic annotation of move and step types based on their rhetorical functions, which involves "making qualitative judgments on the communicative purposes of different parts of a text" (Upton & Cohen 2009: 600). However, as mentioned earlier, the situation is rapidly changing due to AI and LLMs, which are transforming traditional research methods, including corpus annotation. This disruptive technological advancement has the potential to facilitate more efficient and automated methods of analysis by incorporating expert rhetorical knowledge into automated annotation of extensive corpora (see Sanz-Valdivieso & López-Arroyo, this volume).

2.2. Previous research on English-Spanish contrastive rhetoric in the domain of food and drink

Several studies have examined the rhetorical structure of food and drink descriptions, frequently using a contrastive approach between English and Spanish. These studies can be divided into two groups: those focusing on food products, including cheese, dried meats, and baked goods, and those examining beverages, such as herbal teas and wine. The results of these investigations, outlined in the following paragraphs, offer evidence suggesting the existence of a shared rhetorical structure in food and drink product descriptions, which, as previously stated in the introduction, constitutes the object of our investigation. This line of research is of great importance for understanding the differences in rhetorical structures across languages.

Labrador and Ramón (2015) analyse the cheese descriptions genre, establishing its rhetorical structure and the lexico-grammatical features of each move and step in English. Building on this research, Labrador and Ramón (2020) present a cheese description generator (CDG) developed to assist Spanish professionals in writing promotional cheese descriptions. Their corpus-based analyses identify seven prototypical moves that form the rhetorical structure of the genre. Similarly, Ortego Antón (2019, 2020) presents an English-Spanish contrastive analysis of dried meat descriptions, focusing on their rhetorical structure. One of the main aims of her research is to identify the typical rhetorical patterns in each language, highlighting similarities and differences. Her research reveals that while the rhetorical moves and steps overlap in both languages, there are variations in their sequential order, frequency of use, and length measured by word count. The linguistic data were used to develop a writing generator for English descriptive meat product cards.

López-Arroyo and Sanz-Valdivieso (2020) examine another food-related genre: olive oil tasting notes. Their study investigates the rhetorical structure, phraseology, and semantics of these tasting notes in English, focusing on lexical chunks. The analysis reveals a rhetorical structure consisting of six moves and seventeen steps, similar to that identified by López-Arroyo and Roberts (2014a, 2015b) for wine-tasting notes. Finally,

Pizarro Sánchez and Pérez Ruiz (2024) analyse the rhetorical structure of online baked product descriptions, including cookies, cakes, muffins, crackers, and bread from an English-Spanish contrastive approach, and investigate the use of adjectives as a persuasive element used in this genre.

Concerning the rhetorical structure of beverages, López-Arroyo and Roberts (2014a, 2015b) describe the structure of wine-tasting notes in English and Spanish and identify five different moves with various steps, as a previous stage to their analysis of the key nouns and descriptors of the move 'Taste' and its steps. Izquierdo and Pérez Blanco (2020) examine herbal tea promotional texts (HTPTs), a subgenre of online food descriptions, identifying their rhetorical macrostructure and the main persuasive linguistic features. These findings provide the basis for developing a writing tool specifically designed to assist professionals in creating effective promotional texts (Izquierdo & Pérez Blanco 2020). Based on this work, Pérez Blanco and Izquierdo (2022) compare the emotional engagement in English and Spanish herbal tea advertisements as a promotional marketing strategy.

The investigation of genre-specific rhetorical structures lays the groundwork for further monolingual or contrastive analyses of linguistic features within each rhetorical component. It provides valuable linguistic information for developing genre-specific writing tools, such as the generators designed by the ACTRES research group for the English-Spanish language pair (see Labrador & Ramón, this volume).

3. Materials and methods

The analysis of moves and steps was conducted through a corpus-based approach using the English/Spanish comparable corpus CLANES. Corpus-based methodologies offer significant advantages in contrastive studies, providing a systematic, empirical, and data-driven approach to linguistic analysis and enabling the identification of patterns, similarities, and differences across languages (see Sanjurjo-González, this volume). Corpus-based methods enable researchers to examine real-world language usage in diverse contexts, offering a more precise and comprehensive representation of linguistic features.

Since rhetorical annotation remains infrequent, the ACTRES research group has developed a rhetorical annotation tool, the ACTRES Tagger,[1] and a browser, the ACTRES Browser.[2] This browser automatically extracts linguistic and statistical data from the annotated corpus. The tools offer advanced analytical techniques, including concordance and frequency analysis, thus integrating traditional rhetorical analysis with modern corpus linguistics.

3.1. CLANES Corpus

3.1.1. Features

CLANES is a bilingual comparable corpus encompassing English and Spanish texts in the food and drink industry compiled by the ACTRES research group. This corpus consists of a finite collection of texts sourced from the web. It is structured into seven distinct subcorpora, each representing different genres and textual varieties related to this domain. The texts included are carefully selected to ensure relevance to the specific field, genre, and variety, as emphasised by Corpas Pastor (2008: 91).

A key feature of CLANES is its comparability. According to the EAGLES guidelines (Sinclair 1996), a comparable corpus consists of similar texts across more than one language or linguistic variety, facilitating cross-linguistic analysis. This aspect ensures that the corpus provides an ideal foundation for contrastive linguistic studies, as it allows for the identification of linguistic patterns and phenomena across languages within a shared context.

Regarding the size, the total word count of the CLANES corpus is approximately 1.8 million, distributed across both English and Spanish texts. Table 15 offers a detailed breakdown of the corpus composition by subcorpus and language. The corpus is annotated on multiple levels—PoS, rhetorically, pragmatically and semantically—enhancing its utility for in-depth linguistic analysis across different dimensions of language (see Sanjurjo-González, this volume).

---

1 https://actres.unileon.es/web/en/tagger.html

2 https://actres.unileon.es/web/en/browser.html

Table 15: CLANES subcorpora and number of words in each language.

Name	Tokens (EN)	Tokens (ES)
BiTeX: Culinary recipes	307,161	275,115
C-FITECVI: Wine technical sheets and C- FIVI: Wine tasting notes	124,446	220,061
C-GDQ: Cheese descriptions	135,213	145,254
ACTEaS_Promo: Promotional texts for herbal teas	130,046	125,218
C-GEFEM: Sausages and cured meats	97,078	50,181
C-BakedGoods: Bakery and pastry descriptions	111,143	99,511
Total	**905,087**	**915,340**

By utilising CLANES, researchers can gain insights into cross-linguistic differences and similarities in the domain of food and drink, benefiting from the dataset's structured, annotated, and comparable nature. The subcorpora within CLANES share a communicative function, consisting primarily of online food and drink descriptions. The focus on this specific textual genre ensures the homogeneity of the corpus and allows for a more precise analysis of the rhetorical and lexico-grammatical features in these texts.

It is important to note that the BiTeX subcorpus, which contains culinary recipes, has not been considered in analysing the rhetorical structure of the product description genre. Culinary recipes constitute a distinct textual genre with its own communicative purpose—providing step-by-step instructions for preparing a dish. This instructional function is reflected in their unique rhetorical structure and lexico-grammatical patterns. Recipes tend to follow a fixed sequence of instructions and rely on imperative verbs and specific quantifiers. In contrast, product descriptions often use descriptive and evaluative language to highlight the attributes of the products. Given their distinctive nature, culinary recipes were excluded from the rhetorical analysis to maintain the genre-specific focus of the study.

3.1.2. Compilation protocol

The CLANES corpus was compiled following a four-phase protocol, which has been employed in previous studies (Seghiri 2017; Ortego Antón 2024b, 2024c; Sánchez Carnicer 2022; Peñuelas Gil & Ortego Antón 2024; among others):

1. Search: Texts were collected from various agri-food websites, ensuring a wide range of products and companies were represented in Spanish and English.
2. Download: Webpages were manually downloaded and saved in HTML on a local computer.
3. Formatting: The downloaded HTML files were converted into TXT format using UTF-8 encoding to facilitate analysis using corpus management software.
4. Storage: Each file was systematically coded and stored in separate English (EN) and Spanish (ES) folders. The coding system followed a specific structure based on subcorpus, product type, source, date, domain, and language. For example, in the C-GEFEM subcorpus, files were numbered (e.g., 001, 002) and tagged with codes indicating the product category (e.g., DM for dried meats), the source (e.g., ws for web-sourced), the company (e.g., MR for Morrisons), the download date (yymmdd), the domain (e.g., Foodie), and the language (EN for English or ES for Spanish). This coding structure ensures clarity and allows for future expansion of the corpus. An example of a file code might be 001DMwsMR160624FoodieEN.

The corpus achieved qualitative representativeness through a compilation protocol designed to ensure the inclusion of online food and drink descriptions of different products from different geographical areas. Quantitative representativeness was determined using the ReCor software (Seghiri 2006; Corpas Pastor & Seghiri 2010), a statistical tool that determines the minimum number of words required to represent the essential terminology of a given genre.

Having outlined the protocol employed to compile CLANES, the following section details the methodology used to analyse the corpus. A top-down approach, as proposed by Biber et al. (2007: 13), was adopted to identify the rhetorical structure of the genre.

3.2. Identification of the rhetorical structure

To identify the primary moves and steps of the genre, an initial pilot-coding test was conducted following the methodology outlined by Upton and Cohen (2009: 59). A specific tagset was developed for each field—i.e. baked goods, wine, dried meats, cheese and herbal teas—and a random sample of ten texts each was manually tagged. This process enabled the researchers to ensure a shared understanding of move definitions and how moves and steps were realised in the texts. It also helped identify additional moves and steps that had not been initially considered, leading to the redefinition of categories where necessary. The coding protocol was revised to resolve any discrepancies revealed by the inter-rater reliability check or by the newly identified moves and steps, and problematic areas were recoded accordingly.

Next, using the ACTRES Tagger (Figure 16), the various moves and steps within each text were annotated. Dividing texts into moves and steps is a complex task, as these functional elements do not always have clear boundaries, such as punctuation marks. A range of formal hints was employed to address this issue, including content and linguistic clues, such as section headings, titles, subtitles, keywords, verbs, and non-verbal elements (e.g., bold or italicised text, layout). A functional-semantic approach was adopted for the annotation (Pizarro Sánchez & Pérez Ruiz 2024: 91).

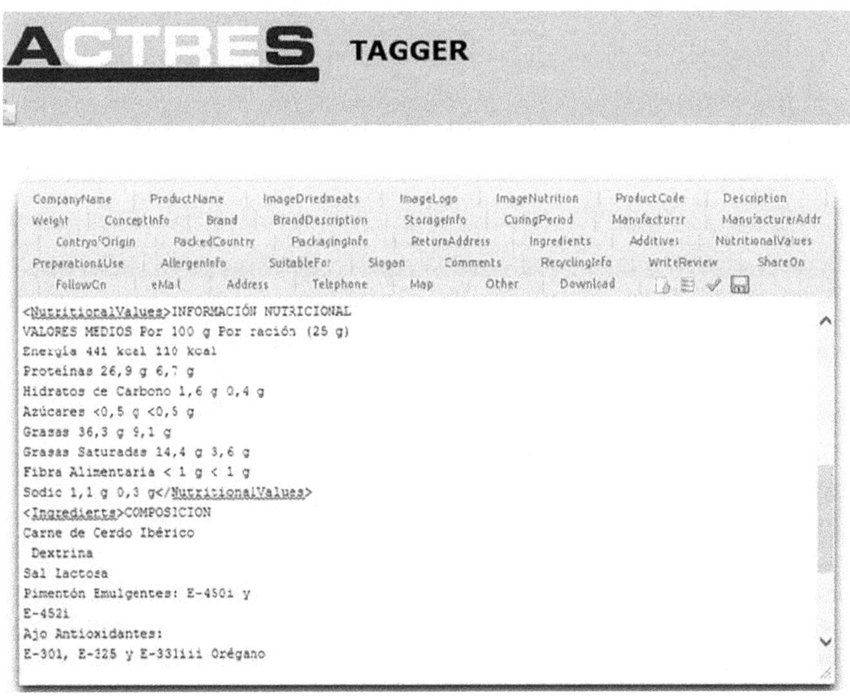

Figure 16: Screenshot of the ACTRES Tagger.

Although the tagging process was time-consuming and not fully automated, the coding, once electronically inserted using the ACTRES Tagger, could be reused with other linguistic analysis tools. Each move or step was subsequently retrieved using the ACTRES Browser, which provided concordance lines and statistical information, such as the frequency of use and the number of tokens, as illustrated in Figure 17.

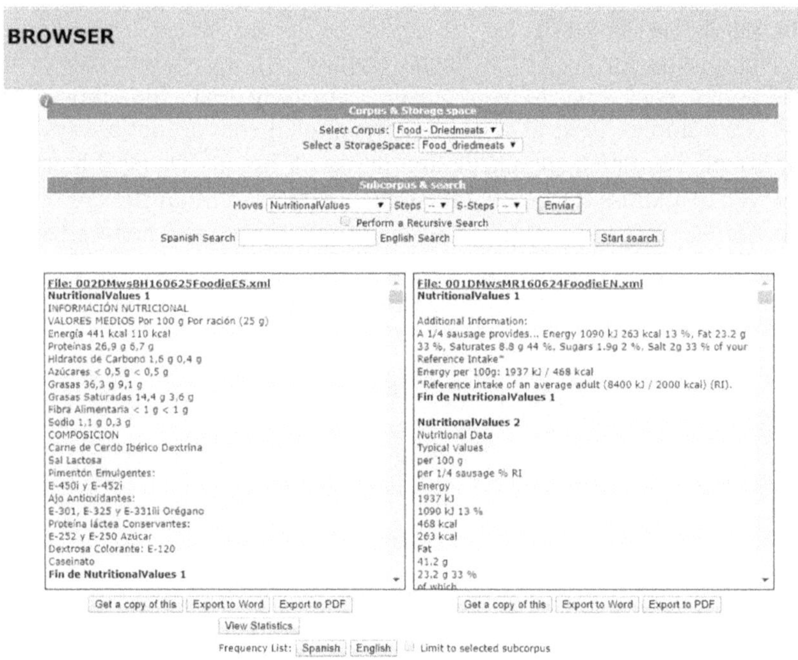

Figure 17: Search for the step <Nutritional Value> using the ACTRES Browser.

The ACTRES Browser enables researchers to examine the percentage of moves and steps in each annotated subcorpus, the occurrences of such moves and steps, and the percentage of texts containing these rhetorical structures. This allows for the identification of linguistic patterns associated with moves and steps, as well as the total number of words per move or step. The resulting data facilitated the development of a prototype rhetorical structure comprising moves and steps in both Spanish and English (Rabadán et al. 2016; López-Arroyo & Sanz-Valdivieso 2022; Pérez Blanco & Izquierdo 2022; Peñuelas Gil & Ortego Antón 2024; Pizarro Sánchez & Pérez Ruiz 2024; among others).

In terms of rhetorical patterns, the frequencies of occurrence (based on 100 files per language) were used to classify moves and steps into five categories: compulsory (>80%), high priority (80–60%), medium priority (59–40%), low priority (39–20%), and occasional (<20%). It is important to note that there is no universally agreed-upon threshold defining these categories (Connor 2000; Biber et al. 2007; López-Arroyo & Roberts 2014b; Rabadán 2016; Pizarro Sánchez 2017; Ortego Antón 2024a, 2024c; Pizarro Sánchez & Pérez Ruiz 2024). Similarities and differences in the use of moves and steps were contrasted, their frequency of use was determined, and the position of moves and steps within descriptions in both languages was established.

The latest subcorpora added to CLANES were annotated using the innovative tool OpenTagger, a user-friendly software developed by Sanjurjo-González and Andaluz-Pinedo (2021). OpenTagger is an open-source linguistic tagger written in JavaScript, which allows users to include various types of information in paragraphs, sentences, or words within a text. It is web-based, supports custom and multi-layered annotation, and is noted for its user-friendliness (see Figure 18 for a screenshot).

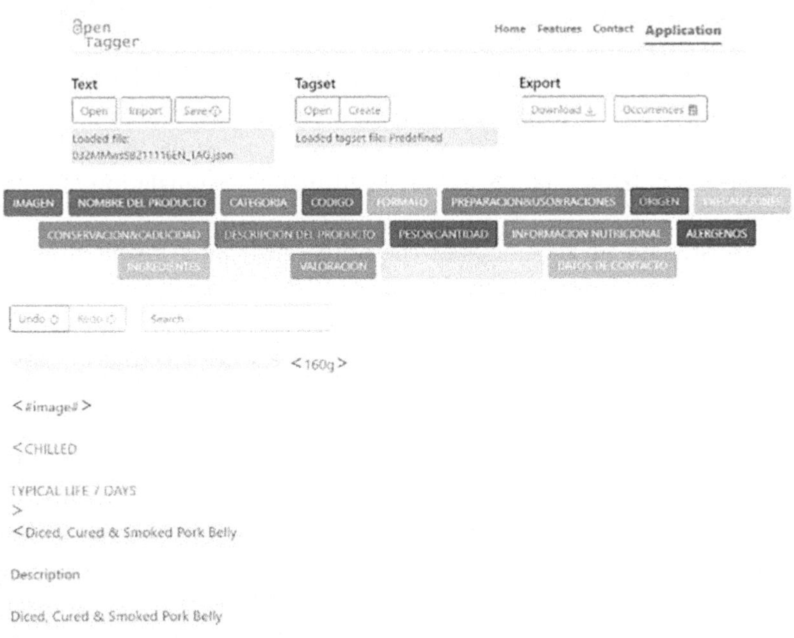

Figure 18: OpenTagger interface with the tagset for cured meats.

A tagset was first created using the protocol described above. This tagset was uploaded via the *Create* function, which allows users to manually introduce tags by selecting the *Visual* option and writing tags separated by semicolons or by choosing the *Text* option and writing a category per line. Once the tagset was prepared, the text was uploaded and manually labelled following the same procedure as with the ACTRES Tagger. Once the rhetorical structure was established for each subcorpus in CLANES in both Spanish and English, a gold standard was developed for universal application to food and drink descriptions.

3.3. Development of a rhetorical gold standard

After rhetorically annotating the English and Spanish subcorpora of each food and drink domain (cheese, wine, herbal teas, baked goods and dried meats), it became apparent that many of them share common moves, albeit designated by different terminologies. This inconsistency highlighted the need to develop a gold standard to provide a unified framework for categorising these rhetorical moves across languages and domains. Such a standard would facilitate greater consistency and comparability in the analysis of discourse in this domain. In addition, a rhetorical gold standard would streamline the annotation process, making it easier to annotate product descriptions. This would create a more systematic approach to studying these texts across languages, support research in applied linguistics, and enhance the effectiveness of machine translation and NLP systems.

The process of harmonising rhetorical structures involved several stages. Initially, the team developed broader categories of moves and steps based on the rhetorical structures identified for different product descriptions, classifying moves and steps accordingly. Some moves and steps were always present, others did not appear in some subcorpora, and some moves and steps were given different names. For instance, the move on nutritional values, which describes the nutritional properties of a product in terms of calories, sugars, fats, proteins, vitamins, etc., was considered a step (M3_S3 Nutritional Values) in the move M3 Main Product Description in C-BakedGoods. In contrast, in C-GEFEM and ACTEaS_Promo it was considered a move (M9 Nutritional values and M5 Nutritional facts, respectively). This information was not included in C-FIVI nor in C-GDQ. Consequently, adjustments were made, and a reclassification was undertaken. This reclassification process involved a careful comparison and review, ultimately establishing a gold rhetorical standard common to all.

After the manual establishment of correspondences, the CLANES corpus underwent an automated reannotation process. This process involved, for example, reassigning segments initially labelled as M3_S2 Ingredient in the C-Baked Goods corpus, M8 Ingredients in the C-GEFEM corpus, M2_S2 Ingredients in C-GDQ corpus or M2_S8 Ingredients in ACTEaS_Promo corpus to a newly designated tag, M5 Components. The automated reannotation of the CLANES corpus, in alignment with the rhetorical gold standard, enables researchers to extract quantitative data regarding the rhetorical structure of CLANES or its subcorpora through straightforward search queries, as depicted in Figures 19 and 20.

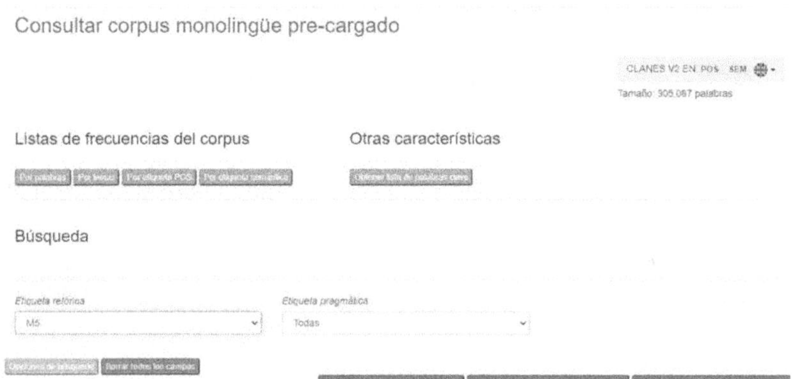

Figure 19: Example of a rhetorical search in ACM.

ACM currently only allows searches by moves, not by steps. Implementations are planned to enable searches by steps and display them embedded in a specific move. For the time being, the search results offer the move and the pragmatic category associated with it, providing a more comprehensive view of the data.

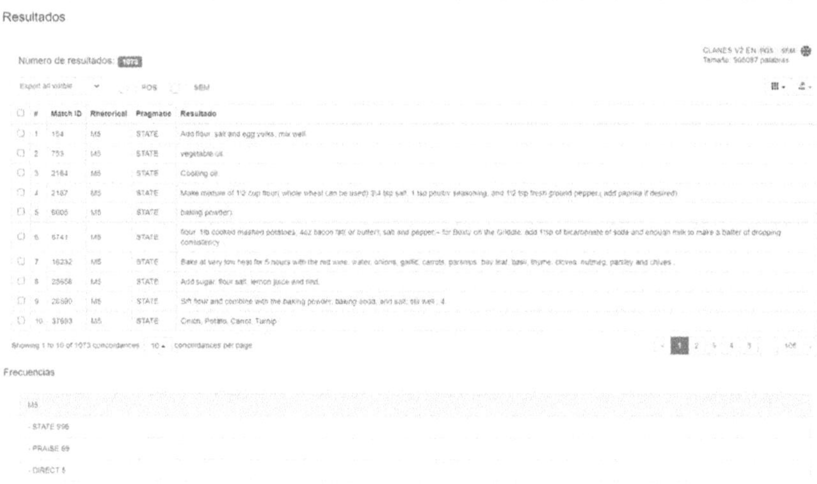

Figure 20: Excerpt of search results using the M5 rhetorical tag in ACM.

4. Rhetorical gold standard

Following the procedure outlined earlier, the moves and steps for each sub-corpus (C-FIVI, C-FITECVI, C-GDQ, ACTEaS_Promo, C-GEFEM, and C-BakedGoods) were meticulously classified into broader categories and correspondences were established. The result is illustrated in Table 16.

Table 16: Rhetorical gold standard proposal.

Moves	Steps
M1 ProdPres (product presentation)	
M2 ProdDesc (product description)	
M3 BackInfo	
M4 TechInfo	M4_S1 Nutrition facts
	M4_S2 Dietary requirements
	M4_S3 Equipment
	M4_S4 Contact details
	M4_S5 Product tracking/ Quality control
	M4_S6 Recycling info

Moves	**Steps**
M5 Components	
M6 Procedure	
M7 (Att)goal/ Result/ End-prod	M7_S1 Serving suggestions
	M7_S2 Pairing
	M7_S3 Storage
M8 Product liability waiver/ disclaimer	

The rhetorical gold standard consists of eight moves, some of which encompass several steps, which we will now outline in detail, providing examples extracted from CLANES using ACM.

4.1. M1 ProdPres (product presentation)

This move includes data about the product name, images of the product, the packaging, the code, the weight, the company name, a slogan, a video, opinions, links to social media, and flavour data.

Table 17: Example of *M1 ProdPres* in C-GDQ.

Language	**Move**	**Pragmatic**	**Left context**	**Result**	**Right context**
EN	M1	STATE	*Colston Bassett*	*Stilton*	.
ES	M1	STATE	*Crema de*	*queso*	*de Valdeón Garganta del Cares.* (Valdeón Garganta del Cares cream cheese.)

The results presented in Table 17 highlight the occurrence of *M1 ProdPress* in both English (EN) and Spanish (ES) within product descriptions, where it introduces specific product information, including brand names and descriptions. This alignment across languages indicates the universality of this rhetorical move in establishing product identity despite cultural and linguistic differences. Consequently, the findings demonstrate how M1 is essential in online food and drink descriptions.

4.2. M2 ProdDesc (product description)

As its name suggests, this move encompasses information about the product descriptions, including features, promotional details, conceptual information, tasting notes, flavour characteristics, marketing details, wine-tasting sheets, etc.

Table 18: Example of *M2 ProdDesc* in C-BakedGoods.

Language	Move	Pragmatic	Left context	Result	Right context
EN	M2	STATE	*Crunchie Rocks are perfect combinations of crispy*	*crunchie*	*honeycomb pieces and golden cornflakes tumbled in Cadbury milk chocolate.*
ES	M2	PRAISE	*Deliciosos* (Delicious	*barquillos* wafers	*bañados en dos chocolates: negro y leche.* coated in two chocolates: dark and milk)

The data in Table 18 exemplifies the use of *M2 ProdDesc* in English (EN) and Spanish (ES) for product descriptions. In the English example, M2 highlights specific features of *Crunchie Rocks*, a type of biscuit, emphasising the combination of ingredients. In contrast, the Spanish instance takes a promotional approach, focusing on the deliciousness of the *barquillos*. This comparison illustrates that while the purpose of *M2 ProdDesc* is to provide descriptive product information, its pragmatic realisation can vary, with the English favouring a more neutral tone and the Spanish leaning towards an expressive promotional style. The findings suggest that *M2 ProdDesc* adapts to different rhetorical and marketing strategies depending on the language and cultural context.

4.3. M3 BackInfo

Background information is a move comprising the description of the product's provenance, details about the packaging country, and the brand description and the values that it would like to transmit with the product.

Table 19: Example of *M3 BackInfo* in C-FIVI.

Language	Move	Pragmatic	Left context	Result	Right context
EN	M3	STATE	*Our Willamette Valley Pinot Noir is predominantly from the Yamhill-Carlton AVA with certified organic fruit from the Lemelson*	*Vineyards;*	*and from the Eola-Amity Hills AVA with fruit from the old vines of Eola Springs Vineyard.*
ES	M3	STATE	*Viñedos seleccionados con una producción controlada de 1–1.5 kg por* (Selected vineyards with a controlled production of 1–1.5 kg per	*cepa* vine	*que crecen en terrenos cascajos compuestos de piedra silícea y arcilla a 630 m de altitud.* growing on gravelly soils composed of siliceous stone and clay at 630 m altitude).

The examples in Table 19 demonstrate the use of *M3 BackInfo* in online product descriptions in both languages. The English instance provides detailed information about the provenance of the wine, mentioning specific vineyards and cultivation practices. Similarly, the Spanish example offers a technical description of selected vineyards, focusing on controlled production and geographical details. Both instances enhance the product's authenticity and quality by highlighting its origin and specific production conditions. Thus, *M3 BackInfo* is crucial in building credibility and reinforcing the product's brand identity across languages by foregrounding its heritage and production values.

4.4. M4 TechInfo

Technical information is a move that includes several steps:

- M4_S1 focuses on nutrition facts, which comprise a list of percentages and may include nutritional values related to flavour components.

- M4_S2 corresponds to dietary requirements, i.e. allergens, images about allergens, flavour allergen information, or for whom the product is suitable.
- M4_S3 is related to equipment.
- M4_S4 describes the contact details, that is, data about the manufacturer, the email, the address, the telephone, or order details.
- M4_S5 is the product tracking/quality control, for example, brand standards, warnings, or code control.
- M4_S6 describes the recycling information.

An example of M4_S1in both languages is provided in Table 20.

Table 20: Example of *M4 TechInfo* in C-GEFEM.

Lang.	Move	Pragmatic	Left context	Result	Right context
EN	M4 (S1)	STATE	*A ¼ provides... Energy 1090 kJ 263*	*Kcal*	*13%, Fat 23.2 g 33%, Saturates 8.8 g 44%, Sugars 1.9 g 2%, Salt 2 g 33% of your Reference Intake*.*
ES	M4 (S1)	STATE	*Azucares: 1.1 g. Sodio/Sal: 1610 mg. Valor* (Sugars: 1.1 g. Sodium/Salt: 1610 mg.	*Energético:* Energy Value:	*306.2 Kcal.* 306.2 Kcal.)

The data in Table 20 illustrates the use of *M4 TechInfo* and, more specifically, the step *M4_S1 Nutrition Facts* in both languages. The English example describes a detailed breakdown of energy, fat, sugars, and salt content, along with their respective percentages of the recommended daily intake. Similarly, the Spanish example straightforwardly presents nutritional values such as sugar, sodium, and caloric content. Both examples perform the same pragmatic function of informing consumers about the product's nutritional composition, reinforcing transparency and compliance with regulatory standards. The consistency across languages underscores the universal importance of this move in conveying essential health-related data to consumers.

4.5. *M5 Components*

This move mainly comprises ingredients and data related to them, such as names, percentages, and constituents. In the case of C-FIVI, varieties are also included in this move.

Table 21: Example of *M5 Components* in C-BakedGoods.

Lang.	Move	Pragmatic	Left context	Result	Right context
EN	M5	STATE	*Milk chocolate (Sugar, Cocoa butter, Dried whole milk, Cocoa mass, Dried whey, Vegetable Fat, Emulsifiers (E442, E476)), Flavouring), Cornflakes (16%) (Maize, Sugar,*	*Salt,*	*Barley, Emulsifier (Sunflower lecithin)), Honeycombed pieces (16%) (Sugar, Glucose syrup, Raising agent (Sodium bicarbonate)). ALLERGEN INFORMATION*
ES	M5	STATE	*Harina de espelta (86%), aceite de oliva virgen extra (9%)**, (Spelt flour (86%), extra virgin olive oil (9%)*,	*sal* sea salt,	*marina, emulsionante: lecitina de soja IP, levadura.* emulsifier: IP soy lecithin, yeast).

The data analysis in Table 21 reveals that the move *M5 Components* predominantly comprises lists of ingredients, often accompanied by additional details such as their respective percentages and specific features. Notably, while both languages follow a similar structure, the inclusion of allergen information is more explicit in the English example, whereas the Spanish version lacks such detailed disclosure. This contrast highlights the varying degrees of specificity in ingredient labelling practices between the two languages, potentially reflecting different regulatory or cultural approaches to product transparency.

4.6. *M6 Procedure*

This move describes the processing of teas in the ACTEaS-Promo corpus and the preparation and ageing process of cheese in C-GDQ. It is also a popular move in wine texts (C-FIVI corpus) because it describes the weather conditions, the season, the grape harvest, the date, the fermentation method, and the ageing period. This move has not been found in C-BakedGoods or C-GEFEM.

Table 22: Example of *M6 Procedure* in C-FIVI.

Lang.	Move	Pragm.	Left context	Result	Right context
ES	M6	PRAISE	*Ha sido hecho con el método tradicional de elaboración en rosado siguiendo las más modernas tecnologías y sometido a los más esmerados cuidados en su transformación y posterior estabilización,*	*conservación*	*y embotellado, adquiriendo un color característico.*

The results in Table 22 illustrate the use of *M6 Procedure* in the C-FIVI corpus. The absence of examples in English is because no results are obtained, except for the BiText subcorpus for culinary recipes, which is not included in this study. Regarding the example in Spanish (It has been made with the traditional method of rosé production following the most modern technology and subjected to the most careful care in its transformation and subsequent stabilisation, conservation and bottling, acquiring a characteristic colour), it highlights the emphasis on traditional methods, modern technologies, and meticulous care in production, aiming to enhance the perceived quality of the product. In contrast, *M6 Procedure* is notably absent from the C-BakedGoods and C-GEFEM corpora, suggesting that while the move is common in sectors where craftsmanship and production processes are pivotal to product value, it is less relevant or utilised in more standardised or less process-focused industries.

4.7. M7 (Att) goal/result/End-product

This move is composed of three steps:

- M7_S1 comprises serving suggestions, preparation and use, the use-by and the best-before dates.

- M7_S2 describes the product pairing with other food or wine.
- M7_S3 explains the storage instructions and conditions.

An example in both languages about *M7* is provided in Table 23.

Table 23: Examples of *M7 (Att)goal/result/End-product* in ACTEaS_Promo.

Lang.	Move	Pragmatic	Left context	Result	Right context
EN	M7	DIRECT	*Brewing instructions. Use filtered or bottled*	*water*	*Just off the boil, and brew for 3–4 minutes.*
ES	M7	DIRECT	*Modo de empleo: Poner una* (Instructions for use: Put a	*bolsita* sachet	*en la taza, añadir agua hirviendo y dejar tapada en reposo durante 5 minutos.* in a cup, add boiling water and let it stand covered for 5 minutes).

The data in Table 23 show that the *M7 (Att)goal/result/End-product* is used directly to provide instructions for the use of the product, focusing on essential information such as brewing techniques and timeframes. The instructions are concise and to the point in English, while in Spanish, they are more detailed and explicit. In addition, the English instructions use a more idiomatic way of saying that the water should be very hot but not boiling (*just off the boil*). In contrast, the Spanish instructions are more literal and less idiomatic. The left-hand context introduces the preparation process in both languages, while the right-hand context concludes with specific time instructions.

On the other hand, the consistency in structure suggests that this move is effectively used to deliver precise and straightforward guidance in online food and drink product descriptions. These findings underscore the cross-linguistic similarities in functional texts aimed at consumers.

4.8. M8 Product liability waiver/disclaimer

The final move represents text strings that provide instructions for consumers who are not satisfied with the purchased product, such as a return address or options to write a review or leave comments about the product. It is only found in C-Baked Goods and C-GEFEM.

Table 24: Examples of *M8 Product liability waiver/disclaimer* in C-GEFEM.

Lang.	Move	Pragm.	Left context	Result	Right context
EN	M8	DIRECT	*If you have any queries, or you'd like advice on any Tesco brand*	*products,*	*please contact Tesco Customer Services, or the product manufacturer if not a Tesco brand product.*
ES	M8	DIRECT	--	*COMPARTIR* (SHARE)	--

Data shown in Table 24 demonstrate that *M8*, which addresses consumer instructions in cases of dissatisfaction, is achieved through the pragmatic function <DIRECT> in English. However, while the English example provides a detailed, customer-focused statement including contact details and further instructions, the Spanish one remains incomplete, with only the term *compartir* (share). This disparity suggests that while both languages aim to guide customers, the Spanish text may omit details and require additional context for full comprehension.

The analysis of examples from the ACTRES rhetorical gold standard shows a balance between universality and cultural specificity in online product descriptions. While certain moves, like product presentation and technical information, are essential across languages, others, such as product descriptions and customer service information, reflect distinct cultural and market practices. The ACTRES rhetorical gold standard contributes to standardising online food and drink product descriptions.

5. Conclusions

This paper explores the rhetorical structures used in online food product descriptions in Spanish and English, identifying a consistent framework of rhetorical moves across various food categories. The study identifies similarities and also cultural and linguistic differences between the two languages, highlighting variations in the frequency and prominence of certain rhetorical moves.

A key outcome of this study is the establishment of a rhetorical gold standard that can be employed to standardise the annotation of food and drink product descriptions. The findings reveal that while certain moves are essential in both languages, other moves differ in usage depending on the language. In addition, the role of cultural influences in shaping product descriptions is emphasised. English texts tend to offer more detailed information. Conversely, Spanish descriptions are often more concise, providing practical insights for writers, translators, and marketers in tailoring content to meet the expectations of consumers in each language group, as previously pointed out by Pérez Blanco and Izquierdo (2021: 148).

The study's methodology is adaptable, offering potential for application in other sectors. This flexibility opens avenues for future research in industries where product descriptions are vital to online marketing strategies. The study potentially offers opportunities for integrating AI and LLMs to automate rhetorical analysis and generate product descriptions. These technologies could improve efficiency and ensure consistency in multilingual product description writing, improving speed rates and enhancing accuracy.

Future research could delve deeper into the rhetorical differences across specific product types and explore how these structures impact consumer behaviour. Also, integrating AI-driven tools for rhetorical tagging and corpus annotation presents promising possibilities for streamlining the research process, making rhetorical analysis more accessible and scalable (see Sanz-Valdivieso & López-Arroyo, this volume).

In conclusion, this study contributes valuable knowledge to genre analysis in the food and drink domain, offering data for text production (see Labrador & Ramón, this volume) of online product descriptions aimed at better marketing communication.

Lucía Sanz-Valdivieso and Belén López-Arroyo

Human vs. ChatGPT corpus annotation: Data augmentation using LLM fine-tuning

1. Introduction

The relevance of training and fine-tuning datasets to develop text production tools seems apparent, so curation and synthesis of linguistic data are now popular means to obtain quality material. Manual approaches seem to have become outdated, and some authors defend that technology has "paved the way for automation using AI techniques and tools to analyse and extract information from documents, trying to emulate what human beings are capable of doing with a limited volume of text data" (Pillai & Tedesco 2024: 3).

In this chapter, we explore the potential of Pretrained Large Language Models (PTMs) to serve as research and data enhancement tools towards the future development of multilingual text production applications. We aim to test ChatGPT's ability to provide automatically annotated high-quality data compared to human manual annotation. The focus of the experiment is on rhetorical annotation for two reasons: first, data availability, since the CLANES project already had manually annotated comparable data; and second, the close relationship between rhetorical annotation and other Natural Language Processing (NLP) tasks of interest, such as Named Entity Recognition or sentiment analysis, which are complex semantic tasks that cannot rely on language form exclusively. The result could be fine-tuned datasets for the subsequent development of specialised neural tools for language generation. Our long-term purpose is to leverage low-data availability contexts and the undeniable need for language tools in all sectors of human activity.

Computational power and NLP research have brought about developments in language technologies which we could only have dreamed of ten years ago: "If we take the notion of tools for supporting text production to the extreme, we can imagine software that carries out the entire writing process itself, perhaps with a little help from a human in defining the writing task and specifying the audience" (Mahlow & Dale 2014: 222–223).

Tools like ChatGPT by OpenAI have already surpassed everyone's wildest expectations, in whose light tools such as CLANES' generators have naturally fallen behind (see Labrador & Ramón, this volume). Current text production[1] tools are mainly based on machine learning, i.e., "algorithms and statistical methods that computer systems use to effectively perform a specific task" (Pillai & Tedesco 2024: 4). Deep learning, found in neural networks, is the technique employed in state-of-the-art systems such as ChatGPT (Joseph & Eapen 2024: 33) and this approach "makes it possible to build complex computer programs from examples" (Eisenstein 2019: 2).

Since the advent of PTMs, neural machine translation and bilingual text generation can be considered the most popular means of achieving multilingual text production. The current trend is pre-training with self-supervised learning on massive unannotated data to then make the Large Language Model (LLM) specific for a task or domain "via fine-tuning or few-shot learning" (Wang et al. 2022: 51).

These technologies require a shift in the conceptualisation and operationalisation of linguistic data.[2] Training corpora must have features according to how deep-learning techniques process language, mainly in terms of their huge size (Zhou et al. 2023). Otherwise, "deep neural networks are likely to overfit on these small datasets and do not generalise well in practice", and so dataset size and availability become "a major performance bottleneck" (Li et al. 2022: 2).

For instance, the language used in the biomedical or legal domains has been extensively researched. It is not difficult to find enough parallel data to train LLM-based systems (Anesa 2022). Nevertheless, the

1 We use text production to refer to genre-specific production in the food and drink domain, where linguistic and discourse constraints are observed.

2 In NLP, "datasets are called corpora" (Pillai & Tedesco 2024:12), and both are used interchangeably in this study.

agri-food domain and sub-fields, such as the wine industry, are domains where authentic linguistic data become scarce (Sanz-Valdivieso & López-Arroyo 2023). Therefore, compiling a high-quality, specialised corpus large enough to train an LLM becomes a virtually impossible task. In fact, the manual compilation and annotation of CLANES was a labour-intensive process that spanned several months. If we take wine tasting notes (TNs) as a case study, the resulting corpus consisted of 54,452 words and 716 samples in English, and 52,413 words and 751 samples in Spanish. Despite the meticulous effort invested in creating this corpus, its size is not substantial enough to effectively train an LLM. Fortunately, fine-tuning a PTM, i.e., a trained LLM, is a suitable alternative when smaller but annotated datasets are available (Zhang et al. 2023).

We start this chapter by describing the relevance and context of this study. Then, the latest developments in the field of NLP, specifically PTMs and fine-tuning applied to text production, are detailed. We overview previous studies on PTMs as research tools and then develop a methodology to automatise corpus annotation through prompt engineering. Results are compared against high-quality, human-annotated samples. We conclude that ChatGPT is fairly accurate in identifying rhetorical moves established according to the writer's purpose (Swales 1990), i.e., the taste, aroma and appearance in a tasting note. However, ChatGPT struggles with more intricate moves or steps, such as aroma development or astringency within taste, which become challenges that prevent ChatGPT from being a reliable automatic annotation tool for this specialised domain. The quality of neural text production tools can be jeopardised since the quality of PTMs applied to language generation highly depends on the quality of the data used to train them.

2. Natural Language Processing and Text Production Tools

NLP is "a sub-field of computer science, information engineering, and Artificial Intelligence (AI) that deals with the computational processing and comprehension of human languages" (Pillai & Tedesco 2024: 3). Core areas of NLP involve language modelling and morphological, syntactic and semantic processing (Otter et al. 2021: 604–605). NLP application areas include information extraction, translation, summarisation, question answering and classification, among others (Otter et al. 2021: 605). NLP can be divided into two fundamental branches: Natural Language Understanding (NLU), "which aims to disambiguate an input text to produce a single normalised representation of the ideas expressed in the text" (Wang et al. 2022: 1) and Natural Language Generation (NLG), which "mainly focuses on transforming the potential representations into specific, self-consistent natural language text" (Zhang et al. 2023: 1; Horacek 2000).

NLG applications meet a myriad of communicative needs from different discourse communities around the world, but one of the most common is the development of writing assistance tools (WATs). WATs are "a range of products designed to assist users with written text production in their mother tongue or a foreign language" (Fuertes-Olivera & Tarp 2020: 262). However, few WATs can be used in professional, product-oriented settings (Sanz-Valdivieso 2024), less so for L2 English speakers with basic competence in the language (Rabadán et al. 2021b: 672).

Most current WATs applicable in professional and technical domains are based on LLMs. LLMs "are able to learn from large amounts of data and build models to perform different tasks with a level of success never reached previously by other solutions" (Montejo-Ráez & Jiménez-Zafra 2022: 1). What is new from previous NLG techniques is that in LLMs, "no prior knowledge on language is needed, although only when a massive amount of data is available" (Montejo-Ráez & Jiménez-Zafra 2022: 1).

2.1. Large Language Models, Pre-Trained Models and Fine-tuning

A language model "is just a discrete probability distribution that permits to assign a probability value to any sequence of words," or, put simply, the numerical way of capturing and representing language so that computers can understand and process it (Pillai & Tedesco 2024: 4–5).

Large-scale PTMs have improved NLG tasks because they do not require annotated data to learn language patterns and generate fluent and coherent language (Wang et al. 2022: 58). They have been applied to multiple content-creation tasks such as "ad generation, AI copywriting, book writing, code generation, customer service, and so forth" (Wang et al. 2022: 60; also Zhang et al. 2021; Radford et al. 2019; Agarwal & Kann 2020).

Model pre-training is related to transfer learning, i.e., using knowledge learned for a given task and applying it to a different task. (Dai & Le 2015; Wang et al. 2022: 51). Generative pre-training (GPT) uses "unidirectional transformers as the backbone of the GPT language model" (Wang et al. 2022: 52). A transformer is a kind of neural network architecture characterised by its attention mechanism (Zhang et al. 2024: 6). Bidirectional transformers were introduced as BERT (Bidirectional Encoder Representations from Transformers), capable of learning bidirectional contexts by considering both left and right contexts (Devlin et al. 2019; Wang et al. 2022: 52).

These models show that "the use of large-scale unlabelled data can provide […] a better grasp of the diverse knowledge (e.g., linguistic knowledge, commonsense, facts, expertise, etc.) in the data" (Zhang et al. 2023: 6). While traditional transfer learning is done using annotated data, current deep learning techniques use massive unannotated data in self-supervised learning processes and can be applied to different tasks through fine-tuning or few-shot learning approaches (Wang et al. 2022: 51; Chowdhery et al. 2023). Nevertheless, their success "relies heavily on large-scale datasets, posing a challenge for supervised and cross-domain text generation tasks" (Zhang et al. 2023: 3), so controllability and explainability become major issues of this technology. Hence, when massive amounts of data are not available for training, as in the agri-food domain, annotated data becomes a suitable solution instead.

PLMs have been adapted to specific tasks or domains in a variety of ways, including fine-tuning, model refactoring, and postprocessing. In fact, state-of-the-art results have been achieved by fine-tuning PTMs using small-size supervised data (Zhang et al. 2023: 6). In sum, more human intervention is needed as the desired output becomes more specialised since these systems show deficient performance regarding controlled production such as following a specific structure or style (Otter et al. 2021: 614; Wei et al. 2018; Hopkins & Kiela 2017).

Especially interesting is the fact that providing models with general knowledge data increases the quality of desired specialised output (Otter et al. 2021: 614; Chippada & Saha 2018; Yu et al. 2018). Because of this, fine-tuning PTMs using annotated data becomes a promising pathway to leverage low-resource specialised contexts and the latest NLP technology (see Sanjurjo-González et al., this volume).

Fine-tuning has become the current paradigm in NLG tasks since a fine-tuned PTM "can perform the CTG [Controllable Text Generation] task at a lower cost" (Zhang et al. 2023: 9). It works as follows:

> A large amount of training data (usually unlabelled samples) and model parameters are used to learn general knowledge from the data and encode the learned knowledge into a PLM. Then a domain/task-adapted model will be obtained [...] by fine-tuning the PLM based on a small amount of labeled data for the specific downstream task (Zhang et al. 2023: 9)

There are different approaches to fine-tuning, such as Adapted Module, Reinforcement learning approaches, or the Prompt method (Zhang et al. 2023: 9–10; Gao et al. 2021; Lester et al. 2021; Zou et al. 2021; Carlsson et al. 2022). Similarly, the recent Instruction Tuning, such as the FLAN model (Wei et al. 2022) or InstructGPT (Ouyang et al. 2022), involves using natural language and annotated datasets as examples to be "used as instructions to fine-tune GPT" (Zhang et al. 2023: 12). Instruction Tuning is especially useful in low resource-contexts such as the CLANES project: small available datasets may be enhanced through annotation and data augmentation procedures to achieve sufficient samples, and therefore obtain satisfactory controlled text generation performance through fine-tuning (Lee et al. 2023; Peng et al. 2023; Jha et al. 2023; Wu et al. 2023; Chung et al. 2022).

2.2. Data Augmentation Through PTM-based Automatic Corpus Annotation

Language datasets or corpora need to be annotated so their subsequent analysis can be operationalised and become useful (Garside et al. 1997; Csomaym & Crawford 2024). Annotation consists of making explicit the information implicitly present in the corpus (McEnery & Wilson 2001, McEnery & Hardie 2012, Bowker & Pearson 2002). There are multiple types of annotation, such as tagging or labelling, lemmatisation or parsing (Leech 1993). Rhetorical annotation consists of adding tags that identify and delimit specific functional units within a text.

The cost of data collection and cleaning needed for a neural network-based linguistic tool becomes a significant challenge since these systems "heavily rely on large amounts of labelled data" (Zhang et al.

2023: 5), especially in low-availability contexts. In this sense, since "recent neural network models are capable of generating near-realistic text, it is possible to utilise them to expand existing datasets and even create new data" (Zhang et al. 2023: 5). In fact, generative AI has emerged as a data augmentation tool, particularly in the context of data processing by LLMs like GPT.

To evaluate their usefulness, part of NLP research focuses on the comparison of manual human versus LLM-based automatic linguistic analysis. For instance, Curry et al. (2024) use ChatGPT-4 to replicate previous manual corpus-based discourse analyses, including semantic categorisation and concordance analysis. Their study concludes that, while ChatGPT does not meet human standards, it can support a human-led analysis (Curry et al. 2024: 8). In a similar vein, Uchida (2024) compares the effectiveness of five different LLMs with manual searches based on COCA to generate quantitative and qualitative corpus-based analysis. The study concludes that the use of LLMs for quantitative analysis is an advantage for corpus research. Ostyakova et al. (2023) used ChatGPT for data augmentation, more specifically, for discourse structure annotation in casual dialogue, where low accuracy and stability of the output were the main limitations of the approach. Other studies suggest that even previous versions of GPT can be used as data augmentation tools (Kumar et al. 2020; Kobayashi 2018).

Previous studies have predominantly focused on general language usage, overlooking a critical dimension: the exploration and analysis of linguistic data within professional texts, such as promotional genres in the agri-food industry, as those analysed in CLANES. Despite their significance, there is a notable gap in our understanding of how well LLMs can annotate, analyse, interpret, and generate content within these specialised domains. Therefore, PTMs like ChatGPT could be used to synthesise further annotated linguistic samples from few high-quality, manually annotated texts. Like this, enough annotated data could be obtained for fine-tuning a subsequent PTM for NLG, avoiding the cost and time required to annotate a whole fine-tuning dataset by human experts (see Section 3). In essence, this study will inform the prospective development of specialised tools to meet the demands of international professional linguistic production and communication in the food and drink domain.

3. Methodology

To explore PTMs' potential in data augmentation tasks such as automatic corpus annotation, ChatGPT 3.5 was selected due to its popularity among academics and end-users alike, which fosters comparability of results with other similar studies. The baseline against which to compare ChatGPT's annotated data are samples part of the CLANES project, specifically human-annotated wine TNs. The human-annotated samples are deemed to be of the highest quality since annotators were both language and domain experts (see Sanjurjo-González, this volume).

The following sections describe the sample selection used for this experiment, as well as the design criteria followed to build the prompt fed to ChatGPT and the analytical procedure employed to compare CLANES human annotation empirically and objectively to ChatGPT's annotation.

3.1. Human-annotated Dataset

The rhetorical annotation in this project was based on tags that follow the rhetorical structure of wine TNs where information is organised hierarchically into functional units, which Swales (1990) refers to as moves and steps. Even though genres and their expectations may evolve and change, we adhere to Swalesian terms since the hierarchical and fixed structure of moves and steps allows for a stable analysis of the data. Before developing the rhetorical gold standard (see Pizarro Sánchez & Ortego Antón, this volume), the structure for wine TNs included five moves, often with several steps, each occurring at different frequencies and shared in both Spanish and English TNs. The most common moves and steps in the wine TNs appear underlined in the rhetorical structure and tags presented below:

- Introductory remarks <IR>.
- Appearance <AP>
  - Colour hue and depth <CD>
  - Viscosity <VI>
  - Clarity <CL>
  - Effervescence <EF>

- Aroma <AR>
  - Fragrance <FR>
  - Intensity <IN>
  - Development <DV>
- Taste <TA>
  - Flavour <FL>
  - Finish <FI>
  - Astringency <AS>
  - Mouthfeel <MF>
  - Body <BO>
  - Balance <BA>
- Concluding remarks <CR>

These 18 tags (5 moves, 13 steps) were assigned in Extensible Markup Language during the human annotation of the corpus using the ACTRES Tagger, a software built for this purpose by the ACTRES research group (see Labrador & Ramón, this volume). Below are two short annotated examples, one in English (1) and one in Spanish (2):

(1) <?xml version="1.0" encoding="utf-8"?><xml>003FcAKCH000000OenoEn
AKARUA CHARDONNAY 2011
<AP>APPEARANCE
<CD>Golden, straw colour</CD></AP>
<AR>BOUQUET
<DV>A full bodied wine</DV> <FR>showing citrus and tropical aromas</FR>.</AR>
<TA>PALATE
<FL>The palate is rich with stonefruit and vanillin</FL> <AS>supported by a lingering minerality typical of the region,</AS> <FI>which provides great length.</FI></TA>
</xml>

(2) <?xml version="1.0" encoding="utf-8"?><xml>023FcLBR000000EnoEs
Bodegas Luna Beberide LB Reserva Cata
<AR><FR>*Balsámico, floral y terroso en nariz* [Balsamic, floral and earthy on the nose]</FR><DV> *va desgranando su profundidad aromática después de un cierto hermetismo inicial* [its aromatic depth unravels after a certain initial hermetism]</DV></AR>
<TA><BO>*En boca es compacto, opulento*</BO><MF>*y muy fino* [The palate is compact, opulent</BO><MF>and very fine.]</MF><AS>*con taninos de seda y un carácter rectilíneo.* [with silky tannins and a straight character.] </AS> <FI>*Excelente longitud.* [Excellent length]</FI></TA>
</xml>

From the whole corpus of wine TNs, a smaller sample was selected for this experiment based on text length: the mean for Spanish wine TNs is 70 words and 75 for the English sub-corpus. Hence, those TNs ranging from 70 to 75 words long were selected, resulting in 45 Spanish and 50 English TNs. Five of the 50 English TNs were randomly discarded in order to employ a balanced dataset for the experiment consisting of 45 TNs in Spanish and 45 in English.

3.2. Experiment and Analytical Procedure: Prompt-Based Automatic Annotation

The prompt used to obtain automatically annotated TNs is based on the widely used principles for effective prompting by Bsharat et al. (2023), designed aiming at conciseness and clarity, contextual relevance, task alignment, and avoiding bias, among others.

The main principle followed in the design of this experiment's prompt is the combination of Chain-of-thought and Few-shot prompting since automatic rhetorical annotation is a complex language task (Bsharat et al. 2023). This involves, on the one hand, breaking down a complex task into simpler ones and, on the other, providing some examples of the desired completion of the task together with the instructions. Other principles involve structuring the instructions, using delimiters (e.g., ###EXAMPLES###, ###TASK###), using affirmative imperatives and phrases such as "your task is", employing consistent terminology throughout the prompt, specifying the expected format of the desired output, and clearly stating requirements for the task. Other approaches, such as the use of emotional language (politeness, threats, offering rewards, etc.), were left out of the prompt for this experiment not only in favour of synthesis but also due to contradictory evidence on the usefulness of such language when prompting ChatGPT (Li et al. 2023).

The prompts employed were structured as follows: a definition of a TN was provided, followed by the task instructions. Then, the tagset and its correspondence to the moves and steps above were presented. Next, an example demonstration was included by "showing input-output pairs" (Bsharat et al. 2023: 7) or original samples paired with human-annotated TNs. Finally, original texts for the task were included, separated by delimiters. The prompt shown below was translated and adapted to Spanish to generate the automatic annotation of the Spanish samples (only one example-expected output pair is included for clarity, although the original prompt provides five):

"A tasting note is a text containing descriptions and evaluations of a food/drink product's appearance, aroma, taste, and other features. Your goal is to infer which parts of a tasting note represent appearance, aroma, taste, or other features descriptions. Tags to base your task on are

"Introductory remarks" = <ir>;

"Appearance" = <ap>, and within Appearance, "Color hue and depth" = <cd>, "Viscosity" = <vi>, "Clarity" = <cl>, and "Effervescence" = <ef>;

"Aroma" = <ar>, and within Aroma, "Fragrance" = <fr>, "Intensity" = <in>, "Development" = <dv>;

"Taste" = <ta>, and within Taste, "Flavor" = <fl>, "Finish" = <fi>, "astringency" = <as>, "Mouthfeel" = <mf>, "Body" = <bo> and "Balance" = <Ba>; and "Concluding remarks" = <cr>.

I present some examples and then I provide the texts for your task. Your answer must be in xml format.

EXAMPLES

#Original text#

"029FcARKG000000OenoEn

2011

The 2011 Kahu has intense aromas of mandarin, butterscotch, apricot and melon overlaid with hints of hazelnut. The palate is rich, full and velvety with hints of spicy tamarind. The tight finish with a residual sugar of 120g/l results in a rich but fresh expression of Ali's favourite wine! Kahu makes a lovely after-dinner drop, delicious with the classic combination of blue cheese, a few nuts and a slice of fresh, creamy pear."

#Expected output#

"<?xml version="1.0" encoding="utf-8"?><xml>029FcARKG000000OenoEn

2011

<ar><in>The 2011 Kahu has intense aromas</in> <fr>of mandarin, butterscotch, apricot and melon overlaid with hints of hazelnut.</fr></ar> <ta>The palate is rich, full and velvety with hints of spicy tamarind. <fi>The tight finish</fi> <as>with a residual sugar of 120g/l results in a rich but fresh expression of Ali's favourite wine!</as></ta> <cr>Kahu makes a lovely after-dinner drop, delicious with the classic combination of blue cheese, a few nuts and a slice of fresh, creamy pear.</cr></xml>"

[Four more examples of the expected output]

ORIGINAL TEXTS FOR THE TASK

#Text 1#

"464FcBST000000EnoEn Bressler 2002 Bressler Cabernet Sauvignon Broad and fleshy on the palate, with beautiful purity, nicely integrated acidity and tannin, and a succulent, concentrated finish, this 2002 should be accessible young, yet age nicely for 10–15 years. This is an estate-bottled 100% Cabernet Sauvignon that is aged in 100% new French oak for 25 months prior to bottling. This wine can be enjoyed now or will continue to evolve in the cellar."

#Text 2#

[The prompt continues until all samples for annotation are included]"

Incremental prompting was also applied since several iterations of the experiment were performed to obtain the most homogeneous and comparable output possible. Incremental and iterative prompting means that the dataset described above had to be divided into a training dataset (example pairs) and a testing dataset (unseen samples). The final training dataset consists of five TNs in each language because when ten samples were used in initial iterations, ChatGPT apparently became *distracted* by the examples in what could be an instance of overfitting: preliminary output consisted of some regularly annotated samples, partial repetitions of unannotated samples and other forms of hallucination (Huang et al. 2023; Rawte et al. 2023). For instance, TN (3) below was part of an incomplete output (i.e., not all TNs from the prompt were annotated, and this TN was incomplete as well), where concluding remarks <cr> are annotated in the slot for the name of the wine, which appears at the beginning:

(3) *"<?xml version="1.0" encoding="utf-8"?> <xml> <ir> <cr>Angels Gate 2007 Angels III Red</cr> <ar> Our premium flagship"*

In contrast, providing five example pairs out of the forty-five selected TNs resulted in more homogeneously annotated samples, even if there were some inconsistency issues, which will be discussed later (see Section 4). Similarly, the remaining forty samples that composed the testing dataset had to be fed in four batches of ten since including all forty in a single prompting would result in useless output as well. The specifics of these iterations are beyond the scope of this paper.

The output resulting from prompting ChatGPT was stored for comparison with the human, high-quality annotated samples. The automatic and human-annotated samples were analysed in parallel to determine to what extent they differed. Layout and formatting inconsistencies prevented us from performing an automatic comparison, so a spreadsheet was used to record the similarities and differences between the samples manually.

Taking the human-annotated texts as the baseline, we recorded a) whether a move/step was included or omitted by ChatGPT in the automatic annotation and b) whether it was acceptably or unacceptably included/omitted. This approach allows for the quantification of results regardless of the different moves or steps present in each sample so that our attention is on each 'annotation chance' faced by ChatGPT: each tag, annotated or omitted correctly or incorrectly by ChatGPT, is here considered as an item for analysis. Hence, since there are 18 tags in the tagset, and the sample amounts to 40 samples in each language, we examined 720 annotation chances. A comment cell was habilitated so that other remarkable qualitative aspects of the comparison could be taken into account when analysing the results (Figure 21).

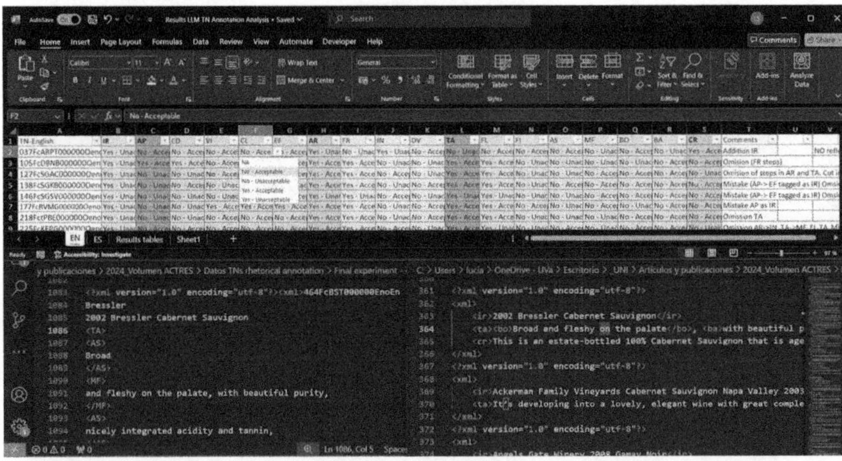

Figure 21: Screenshot of the analysis. The top half is an Excel file where results for each comparison were recorded. The bottom half is divided into the TNs being compared: human-annotated (left) and automatically annotated (right).

After obtaining all the automatically annotated samples and comparing them to the human-annotated TNs as described in this section, the results of the comparison were aggregated, and percentages were calculated to report results in the Results and Discussion section.

4. Results and Discussion

The experiment's results were analysed considering the hierarchical levels within the rhetorical structure reflected by tags. Hence, the following results show ChatGPT's performance in rhetorical annotation at the textual, move and step levels.

4.1. Quantitative results

At the general level (Figure 22), ChatGPT's total acceptable annotations (69.17% in Spanish and 72.92% in English) outnumber unacceptable ones (30.83% in Spanish and 27.08% in English).

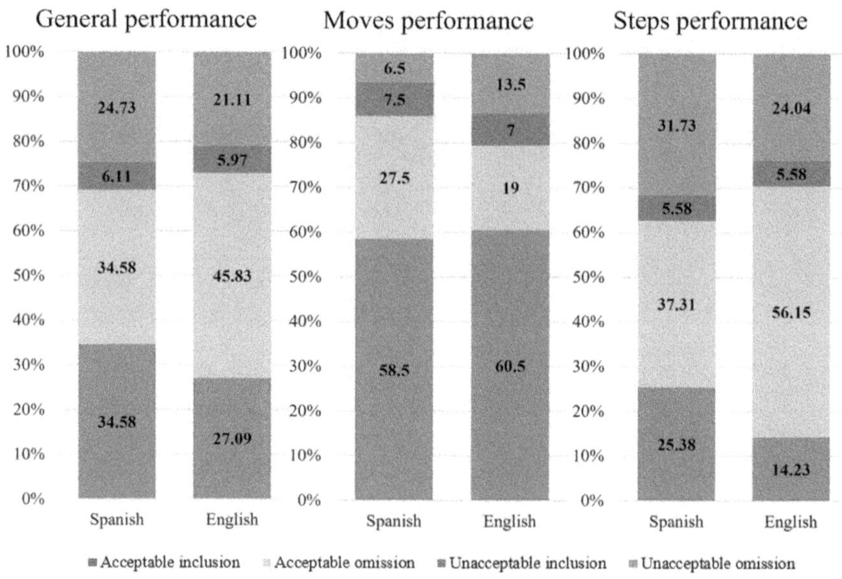

Figure 22: ChatGPT's performance in rhetorical annotation tasks at the textual, move, and step level of Spanish and English TNs.

Besides, at the general, move, and step levels, the most salient annotation mistake is the unacceptable omission of tags, with unacceptable inclusions being less numerous. The only exception is the move level in Spanish, where unacceptable inclusions outnumber unacceptable omissions. Sample (4) below shows how humans annotated the Appearance move and the Viscosity and Effervescence moves, but ChatGPT mistakenly annotated the same span of text as Introductory remarks.

(4) Manual annotation:
<ap><vi>Lively energetic mousse</vi> <ef>forms a crown of bubbles in the glass</ef>.</ap>

ChatGPT annotation:

<ir>Wine Description
Lively energetic mousse forms a crown of bubbles in the glass.</ir>

Other aspects related to move and step annotation are presented itemised below. Figure 23 shows the annotation performance at each of the five main moves within the tagset.

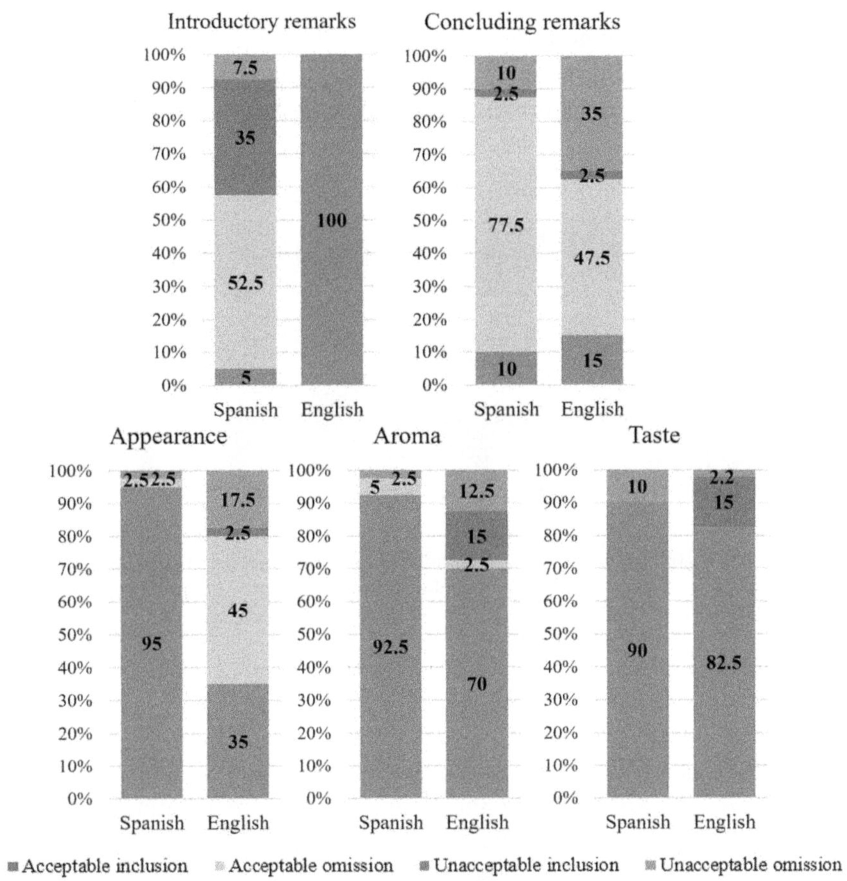

Figure 23: Itemised results at the move level, i.e., Introductory and Concluding remarks together with the three main tasting phases.

Introducing and Concluding remarks (IR and CR, respectively) need to be looked at separately from the three moves linked to the three tasting phases (Appearance, Aroma and Taste). On the one hand, IRs are consistently accurately recognised in English, while, in Spanish, the IR tag is often mismatched to text segments alluding to different aspects. Conversely, CRs in Spanish are less accurately annotated than in English, where the CR tag is often unacceptably omitted. On the other hand, the annotation of the main three tasting moves shows quite a comparable high accuracy in both languages, especially in Spanish.

The automatic annotation of the steps that make up these three tasting moves is explored next. Figure 24 shows ChatGPT's annotation performance of the steps within the Appearance move.

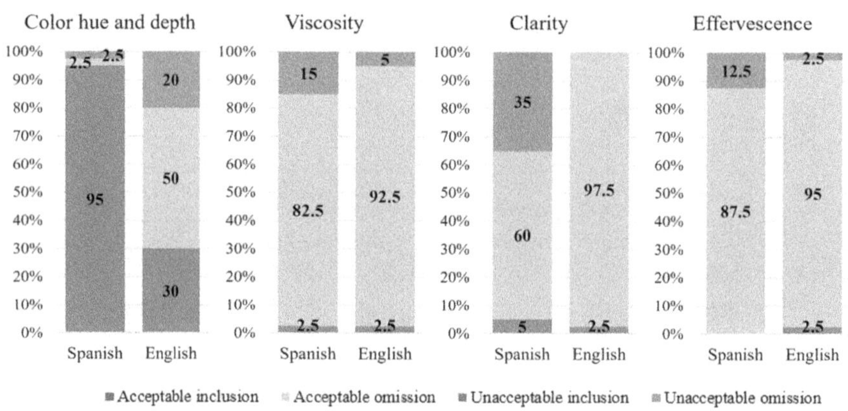

Figure 24: Itemised results at the step level within the Appearance move.

The most frequently occurring step, Color hue and depth, is acceptably included or omitted in over 80% of the cases, even though English samples suffer unacceptable omissions more often. The three other less frequent steps, Viscosity, Clarity and Effervescence, are accurately omitted in most cases. However, in these cases, ChatGPT fails to include the Viscosity, Clarity and Effervescence tags in the Spanish samples to a greater extent than in English.

A similar pattern is found in the steps that make up the Aroma move (Figure 25).

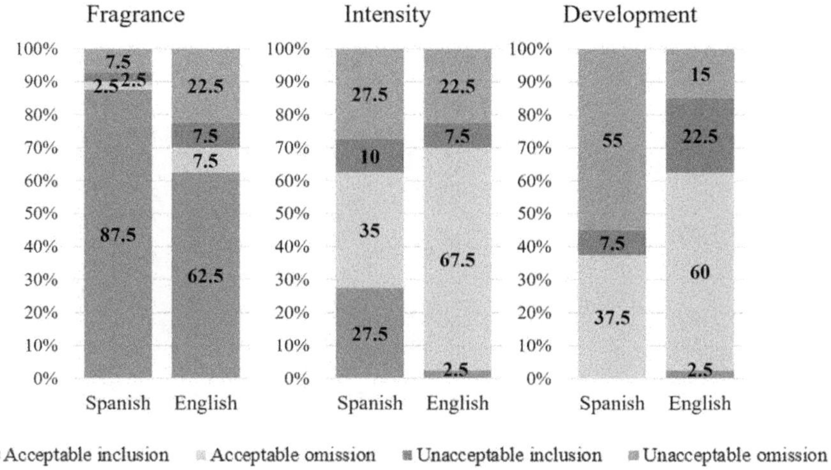

Figure 25: Itemised results at the step level within the Aroma move.

Fragrance, the most frequent step within the move, is accurately annotated (or omitted) most of the time, with Spanish samples being processed more accurately than English, possibly due to higher unacceptable inclusions and omissions. Similar to the annotation of Appearance steps, the less frequent Intensity and Development in Aroma are better recognised in English. However, these Aroma steps pose a greater difficulty to ChatGPT than Appearance Steps: more annotation mistakes are produced due to inaccurate inclusion and omission of the Intensity and Development tags.

Finally, itemised Taste steps show these steps are the most problematic for ChatGPT (Figure 26), even if the move Taste itself is one of the better-annotated items among moves and steps (Figure 22).

There are differences in accuracy when annotating both languages; however, the fact that this is the move with a higher number of steps may play a role in the relatively comparable performance of ChatGPT annotating taste steps in Spanish and English samples. Finish is the only step where Spanish is more accurately annotated than English: 52.5% of the Spanish samples that contain this step are correctly annotated versus 42.5% of the English samples. Steps in the Taste move are the most unacceptably annotated over the Aroma and Appearance steps (Figures 24 and 25).

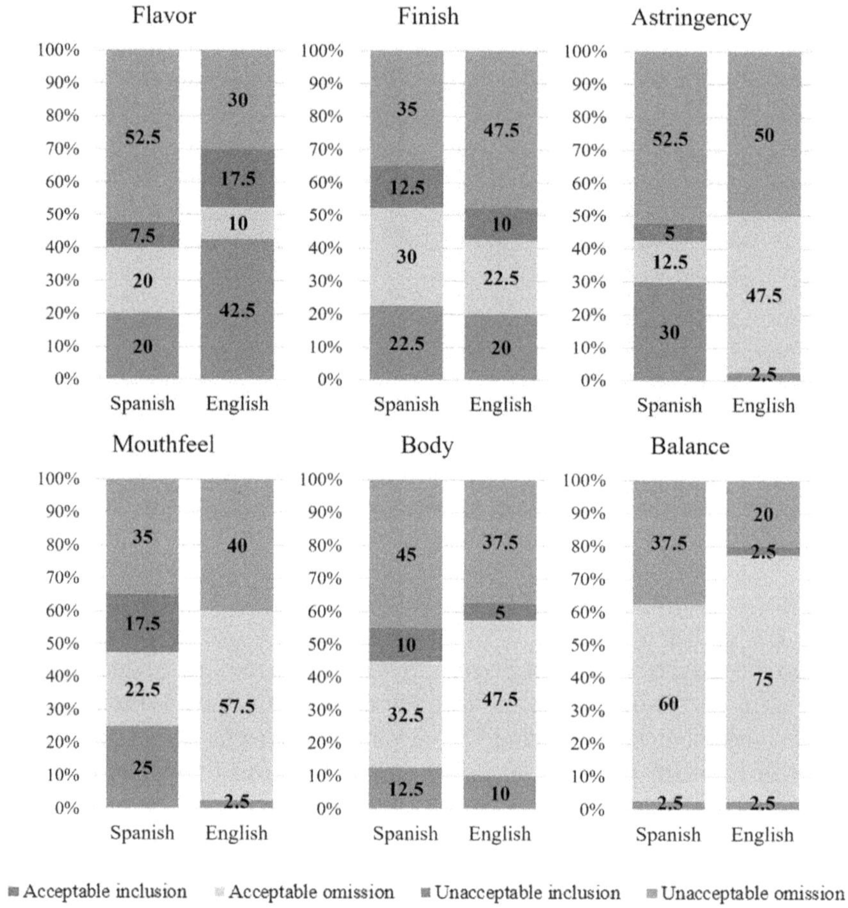

Figure 26: Itemised results at the step level within the Taste move.

4.2. Qualitative observations

A qualitative look at the rhetorical annotation using ChatGPT reveals inconsistencies and reliability issues across multiple dimensions, which are often pervasive and below human standards. Notably, at the step level, where text analysis occurs on a finer granularity, ChatGPT annotation tends to exhibit remarkable unreliability.

To begin with, ChatGPT struggles to identify or accurately interpret nuanced textual cues at the step level, leading to inconsistent annotation.

While it successfully identifies the move and one step, such as Flavour (FL) within Taste (TA) (5), ChatGPT often misses crucial cues that could have led to the identification of other steps within the move:

(5) *<TA><FL>The palate is just off dry and gives flavours of sweet Winter Cole pear and cardamom spice. </FL> Vibrant and elegant the finish lingers with refreshing pear, spice and honey. A relatively low alcohol style, perfect for summer lunch or with pre dinner snacks. </TA>*

In the annotated sample (5), ChatGPT does not identify the steps Mouthfeel (MF), Balance (BA) and Finish (FI) in Taste. Similarly, it does not recognise that expressions like *perfect for* could indicate the move Concluding remarks (CR). In other instances, ChatGPT misses even straightforward cues, such as the word *colour* as identification of the step Colour hue and depth (CD) embedded in the move Appearance (AP), and misidentifies it as the move Introductory remarks (IR) (6), affecting layout and tag capitalisation as well:

(6) *<ir>*
Wine Description
Enticing pale straw colour.
</ir>

Similarly, ChatGPT tends to focus on the sentence as the annotation unit, so it often fails to recognise steps within a move if several steps are expressed together. In the example below, it misses *aterciopelados* [silky] as a cue for the Mouthfeel (MF) step (7), identifying the whole sentence as a single step when Finish (FI) should be embedded within FI:

(7) <FI>*De taninos aterciopelados que aparecen pulidos y firmes, con final largo y suave.* [Firm and silky tannins followed by a smooth and long aftertaste]</FI>

In sum, ChatGPT's annotation process at the step level exhibits inconsistencies in the assignment of rhetorical tags. Conversely, move-level analysis offers a higher reliability (Figure 23).

Other problems have also been observed, such as annotation mistakes at both levels and in both languages and instances of text invention by ChatGPT. Annotation errors range from misidentification of rhetorical moves, as shown above, to the creation of new texts, compromising the accuracy and integrity of the annotation outcomes, such as (5). In (8), ChatGPT joins the sentences about aromas and flavours into one that leads to the omission of the move Taste (TA).

(8) Manual annotation:
<AR> <FR> The wine has a great diversity of aromas including [...] </FR> </AR>
<TA> <FL> The wine has a great diversity of flavors [...]. </FL>

ChatGPT annotation:
<ar> <fr>The wine has a great diversity of aromas and flavors including [...].</fr> </ar>

Similarly, omissions of parts of the TN have also been observed. In (9), the segment *Youthful elegance is an excellent descriptor of the 2006 Reserve Chardonnay* is deliberately omitted.

(9) Manual annotation:
Hafner Vineyards 2008 Reserve Chardonnay
<AR> <DV>Youthful </DV> <IN> elegance is an excellent descriptor of the 2008 Reserve Chardonnay.</IN>
<FR> Sweet grapefruit and melon aromas give the wine its structure; vanilla toastiness and flinty, mineral notes</FR>

ChatGPT annotation:
<ir>Hafner Vineyards 2008 Reserve Chardonnay </ir>
<ar> <fr>Sweet grapefruit and melon aromas give the wine its structure; vanilla toastiness and flinty, mineral notes from its barrel-fermentation and extended barrel-aging enhance its bouquet. </fr>

Improvements in the identification of certain moves have also been observed. The move Introductory remarks (IR) is often left out in the human annotation. However, in the English sample annotation, ChatGPT systematically identifies the name of the wine and vintage as IR (10). Unfortunately, that is not the case in the Spanish corpus (11), where ChatGPT creates a new tag:

(10) English sample:
<ir>Kestrel 2008 RAPTOR RED</ir>

(11) Spanish sample:
<*nombre_bodega* [winery_name]> *Abadía Retuerta* </*nombre_bodega*>
<*nombre_vino* [wine_name]> *Pago de Valdebellón 2009* </*nombre_vino*>

In general, results show that Spanish samples are more accurately annotated due to the better recognition of the most frequent steps. However, English samples are better annotated for those steps that are less frequent within a move. Most unacceptable annotation items are due to incorrectly omitted tags. Besides, there is no direct relationship between the accurate recognition of a move and that of its constituent steps. For instance, the Taste move is the best annotated, but its steps are the least accurately annotated. Also, moves and frequent steps are better annotated in Spanish samples, but less frequent steps are more accurately included or omitted in English samples.

These automatic tagging results may be explained because moves represent coherent, meaningful units in the genre of TN. At the move level, ChatGPT can leverage contextual cues and linguistic patterns to identify rhetorical moves more accurately. This may be related to the fact that ChatGPT predominantly segments the TNs at the sentence level, as shown in our examples. Unlike the step-level analysis, move-level annotation minimises the fragmentation of rhetorical moves, preserving the coherence and continuity of the rhetorical analysis. By treating each move as a holistic unit, ChatGPT captures the overarching rhetorical patterns, resulting in a more consistent annotation.

Phenomena such as the omission and invention of text, the creation of new tags, and the inability to recognise non-literal cues for step annotation may be due to a myriad of factors. For instance, a different prompt could lead to better results. Possibly, using the latest version of ChatGPT could throw more accurate step annotation. Nevertheless, the lack of explainability of PTMs may lie at the bottom of those undesirable results. This black-box problem entails a lack of interpretability and traceability of results from PTMs, which may explain the pervasive issues and inconsistencies found in this study.

In any case, given the purpose of automatic specialised annotation, which is to save time while maintaining quality, it seems ChatGPT cannot be considered a fully reliable automatic annotation tool. With outputs like the ones presented here, it is hard to see how this process, which requires human manual supervision and revision, could serve as a better alternative to manual annotation in terms of cost or efficiency. These findings go in line with previous studies on the matter (Curry et al. 2024; Uchida 2024; Ostyakova et al. 2023), which argue that PTMs may become valuable tools to different extents but, more often than not, require human supervision to guarantee the desired quality output.

5. Conclusion

This study has attempted to test the usefulness of PTMs as automatic rhetorical annotation tools applied to specialised texts belonging to the food and drink domain in the CLANES project. After designing a prompt to use the few-shot technique with ChatGPT 3.5, a quantitative and qualitative analysis of its output revealed findings similar to those of previous studies on the matter. In the specialised genre of Spanish and English wine TNs, results have yielded the following insights regarding ChatGPT-based automatic annotation:

- Spanish samples match human annotation to a larger extent, possibly due to the greater number of Spanish wine tasting data present in the dataset used to train ChatGPT.
- Globally and distinctively cohesive information (moves) matches human annotation to a larger extent in both languages than that of steps.
- Granular information (steps) in English matches human annotation to a greater extent, possibly due to the higher amount of total training data of ChatGPT in English, which may be reflected in better reasoning performance on unseen data.
- Human annotation relies to a lesser extent on language form; the sentence is the most common annotation unit, and the presence of transparent keywords related to a given move/step enables more accurate annotation.
- Automatic annotation is uncontrollable as the output is often riddled with inconsistencies at the format and layout levels, as well as in the treatment of original text and the annotation task itself.
- ChatGPT for automatic rhetorical annotation lacks quality warranty to be an objective and reliable scientific tool.

These findings may be a consequence of the "fundamental tension between computer science and humanistic approaches to text data" (Marcellino 2023: 149). In essence, computers outperform humans at finding patterns in large amounts of data, while humans excel at fine-grained semantic analysis (Moretti 2005). Nevertheless, PTMs as annotation tools cannot be rendered useless just because of that. Instead, their conscientious use in combination with human judgement can result in improved methodologies: humans and computers ought to apply their strengths to tasks where such abilities are required, attempting to act complementarily and not in opposition (Marcellino 2023: 149).

Hence, while the complete automation of annotation tasks is a distant reality, the application of PTMs to such tasks may be regarded as a valuable semi-automatic data-augmentation technique. These conclusions entail that the low availability of training and fine-tuning datasets is a defining condition for the development of specialised language generation tools since the process of synthesising and augmenting adequate datasets cannot be automated just yet. One thing is certain: human expertise is very likely irreplaceable by machines, but humans cannot match computers' performance quantity-wise. Therefore, the roles of humans and computers need to be rethought as complementary instead of exclusive in a way that machines can enable unimagined applications of human skill.

Belén Labrador and Noelia Ramón

Technology-assisted professional writing for Spanish-speaking users

1. Introduction

The first stage in the research carried out by the ACTRES team on English-Spanish corpus-based contrastive studies made use of large monolingual reference corpora to retrieve the empirical data required for these contrastive studies, Cobuild-Bank of English and CREA (*Corpus de Referencia del Español Actual*) (Labrador 2003a, 2003b, 2004, 2007; Rabadán 2006, 2007; Ramón 2004, 2006a, 2006b). Later, an English-Spanish parallel corpus was built by the ACTRES research group to continue with translation-based contrastive studies with our particular language pair (Izquierdo et al. 2008). This corpus was called P-ACTRES (Parallel ACTRES) and included first only English original texts with their corresponding Spanish translations, and in later stages, it was enlarged to become bidirectional: P-ACTRES 2.0 (Sanjurjo-González & Izquierdo 2019). Some English-Spanish contrastive studies derived from this corpus, still in use, include Izquierdo 2010, 2012a, 2012b, 2014, 2015; Labrador 2011, 2016, 2021, 2023; Ramón 2009, 2023; Rabadán 2009, 2011, 2015; Rabadán & Izquierdo 2013a, 2013b. The purely descriptive studies carried out in these first stages based on monolingual and parallel corpora provided useful information for foreign language teaching and learning, as well as for translation practice and translator training.

After several years engaged in this type of research, the team realised that a closer connection between academia and the professional world was becoming more necessary. Therefore, we decided to focus on the transfer of knowledge obtained from university research to actual real-life situations by means of developing computerised applications in the fields of translation quality assessment (PETRA 1.0©) and assisted writing in specialised domains (ACTRES text generators).

In this paper, we will describe the steps followed in the construction of different types of text generators where academia meets the industry. First, we selected a number of professional genres where native speakers of Spanish might need assistance in writing specialised texts. Then, we compiled comparable corpora in English and Spanish of original texts belonging to these genres, such as online advertisements of electronic products (Labrador et al. 2014), technical brochures (Ramón & Labrador 2015), appliance instruction manuals (Cristobalena 2016), meeting minutes (Rabadán 2016; Pizarro Sánchez 2017), audit reports, director's reports (Rabadán et al. 2021b), football match reports (Díez Fernández 2009), scientific abstracts (Rabadán et al. 2011), opinion articles (Pérez Blanco 2013), and clinical trials. The retrieval of information from these corpora led to the construction of the first set of ACTRES text generators.

The experience gained in this first stage made us decide to expand our research, focusing on the specific needs of the professionals working in small and medium-sized companies in our region of Castile and Leon. The analysis of the local trade narrowed down the potential end users to those working in the food and drink industry. In this sector, 97.2% of the companies are small or medium-sized (*El Adelantado de Segovia*, 14/02/2024). Many of these local companies are expanding their business internationally, with exportations growing by 13.1% from 2021 to 2022. Considering all the exportations of Castile and León, the food and drink industry represents 19.5% of the total. Food and drink companies are required to write promotional texts in English to export their products. With this need in mind, we built a new set of text generators for assisting Spanish speakers in the writing of these promotional texts in the food and drink industry, especially manufacturing companies producing and selling wine, cheese, dried meats, biscuits and herbal teas. These writing aids clearly illustrate how academic research can have an impact on local society, particularly in trade and business. Summing up, our lines of contrastive research moved from exploring monolingual reference corpora in English and Spanish to parallel corpora in these languages, and further on to comparable corpora, sometimes combining several types. The object of study also moved from general language to specialised language, as cultural writing conventions are better identified in original texts and then compared cross-linguistically for applied purposes.

As for research in computer-assisted writing software, in the past thirty years, a wide range of web-based tools have been developed to help native as well as non-native users in the complex task of writing. Some of these tools are spell/grammar-checkers, online dictionaries, machine-translation tools, and corpora. Among the most complete applications for second language writing are Writing Assistance Tools (WATs), which are highly automated suites of tools containing different types of linguistic information, not only grammatical or lexical, but often also rhetorical and/or relevant contextual information. Existing WATs are either general language-oriented, like FLOW (Chen et al. 2012) or specialised, like SWAN (Kinnunen et al. 2012) and arText (da Cunha et al. 2017). For a detailed overview of WATs, see Labrador and Ramón (2020).

The ACTRES linguists carried out detailed contrastive studies on the comparable corpora and provided relevant information regarding online specialised texts: rhetorical, phraseological and lexical. With these linguistic data, the ACTRES computer scientists developed a first set of eight text generators (1.0) for assisting native speakers of Spanish with an intermediate level of English in writing different types of texts in this language in professional domains: a scientific abstracts generator (GAC), a generator for electronic product descriptions (GDPE), a tool for generating meeting minutes (GARE), a generator to write wine tasting notes (FIVI), a technical report generator (GITEC), a directors' report generator (GEDIRE), an audit reports generator (GInA), and a generator of instruction manuals for household appliances (GIT). These generators were developed to assist users in writing only one particular type of technical document. Hence, this software was only valid for the specific communicative goal for which it was built.

As the project evolved into the assistance to write online promotional texts in the food and drink industry, we saw the need to replicate the procedure to build new text generators. The ACTRES computer scientists developed a tool called O-WEAA (Sanjurjo-González et al. 2019), which allowed us to define the main features of any technical document by means of the Acquisition Interface Module. We then produced a second set of seven text generators (2.0) following improved techniques:

a generator for online texts promoting dried meats (GEFEM), wines (FITEVI), herbal teas (PROMOCIONA-Té), cheeses (GDQ), rural accommodation (PROCARU), cookies (GDEGA) and recipes (BiTeX).

In this paper, we will describe in detail the procedure followed to design and construct these two sets of text generators. Section 2 describes the working procedure followed from the compilation of the corpora to the extraction of the information at different linguistic levels. Section 3 shows the results obtained in the form of 14 text-generators. Finally, the implications of this procedure and the challenges imposed by new AI-enhanced tools are discussed in Section 4.

2. Working procedure

Considering the importance of English as a *lingua franca*, especially in all the domains of science and business, non-native speakers are often required to write in English, and this task may be challenging since communication is essential in these areas (Bhatia 2010, 2012). Taking into account the practical needs of small and medium-sized companies in Spain, we selected some text types that are often required to be written in English and initiated the whole process with the compilation of specialised bilingual comparable corpora in English and Spanish.

2.1. Compilation of comparable corpora

The selection of texts for the comparable corpora was carried out ensuring that the English and Spanish texts were similar in several parameters: size (in number of texts and words), balance (from different sources), representativeness (of the genre) and availability (from freely accessible websites). All the texts were originally downloaded in HTML format. We cleaned and saved them in txt format using UTF-8 encoding (machine-readable format) for the subsequent stages of tagging and browsing. A database was compiled in Excel with a list of all the texts, including the titles, the number of words and the ID codes (i.e. names of the files), e.g., [008ChD_140321FoodEN], where the first three figures indicate the number of the text in the corpus, the following letters refer to the corpus, e.g., ChD stands for Cheese Descriptions, then the date when the text was downloaded, then the reference to the field, e.g., Food, and finally the letters in uppercase indicating the language: e.g., EN – English. The complete list of all the texts in our comparable corpora is available at: https://actres.unileon.es/wp/es/corpus-comparables/

All in all, the ACTRES research team compiled a total of 16 English-Spanish comparable corpora in two different stages. The corpora in ACTRES 1.0 comprise a variety of textual genres, and the corpora in ACTRES 2.0 include promotional texts in the food and drink industry under the acronym of the current project CLANES (Controlled LANguage English-Spanish).

ACTRES 1.0: First stage comparable corpora
1. C-GDPE: Electronic products
2. C-GITEC: Technical reports
3. C-GIT: Appliance instruction manuals
4. C-GARE: Meeting minutes
5. C-AuRs: Audit reports
6. C-FMR: Football match reports
7. C-OPRES: Opinion articles
8. C-GAC: Biomedical abstracts
9. C-CT: Clinical trials

ACTRES 2.0: CLANES (Controlled LANguage English-Spanish)
1. C- FIVI: Wine tasting notes
2. BiTeX: Culinary recipes
3. C-FITECVI: Wine technical sheets
4. C-GDQ: Cheese descriptions
5. ACTEaS_Promo: Promotional texts for herbal teas
6. C-GEFEM: Sausages and cured meats
7. C-BakedGoods: Bakery and pastry descriptions

2.2. Tagging of the comparable corpora

Once the subcorpora were compiled, we started with the annotation process. All the texts were tagged for four different linguistic levels:

Part-of-Speech (PoS), rhetorical structure, semantic annotation and pragmatic tagging. The PoS tagging was carried out automatically using TreeTagger. For rhetorical tagging, the ACTRES computer engineers developed a generic tagger customised for each specific corpus so that the linguists could tag their texts manually. The semantic annotation was carried out following the annotation scheme called USAS (UCREL Semantic Analysis System) (Rayson et al. 2004), developed by the University Centre for Computer Corpus Research on Language (UCREL) at Lancaster University (https://ucrel.lancs.ac.uk/usas/). For a full description of the software used for the semantic tagging, see Sanjurjo-González (2020, 2021). For pragmatic tagging, the ACTRES research team devised a specific list of pragmatic functions, which was applied manually on a small number of texts. Later, all the other texts in the corpus were tagged automatically following this model with machine learning techniques (Rabadán et al. 2021a). For more technical information on the tagging process, see Sanjurjo-González (this volume).

Because we are dealing with a specialised genre, it was particularly relevant to tag our corpus with rhetorical labels indicating the main moves and steps in each text following Swales' move-step model (1990, 2004). A move "refers to a section of a text that performs a specific communicative function. Each move not only has its own purpose but also contributes to the overall communicative purpose of the genre." (Biber et al. 2007: 23). After manually analysing a small number of texts, we decided on a provisional list of rhetorical tags to annotate each corpus. These labels were then implemented into the ACTRES tagger by computer engineers in our team so that the linguists could annotate every single text in the corpus, one by one, with their labels. To ensure interrater reliability, the process was carried out separately by two linguists who discussed all the differences encountered during the rhetorical tagging to reach an agreement about the final labels. For more details on the rhetorical tagging of the CLANES corpus, see Pizarro Sánchez and Ortego Antón (this volume). Figure 27 shows the interface of the ACTRES tagger, with the pre-gold standard labels of the moves and steps, in this case, cheese descriptions.

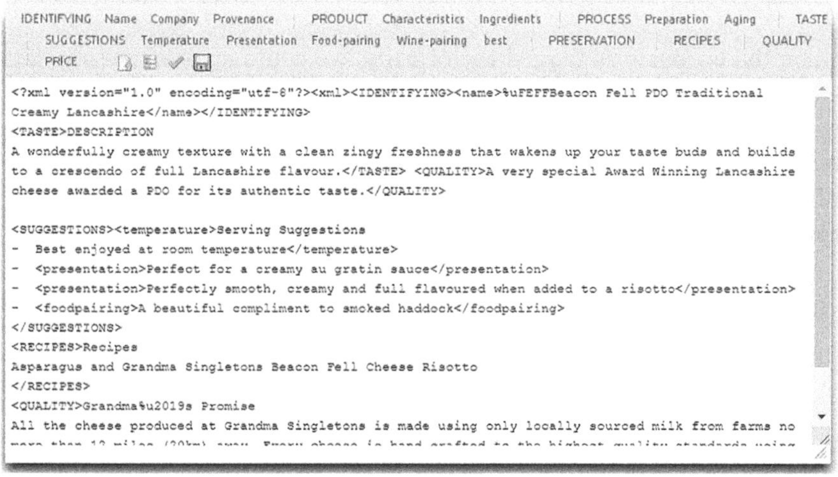

Figure 27: Interface of the rhetorical tagger with an example of an English cheese description.

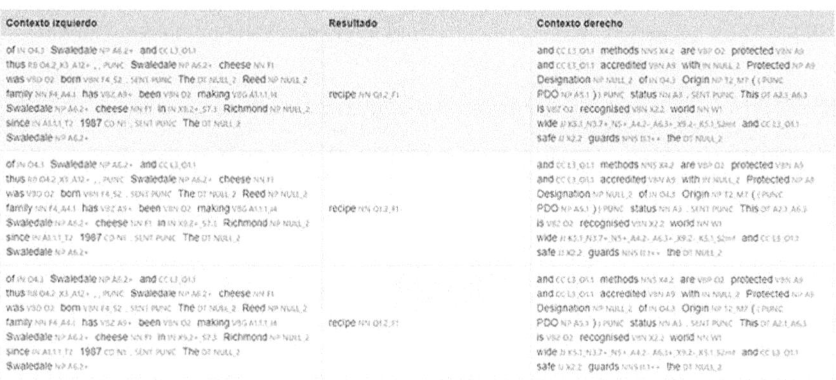

Figure 28: Interface illustrating PoS and semantic tags.

As for examples of PoS and semantic tagging, Figure 28 shows annotations from a corpus of the food and drink industry. The grammatical tagging appears immediately after each word assigning their part of speech. The following label/s refer to the semantic classification of each word following the USAS system mentioned above.

2.3. Retrieving linguistic information

Once the corpus was tagged rhetorically, we could start extracting data according to moves and steps in order to describe the language employed in each text. The browser designed for this purpose was then used to retrieve the concordance lines of the relevant keywords. The interface of the browser (see Figure 29) shows the screen divided into two halves, each one displaying the results of the searches in each language.

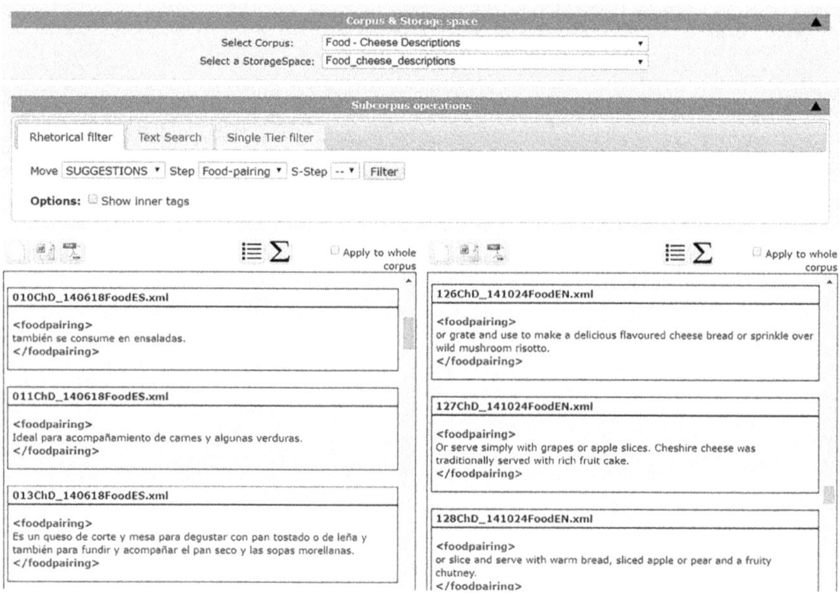

Figure 29: Interface illustrating the ACTRES Browser.

The dual screens allow for comparisons between English and Spanish, although the browser may also be used to search in only one subcorpus as a generic concordancer. It is possible to carry out searches in the whole subcorpus or in particular moves, steps or substeps. It is also possible to extract an entire move/step/substep without searching for a particular keyword or multi-word expression. Another feature of the browser is that it can be used to obtain statistical data: frequency lists, number of words and percentage of texts in that language containing a particular move/step/substep. Finally, the browser can export the results in Word or pdf formats.

The data provided by the comparable corpora enabled the linguists in the ACTRES research team to explore each subgenre cross-linguistically in great detail, gathering the necessary information to build the different text generators. English-Spanish contrastive studies based on these comparable corpora include publications on football match reports (Díez Fernández 2009), biomedical abstracts (Rabadán et al. 2011), opinion articles (Pérez Blanco 2013), electronic products (Labrador et al. 2014), instruction manuals (Cristobalena 2014, 2016), technical reports (Ramón & Labrador 2015), recipes (Rabadán et al. 2016) meeting minutes (Rabadán 2016; Pizarro Sánchez 2017), wine tasting notes (López-Arroyo & Roberts 2014a, 2015a), director's reports (Rabadán et al. 2021b), wine technical sheets (Moreno Pérez & López-Arroyo 2023), online promotional texts describing cheeses (Labrador & Ramón 2015; Ramón & Labrador 2018), herbal teas (Izquierdo & Pérez Blanco 2020; Pérez Blanco & Izquierdo 2022) and dried meats (Ortego Antón & Fernández Nistal 2020; Ortego Antón 2023).

The multilayer linguistic annotation of all the comparable corpora enabled the researchers to conduct in-depth contrastive studies to explore the rhetorical structure of the specialised texts, the recurrent phraseological patterns, and the most frequent technical and semi-technical terms. This information reveals clear and detailed linguistic conventions in English and Spanish for the writing of each of the subgenres studied in this project.

3. From comparable corpora to text generators

The foundation of the ACTRES text generators was the rhetorical tagging of the comparable corpora, as it provided a detailed structure of the moves, steps and substeps of the specialised texts, thus making it easier to guide the user through the writing process in English as a foreign language. Each corpus was tagged using a customised set of rhetorical labels adapted to each subgenre. A statistical analysis of the percentages of occurrence of the various moves/steps/substeps of the texts revealed that they were not present in all the texts.

The first important decision that had to be taken in the building of our text generators had to do with the number of moves/steps/substeps that needed to be included, as some of these rhetorical sections occurred more often than others. Previous authors have classified moves according to whether they are obligatory, conventional, or optional (Biber et al. 2007; Kanoksilapatham 2005; Suter 1993). Because the aim was to construct generators of prototypical texts in English, we established the minimum threshold of occurrence at 20% (Suter 1993). Consequently, any moves or steps occurring in less than 20% of the texts in the corpora were discarded and not included in the generators. For this reason, several moves and steps were excluded from the final rhetorical structure of the generators. Eventually, a prototypical rhetorical dataset was selected for each text generator.

The following step consisted of collecting the most frequent phraseological patterns that were observed in the English subcorpora in each move and step using the browser developed for this purpose. In this process, we identified the recurrent lexico-grammatical patterns used to express one particular communicative function, as "language use in a conventionalised communicative setting [...] gives rise to stable structural forms by imposing constraints on the use of lexicogrammatical as well as discoursal resources." (Bhatia 2004: 23). In specialised texts native speakers of English tend to employ a recurrent range of constructions which seem to have become conventionalised for the expression of a particular function. The patterns selected from the English subcorpora represent common idiomatic expressions to be suggested to the final users – native speakers of Spanish - as prototypical examples. Parts of these patterns may be shared with any texts of the same genre, and other parts need to be edited by the final user to customise the description of each particular product by adapting the suggestions given.

In addition to the rhetorical and phraseological information, we also used the corpora to compile unidirectional Spanish-English bilingual glossaries of terms identified as relevant lexical items in each particular domain. These glossaries include technical as well as semi-technical terms, both single terms and multi-word expressions, with one or more equivalents in the other language. Each entry contains a) the term in Spanish for which the user might need an equivalent in English, b) the equivalent(s) in English, and c) examples of usage. The compilation of these glossaries was carried out to complement the writing assistance offered to the final users.

We took examples from the corpora as prototypes, deleted some words from these authentic examples, and left blanks between brackets with a short indication of what type of information should be inserted there to complete the sentence or paragraph. Our research team coined the term 'model lines' to identify these template-like lexico-grammatical patterns or suggestions with gaps to be filled by each user. For instance, the following sentence extracted from the corpus was considered relevant for inclusion in the text generator: *It has a tangy flavour with a nice touch of salt and a lingering finish*. To adapt this particular sentence to any potential cheese description, we deleted the words *tangy* and *salt* and left gaps to be filled by the end user. In the interface, a generic term in Spanish indicates what type of information is required to complete the sentence, in this case, *cualidad* (quality) and *alimento* (food): *It has a [cualidad] flavour with a nice touch of [alimento] and a lingering finish*.

For various reasons, not all the comparable corpora eventually led to the construction of writing applications. On the other hand, the GEDIRE text generator was built on the basis of a monolingual English corpus, as these texts were not produced originally in Spanish. The 15 semi-automatic text generators resulting from this process, all of them registered as intellectual property by the University of León, are the following:

ACTRES 1.0: First-stage text generators

1. GAC: Biomedical abstracts
2. GDPE: Electronic products
3. GARE: Meeting minutes
4. FIVI: Wine tasting notes
5. GITEC: Technical reports
6. GEDIRE: Directors' Reports
7. GINA: Audit reports
8. C-GIT: Appliance instruction manuals

ACTRES 2.0: CLANES (Controlled LANguage English-Spanish)

1. GEFEM: Sausages and cured meats
2. FITEVI: Wine technical sheets
3. PROMOCIONA-TÉ: Promotional texts for herbal teas
4. GDQ: Cheese descriptions
5. PROCARU: Promotional texts for rural houses
6. GDEGA: Cookie descriptions
7. BITEX: Culinary recipes

4. Results: ACTRES text-generators

In this section, we will describe the type of writing assistance offered by our tailor-made generators to help native speakers of Spanish with an intermediate level of English in writing specialised texts in this language. The user-friendly interface is written in Spanish and is organised according to the rhetorical structure of each text type so that the user can start writing a new text from scratch following the instructions provided for each move, step and substep. Demos of all the writing text generators are available at: https://actres.unileon.es/demos/generadores/applications.html#generators2Section. In each section, the application offers suggestions of prefabricated sentences and authentic examples from our English subcorpora. Our bilingual glossaries are also part of the text generators, and they can be used to check equivalents of key terms in the domain during the writing process.

4.1. Rhetorical assistance

Because the end users are Spanish speakers, the interface with all the guidelines is in Spanish. As can be seen in an example of the cheese descriptions generator (Figure 30), the rhetorical structure of the text type that needs to be written appears in the form of a list on the left-hand side of the interface. A click on a particular section will open a blank box for typing the content required for that specific move, step, or substep. One or two sentences in Spanish are placed at the top of this box to guide the user even before starting to write. These suggestions refer to the number of sentences, the type of format (e.g., lists/phrases/full sentences), and the contents. They are based on the conventions found in the original texts included in the English subcorpora.

The colour code shown in Figure 31 (Director's report generator) refers to the fact that some moves, steps and substeps are compulsory or optional, according to the frequency of occurrence in the English subcorpora. The user can choose the order in which they want to complete the different sections of the text, but the final version will follow the standard prototypical order of this text type in the target language.

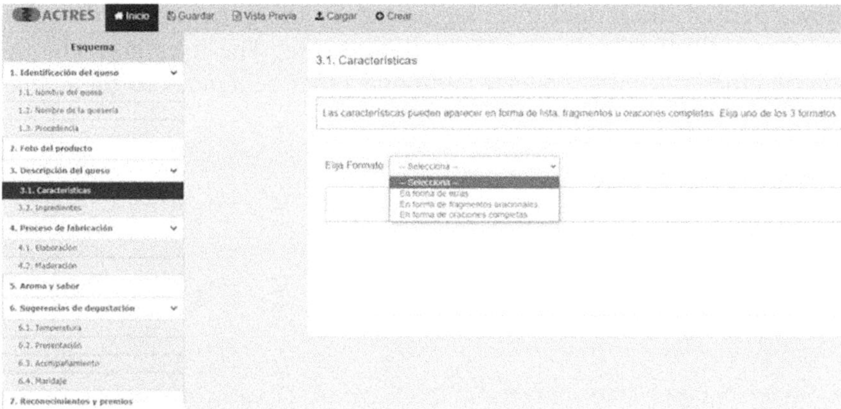

Figure 30: Interface of the cheese descriptions generator.

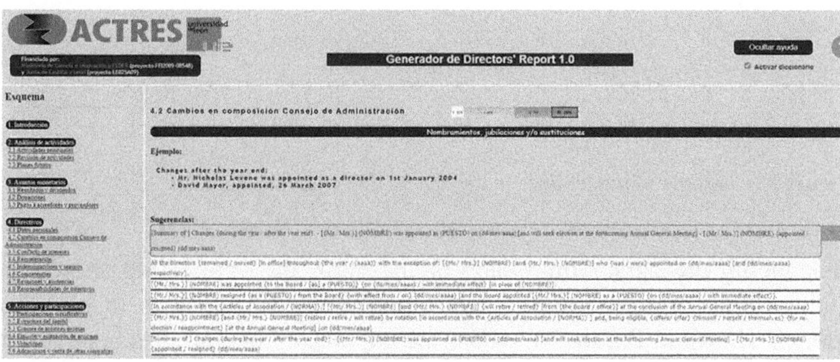

Figure 31: Interface of Director's Report generator.

4.2. Phraseological assistance

In section 3, we introduced the term 'model lines', which refers to the prefabricated sentences offered to the user as prototypical examples in the target language, English. All our model lines have been extracted from authentic texts in English and then edited to include a small number of gaps to be filled by the end user with the information referring to the product they want to promote. These gaps are not empty but contain words in Spanish, which are superordinate terms of the possible fillers in English to orient the user to what needs to be added there. Figure 32 shows part of the model lines suggested by the generator to describe the process followed in manufacturing cheese. The user may choose one or more of these sentences and add other sentences to their final description.

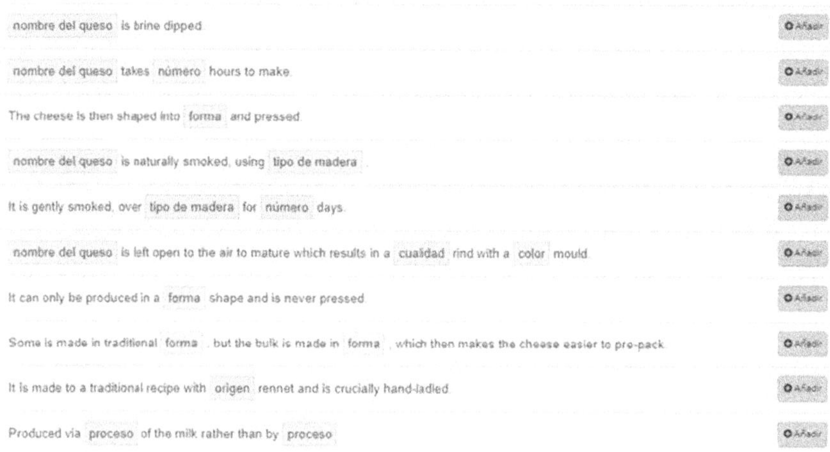

Figure 32: Sample of model lines in the cheese descriptions generator.

By placing the cursor onto each of the gaps, the application shows an authentic example with the entire model line in English to inspire the user, as shown in Figure 33, where the gap *origen* (origin) has been filled with the adjective *animal* used to characterise the origin of the rennet employed.

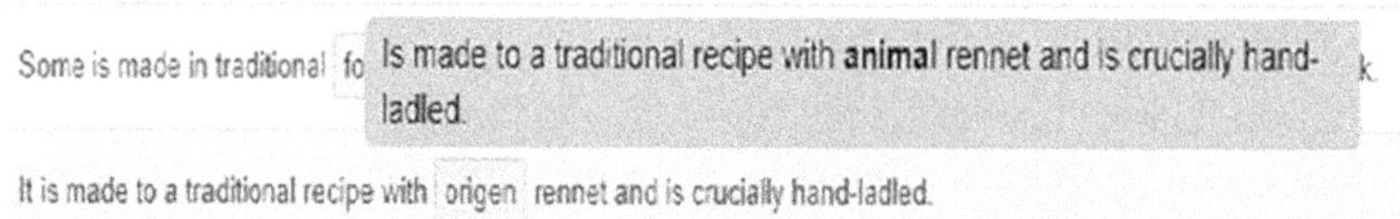

Figure 33: Authentic example from the corpus with a complete model line.

By clicking on the button *Añadir* [add] on the right-hand side of each model line, the application automatically adds the whole sentence to the draft text in order to shorten the typing process. In that case, the authentic example from which the model has been derived will appear to guide the user in filling the required gaps.

Some of the generators have a more complex system of model lines and include three different types of gaps: 1) obligatory gaps, where a lexical unit in English has to be provided to replace the Spanish indication; 2) optional gaps, where one option in English is already available, but not required obligatorily; and 3) selectable gaps, which indicate that one option in English out of two given alternatives must necessarily be chosen to complete the model line. Table 25 shows an example of each type of gap.

Table 25: Type of gap to be filled by the user of the writing aid application.

Type of gap	Meaning	Example
Obligatory	It has to be filled with a specific word in English.	*The use of (ELEMENTO) is recommended.*
Optional	Word or sentence is not obligatory.	*The fan must be clear to work [CORRECTLY]*
Selectable	One choice has to be selected.	*The fan {SHOULD/MUST} be disconnected*

The generators offer a variable number of model lines for each of the moves, steps and substeps. By choosing and completing some of them with the help of the glossaries (see 4.3.), the user constructs their own final text with the assistance provided.

4.3. Lexical assistance

Finally, to complement the phraseological assistance described above, the ACTRES generators feature unidirectional glossaries of technical and semi-technical terms from Spanish into English. These glossaries include single terms as well as multi-word expressions to assist in the filling of the gaps in the model lines.

Each entry contains a) the term in Spanish for which the user might need an equivalent in English, b) the equivalent(s) in English, and

c) examples of usage. An example can be seen in Figure 34, where the application predicts possible words in Spanish that begin with a particular group of letters (*suer-*), shows the English equivalent, and a real example from the corpus.

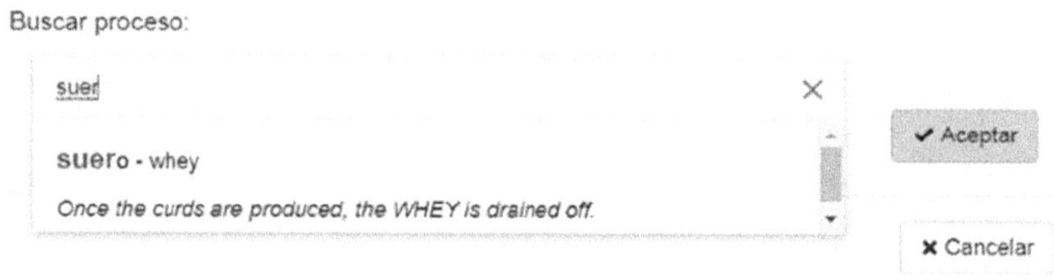

Figure 34: Authentic example of a search of the Spanish word *suero.*

When the glossary includes more than one English equivalent for the Spanish search word, the application displays all of the options with a separate example of each one so that the user can discriminate which one suits their need best. In Figure 35, we can see the English equivalents of the Spanish adjective *blando.*

- **suave, delicado,** blando – MELLOW *Garstang Blue is a unique, rich, MELLOW and indulgent blue cheese with an open body and a velvety, smooth and creamy texture.*
- blando, **húmedo, acuoso** – MOIST *A crumbly MOIST texture with a tang similar to a Wensleydale.*
- **suave, cremoso,** blando, **liso** – SMOOTH *Close and SMOOTH in texture, the cheese contains a minimum of 20% milk fat and a maximum of 60% water.*
- blando, **fresco** – SOFT *Mild and smooth with a slight tang which is creamy in colour with a SOFT moist open texture.*
- **elástico, colante,** blando, **fundente, soluble** – SPRINGY *When young it is SPRINGY and mild but as it matures subtle sweet flavours develop and the texture becomes firmer.*
- blando, **elástico, flexible** – SUPPLE *The result is a sweet flavoured cheese with a SUPPLE texture.*

Figure 35: Examples of the English equivalents for the Spanish adjective *blando.*

It is often the case that semitechnical terms cause more problems in foreign language writing than technical terms, which tend to engage in one-to-one correspondence. Despite the fact that technical terms are generally longer and more complex (from the points of view of morphology, spelling, pronunciation, etc.) than non-technical terms, the latter are usually more problematic to foreign speakers because of their variety of meanings, uses and collocations.

The three types of assistance described in this section, rhetorical, phraseological, and lexical, combine in each of the different generators to help native speakers of Spanish write specialised texts in these domains.

5. Conclusions

In this paper, we have provided an overview of the long-term research project ACTRES, which focuses on exploiting different types of corpora for English-Spanish cross-linguistic studies whose results have led to the construction of writing applications. Writing in a foreign language is a challenging skill, especially in professional contexts involving language for specific purposes (promotional texts in the food and drink industry, meeting minutes, directors' reports, instruction manuals, etc.). This need to assist non-native speakers of English in the writing of specialised texts in this language prompted our research.

After identifying the domains and text types where this need was more prominent in the local companies of our region, comparable corpora were compiled and analysed to extract relevant contrastive data reflecting the rhetorical, phraseological, and lexical conventions of each text type. These prototypical features were used to construct writing aids for non-native speakers. The ACTRES generators are rich template-like applications that include detailed guidelines on the rhetorical structure of each text type, an inventory of ready-made model lines, and a Spanish-English glossary of technical and semitechnical terms. Non-native speakers of English can use these writing aids to produce accurate and idiomatic texts that ensure successful communication in business contexts.

The main features of the ACTRES text generators, as well as the working procedure to obtain the relevant data to build them, can be replicated to improve second language writing in other specialised genres with similar needs. Therefore, there is a high degree of transferability from the domains of our generators to other professional areas, which may also benefit from specific writing aids. The ACTRES generators used by professionals facilitate text production, making end users more confident about the quality of their texts, speeding up the writing process, and reducing costs, as fewer external language services will be needed. These applications provide support for the Spanish industries, particularly small and medium-sized businesses, in expanding their markets more efficiently and increasing their sales worldwide. The ACTRES generators illustrate a way of bridging the gap between corpus-based contrastive research and real-life needs.

Regarding future research in this line, in 2022, the advent of freely available AI-enhanced tools based on large language models (LLMs), such as ChatGPT, Bard, Bing and Bert, poses new challenges in the development of technical writing assistance tools. The ACTRES research team is currently adapting to this new situation and finding ways of integrating linguistic expertise in the finetuning of LLMs (see Sanjurjo-González et al. this volume).

Rosa Rabadán, Ana García-Gallego and Hugo Sanjurjo-González

Post-editing grammatical interference

1. Introduction

In the age of human-machine collaboration, post-editing, i.e., the process of revising and improving a machine translation (MT) output, stands out as possibly one of the most 'traditional' forms of hybrid text production, other being provided by Computer-Assisted (or aided) Translation tools (CAT), Natural Language Processing (NLP) templates (Labrador and Ramón, this volume) and LLM text generation (Sanjurjo-González et al., this volume).

This paper will focus on managing English-Spanish grammatical interference in MT output post-editing using natural language evidence from corpus data. It will also present a plug-in (PEINT) designed to harness the findings in practice.

Human agents usually do the post-editing of machine translation, typically dealing with professional domain- and genre-specific texts where productivity and cost-efficiency are paramount (O'Brien 2011a, Guerberof Arenas 2014, Moorkens & O'Brien 2017) and following guidelines issued by professional bodies (TAUS 2024) and global watchdogs such as the International Standards Organization (ISO 2017). Human post-editing requires considerable cognitive effort (Moorkens 2018), which may partially explain the resistance of translation professionals (Guerberof Arenas 2013, Sakamoto 2019) and the attempts to automatise the process.

Automatic post-editing (APE) (Simard et al., 2007) made good progress for a while, but it has stalled in recent years. It is considered incapable of delivering consistent results (Do Carmo & Moorkens 2021) and not good enough to spare the final human stage. A substantial part of the problem, particularly in neural APE models, lies in the massive amount of training data they need. Training by means of triplets means original language documents, MT outputs and human post-edited versions, which are scarce and hard to come by (Junczys-Dowmunt & Grundkiewicz 2016; Negri et al. 2018). Transfer learning models using a pre-trained LLM add artificial data and reportedly deliver much faster training (Correia & Martins 2019). However, there is little information about the actual linguistic improvements these models offer or whether they discriminate MT errors that would benefit from APE optimisation. To our knowledge, APE is restricted to research environments and has not entered the translation/ text production professional ecosystem. As it is, MT and PE are just part of the workflow, and the agency is with the human translator/ post-editor. Since PE is strategic in the language services industry (Ginovart Cid & Colominas Ventura 2020), the challenge is integrating expert linguistic data into post-editing software and including it in the translation workflow.

Our proposal addresses the problem of source-language interference in MT outputs. It presents a replicable method to obtain fine-grained information that can assist with predicting advisable changes in the text. We also offer a computational add-on to use the findings profitably. This chapter is organised as follows: Section 2 presents an overview of post-editing as a professional practice and in research. Section 3 focuses on interference as a property of translated texts. Section 4 introduces the method and the data. Section 5 presents the results and the add-on designed to aid the post-editing of grammatical interference. Lastly, section 6 summarises the findings, interprets the proposal's improvements and limitations, and outlines future research directions.

2. Post-editing

Post-editing (PE) is the process of revising and improving machine translation "with a minimum of manual labor" (Massardo et al. 2016: 14). With continuous and sustained improvement in MT results, post-editing has become central in translation practice to the point of being considered a type of translation, since the MT output counts as "a set of suggestions and hypotheses" for the final translation (Do Carmo & Moorkens 2021:

35–41). PE guidelines are typically language-independent (Krings 2001, O'Brien 2011b, Flanagan & Christensen 2014, Massardo et al. 2016, ISO 2017, Daems & Macken 2020) and comprise two categories: light (rapid or fast) post-editing and full (or heavy) post-editing. Light post-editing means ensuring the quality is good enough without unduly affecting performance parameters. This is "defined as comprehensible (i.e. you can understand the main content of the message), accurate (i.e. it communicates the same meaning as the source text)" but as "not being stylistically compelling" (Massardo et al. 2016). Full post-editing amounts to human-like translation and revision, but still, Hu and Cadwell's review of available, published guidelines (2016: 350) reveals that parameters such as syntax or style deserve the following: "ignore stylistic and textual problems", "not important", among other similar guidance.

There have also been attempts at producing language-dependent post-editing guidelines, which tend to be formulated as carry-out instructions such as "*LS EN-ES PE Guideline 05*. Correct -ING adjectives by translating them as adjectives or relative clauses" (Rico & Ariano 2014: 310). They largely depend on the rule-based MT software used in the project reported on and, according to the authors, would need to be adapted for different contexts.

These sets of vague instructions are being increasingly questioned (O'Brien 2022, Rico Pérez 2024) because of poor feedback about the MT error types (Daems & Macken 2020) and lack of solid linguistic information to interpret the MT output results (Nitzke & Gros 2021). Also, the preference is for a more realistic understanding of translation, aiming at a "fit for purpose" translation (Bowker 2019), i.e., a translation that fulfils the requirements set by the client. All these remarks call for insights into the place of PE in the workflow to identify the needs of both practitioners (Blagodarna 2018) and trainers (Moorkens & O'Brien, 2017) to facilitate work routines.

PE has also received ample research attention, with a large portion of it focusing on three main aspects: the quality of MT outputs (Gaspari et al. 2015, Guerberof 2017, Way 2018); the evaluation of post-editing, e. g. Moorkens et al. (2018) as well as its consideration by human translators, e. g. (Cadwell et al. 2016, Cadwell et al. 2018), and the analysis of cost-effort and productivity (O'Brien 2011a).

An additional research line is post-editese, which is the difference between the characteristics of human-translated texts and the PE versions concerning the raw MT output. Daems et al. (2017: 90) introduced the term, which the researchers define as "the expected unique characteristics of a PE text that set it apart from a translated text". Toral (2019) conducted computational analyses comparing PE against human translation in five translation directions using three different MT output datasets. He used translation universals to measure simplification, normalisation and interference. Toral's study (2019) is carried out on lexical variety (type-token ratio) and lexical density (ratio between the number of content words and the total number of words), length ratio, i.e. the absolute difference (in characters) between the source and the target text, and part-of-speech sequences (whether the end text is closer to the typical source language PoS sequences or those of the target language). The findings were that MT outputs and post-edited documents are simpler, show more traces of normalisation, and have higher source language interference than human-translated documents. Castilho & Resende (2022) studied the post-editese phenomenon using two Google-translated literary texts and examined whether features in post-edited versions differed from the human translation and the MT output of the same texts. They use the PET tool (Aziz et al. 2012) and focus, with some terminological variation, on identifying simplification through lexical variety (richness here) and density, sentence length, and punctuation. They also track explicitation using the Personal Pronoun Ratio (PPR) and convergence (Baker's levelling out). The results revealed that, at least for one of the texts, the post-edited version was closer to the MT output than the human translation. As a countermeasure, neural MT projects have introduced the so-called "natural language" in the training data, non-translation mediated texts (Freitag et al. 2019, 2022), to minimise language bias owing to human translation data.

This study focuses exclusively on grammatical features in original texts and non-postedited MT drafts to track interference from English to Spanish. Section 3 reviews related work on translated language, translation universals and NLP.

3. Interference

Translated language has long been acknowledged as a "third code" (Frawley 1984, Øverås 1998), showing recurrent characteristics that define it as a separate target language lect, different from the non-translated, original language. Descriptive Translation Studies revealed that translated language had its regularities, regardless of source and target languages (Tirkkonen-Condit 2002). These have been formulated as a series of recurrent properties known as translation universals (TU), namely the distinctive features of translated language that differ from non-translated, original language. This line of enquiry produced abundant literature focusing on translated materials from various languages into one target language based on large-scale corpora such as the *Translational English Corpus* (TEC) (Baker 1998).

Notions such as simplification (Laviosa-Braithwaithe 1997), normalisation (Baker 1996:183, Lefer and Vogeleer 2013), explicitation (Blum-Kulka 1986, Klaudy 1998, Olohan and Baker 2000, Rabadán & Gutiérrez-Lanza 2023), the law of interference and the law of growing standardisation (Toury 1995/2012), as well as the 'unique items hypothesis' (Tirkonnen-Condit 2004) or the gravitational-pull hypothesis (Halverson 2003, 2010, 2017, Marco & Tello 2024), became accepted as the trademark of translated language. Besides being a map of the properties of translated language, TUs are used as a tool to collate and interpret contrastive analysis results (e.g. Martínez Vilinsky 2012, Marco 2018, among others) to empirically identify and verify cross-linguistic interference in applied activities such as translation, human or MT, (e.g. Rabadán 2011, Rabadán & Izquierdo 2013a, 2013b) and to contribute to translation evaluation (e. g. Ramón & Gutiérrez 2018).

From the point of view of NLP, the most popular applications of TUs are discriminating between translated and non-translated language, improving statistical -and neural- MT, and detecting translation direction. One of these discriminating TU features is interference, which can be defined as the transfer of linguistic features of the source language into the target language (Toury 1995: 274–279) in a situation of cross-linguistic contact.[1] In translation studies (TS), interference- or 'translationese'- has been traditionally perceived as a negative outcome of the contact between a source and a target code.[2] However, the fact that it

1 Interference is also relevant in other fields and has received different names (e.g. interlanguage; Selinker 1972) in fields where the phenomenon is relevant, such as language acquisition (Odlin 2005, Jarvis & Pavlenko 2008).

2 Throughout this paper, we will favour interference over translationese, but both terms will be taken to refer to the same phenomenon.

can be found in any target text, independently of the source and target language involved, has earned it the status of "law of translation" (Toury 1995). Interference entails that the source language can be found to 'shine through' any target text (Teich 2003: 207), or, in other words, that a given source language shows its "fingerprints" over one particular target language (Gellerstam 1996: 54), to mention two of the most widespread metaphors in the literature.

Unlike other features of translated language, interference manifests as a directional, language-pair-specific phenomenon. Like other translated language phenomena, it can be empirically identified and used to distinguish translated from non-translated language (Baroni & Bernardini 2006) and improve statistical machine translation (Lembersky et al. 2013). Studies such as Baroni and Bernardini (2006) model translational features computationally, including interference, so that universal hypotheses can be tested for discriminating power. More recently, Rabinovich & Wintner (2015) utilise translationese to feed a fully unsupervised method for distinguishing between original and translated texts that can be applied to different domains; Volansky et al. (2015) present linguistically informed feature sets and use them as a basis to develop robust classifiers able to distinguish between translated and non-translated language (Hebrew) automatically, and Avner et al. (2016) capture word- and sub-word-level properties that are used to boost their -mainly morphological- accuracy.

Improving MT has been and still is one of the most apparent reasons for research into interference. Among others, Lembersky et al. (2013) explore how to operationalise translated language features and use them for improving MT performance, while Twitto-Shmuel et al. (2015) demonstrate that awareness of translationese is an economical way to improve MT results as it allows for a dramatical reduction of the training corpora. Stymne (2017) touches upon the effects of interference patterns on MT, while Tezcan et al. (2020) focus on word-level quality using monolingual information exclusively. Pourdamghani et al. (2019) present a "translationese decoder" based on parallel data to help improve unsupervised neural MT.

Additional work focuses on automatically detecting translation direction (Sominsky & Wintner 2019). Corpora used for studying potential differences should ideally include a reliable indication of translation direction. While academic parallel corpora generally offer this information

(Doval & Sánchez Nieto 2019), this may not be so in multilingual institutional corpora, i.e., the UN Parallel Corpus (Tolochinsky et al. 2018) or Europarl (Rabadán 2019), which is a drawback, particularly when it comes to discriminating translation from non-translation and non-native features (Nisioi et al. 2016).

How interference findings are dealt with in the translation workflow undoubtedly impacts the quality of the translation outcome. Using empirical probabilistic findings to assist in identifying and singling out those linguistic parts that would benefit from human intervention would significantly speed up the post-editing process. This paper contributes beyond existing studies by offering expert linguistic data accompanied by probabilistic scales, which can help to identify problems, save time and curb the cognitive effort involved in PE. To do so, section 4 presents a procedure to identify these areas of interference for the language pair and direction English→Spanish and to conceptualise and operationalise them to be used as "PE nodes" to improve stylistic performance and text flow in post-editing.

4. Method and data

4.1. Tracking language-pair-specific interference

Studies such as Baroni and Bernardini (2006) and Volansky et al. (2015: 25–26) report that, among the TU hypothesis, interference is, by far, the most efficient in the characterisation of translated language and yields robust results, i.e., for some languages, the accuracy of using pronouns alone is over 75%.

We have started with Volansky et al.'s modelling of interference (2015: 16–20) in English. It includes PoS unigrams, bigrams and trigrams, character unigrams, bigrams and trigrams, prefixes and suffixes, contextual function words, and positional token frequency. Additionally, these authors include a miscellaneous section featuring a closed list of function words, with pronouns listed separately, punctuation marks, and the ratio of passive forms to all verbs. Although these classifiers are a great help, for the time being, they lack the accuracy to be expected from a language pair-bound tool, e.g., not all 3-grams are useful for Spanish translated from English, not all Spanish function words are equally relevant to the job, and not all verbal inflections in Spanish are equally affected by interference (see Table 26). A second drawback is that they require a large number of occurrences of a given feature to yield reasonable computational accuracy. Thirdly, proving a robust classificatory power for translated language does not necessarily imply that those features *always* indicate poor translation performance.

To mark the necessary transition from translated language classifier to meaningful interference fingerprint, we will use the concept of "anchor", which refers to "those -language-pair specific resources that can be empirically singled out as recurrent problem-triggers in cross-linguistic communication" (Rabadán 2008 & 2010:10) and reflect the usage of the source language rather than that of the target language. Anchors can be said to be the linguistic interpretation of interference markers and include directionality (Tolochinsky et al. 2018).

Previous work on interference anchors (Rabadán 2007, Rabadán et al. 2009, and Ramón 2009) has relied on a double contrast to unveil cross-linguistic differences between English and Spanish: first, cross-linguistic contrast using comparable corpora or a combination of comparable and parallel corpora; and second, a comparison of translated and non-translated language to verify the target language fit. This double procedure yielded two types of anchors: those that can be processed quantitatively, e.g., Ramón and Labrador (2008), on -ly adverbs into Spanish, as in (1) where the adverb is translated by a formal correspondent *desafortunadamente*, instead of using a prepositional phrase *por desgracia*; and those that are based on qualitative (as well as quantitative) differences and required direct human intervention on the spot, e.g. Rabadán (2006) on *poder* (can) in sensory perception contexts, as in (2), where Spanish would not mark any modality, but state a fact. Also, Rabadán (2011) on *cualquier(a)* (any, anyone, anybody) in negative target contexts, as in (3), where "no one…ever" calls for a full negative *nadie* in Spanish, and Ramón and Gutiérrez-Lanza (2018) on the functions of personal pronouns translated into Spanish, as in (4), where *yo*/I is redundant since it is already present in the verbal inflection, as it is the case with I had/ *tuve*

(1) *Unfortunately*, impending elections in a number of countries…
Desafortunadamente la proximidad de las elecciones en algunos países…/ *Por desgracia…*

(2) And from that need flows a number of characteristics that you *can see* very early in people's lives and in their professional lives.
Y de esa necesidad se desprenden una serie de características que *pueden verse* prematuramente .../ *se ven* prematuramente...

(3) Meredith was sure that *no one* who had seen those eyes *ever* forgot them.
Meredith estaba convencida de que *cualquiera* que hubiese visto esos ojos *no* los olvidaría nunca/...*nadie* que hubiese visto esos ojos los olvidaría *jamás*.

(4) *I* was so frigging cold after two hours, *I* had to go back to my hotel at midnight for hot tea and first aid. Al cabo de dos horas, *yo*/ ∅ tenía tanto frío que *tuve* que volver a mi hotel a medianoche para tomarme un té caliente y pedir primeros auxilios.

The manual qualitative analysis was considered a severe drawback in the potential applicability of the findings, which led to the metalinguistic characterisation of the contexts of occurrence and reformulation of the qualitative anchor format into quantitative processing, sparing the time-consuming analysis. For example, in our early approach, *apenas* followed by a numeral had to be qualitatively processed each time the pattern appeared in the target text by answering a yes/no question: *Significa 'solo'?* (Does it mean 'just, only'?). If the answer was 'yes', it was significant as an anchor; if it was 'no', that occurrence was not computed.

As a result of contextualised reformulation, additional anchors are now coded as metadata (e.g., *adj + adj + N)*. Others rely on a blended cluster of metadata and actual Spanish grams (*sin*/ without + N). A third group consists of grammatical categories, such as certain tenses (imperfect), and another includes Spanish function words, such as conjunctions (*sin embargo*/ however), pronouns (*yo*/ I), or affixes (*-mente*/ -ly). This strategy makes it possible to compute occurrences quantitatively. We apply Volansky et al.'s (2015: 16–20) classification to organise a list of 25 potential anchors obtained by contrastive work using general language corpora. Ten additional candidates were added to the list after a close examination of the texts in the food-and-drink domain (see section 4.3):

- Prefixes and suffixes: *-mente* (an adverb forming suffix, as English -ly), as in *desafortunadamente* (unfortunately).
- PoS unigrams: *imperfecto, infinitivo, soler (imperfecto)*(used to), *poder (ver+ oír, 1ª p.)* (can see, can hear, 1st and 3rd person singular).
- PoS bigrams: *sin* + N (without + N); no + N, no + adj; *apenas* (just)+ numeral, adj + N, *estar* + *gerundio* (be + -ing form), *ser* + Past

Participle (be + Past Participle), *como resultado* (as a result); *adv + adj*, as in *maravillosamente aromática* (wonderfully aromatic).
- PoS trigrams: *no + slot + ninguna, no + slot + ningún, no + slot + ninguno, no + slot + nada* (no + none/ nothing), *adj + adj + N; el hecho de (que)* (the fact that).
- Function words: Conjunctions, such as *sin embargo* (however), *pues* (so, well); pronouns: *esto* (this), *esa* (that), *yo* (I).

It is essential to keep in mind that anchors only signal a different distribution of elements in translated texts, offering probabilistic information (Echeverría Arriagada 2016). The statistical significance of these differences will help us determine which candidates are usable and can contribute to the post-editing of MT outputs. PoS annotation has proven essential in tracking these anchors or interference nodes from English to Spanish. PoS annotated corpora of translated and non-translated language provide the empirical basis to determine whether the differences in the distribution of these elements are significant or otherwise.

4.2. Corpora

Original Spanish (sub)corpus CLANESes and MT translated (from English) TRA_Clanes provide the empirical basis for this study. Both feature the language of the food and drink industries and are PoS annotated using Tree-Tagger in both languages. The original Spanish (sub) corpus (CLANESes) features 915,340 words, sourced from genres in the food-and-drink industries, such as wine tasting notes, cheese descriptions, herbal teas promotional texts, or culinary recipes, among others (see Sanjurjo-González, this volume, and ACTRES 2024). TRA_Clanes is a custom-made corpus containing 30,980 words. Its contents derive from original English texts selected to mirror the genres in CLANESes. They were translated using the free version of DeepL and manually post-edited to ensure intelligibility when:

- The interpretation of the English text results in a meaning change in Spanish, as in rich foods > *alimentos ricos* (*delicious), instead of *alimentos de sabor intenso* (rich, tasty foods).
- Proper names are translated, turning the wine cellar or the manufacturer unidentifiable in Spanish, as in **Níquel y Níquel* < Nickel & Nickel.

- English words are left untranslated in Spanish when there is an equivalent, as in cassis < *grosella negra.*

However, word-for-word renderings producing weird strings have been kept, as in, *roble cremoso* < creamy oak, more acceptable as *toques de roble suave/* soft touch of oak, alternatively, *toque cremoso/* creamy touch.

4.3. Method

As mentioned in section 4.2, translated and non-translated data are collated to determine whether the anchor candidates' use differs significantly between one corpus and the other. As a starting point, we have adopted the 25 anchors identified for general language non-fiction (Rabadán et al. 2014) (files 1 to 25, Table 26) and added ten additional candidates (files 26 to 35, Table 26) for the food and drink corpus. The figures for the general language corpus are not offered here as we only use the anchor list as an input. However, whether anchors' validity -and usability- can be assumed to be cross-sectional or, rather, it depends on and is exclusive of genre cluster is an important question that should be investigated, as it directly impacts the replicability of the method using the same dataset. Table 26 shows the list of candidates to become English-into-Spanish anchors, their raw frequencies in both the original Spanish CLANESes and the translated Spanish TRA_Clanes corpora, and the percentages and frequencies per million words, respectively.

Table 26: Anchor candidates for CLANESes and TRA_Clanes.

Food-and-drink promotional texts	**CLANESes Word number: 915, 340**			**TRA-Clanes Word number: 30, 980**		
Anchor candidate	**Raw freq**	p_1 **%**	**Freq per million words**	**Raw freq**	p_2 **%**	**Freq per million words**
mente/-ly adv	2,954	0.3227	3,227	189	0.6101	6,101
esto	120	0.0131	131	0		0
esa/ that (dem. fem. sing)	95	0.0104	104	1	0.0032	32

(*Continued*)

Table 26: (*Continued*)

Food-and-drink promotional texts	**CLANESes Word number: 915, 340**			**TRA-Clanes Word number: 30, 980**		
Anchor candidate	**Raw freq**	p_1 **%**	**Freq per million words**	**Raw freq**	p_2 **%**	**Freq per million words**
sin /without + N	634	0.0693	693	26	0.0839	839
no + N	5	0.0005	5	1	0.0032	32
no + adj	65	0.0071	71	1	0.0032	32
adj + N	10,598	1.1578	11,578	319	1.0297	10,297
soler/ used to (imperfect)	7	0.0008	8	0		0
Poder/can+(ver/see, oír/hear)	0			0		
sin embargo (however)	25	0.0027	27	1	0.0032	32
imperfect indicative	920	0.1005	1,005	73	0.2356	2,356
estar /be + gerund	5	0.0005	5	3	0.0097	97
apenas/just, only + numeral	2	0.0002	2	0		0
adj + adj + N	18	0.0020	20	2	0.0065	65
N + adj + adj	1,481	0.1618	1,618	78	0.2518	2,518
sido/been + past part	117	0.0128	128	1	0.0032	32
(other) passives	183	0.0200	200	13	0.0420	420
yo/I	183	0.0200	200	5	0.0161	161
no+slot+ninguna/none (f. s.)	0			0		
no + slot + ningún	33	0.0036	36	1	0.0032	32
no + slot + ninguno	0			0		
no + slot + nada	0			0		
no+V+ ning/nada	58	0.0063	63	1	0.0032	32
infinitive	14,399	1.5731	15,731	551	1.7786	17,786
-mente/-ly adv + adj	568	0.0621	621	47	0.1517	1,517
adj + adj+ adj	66	0.0072	72	4	0.0129	129
adj + adj	2,213	0.2418	2,418	106	0.3422	3,422
adj + y + adj	3,775	0.4124	4,124	136	0.4390	4,390
cualquier/any	14	0.0015	15	1	0.0032	32
cualquiera	277	0.0303	303	18	0.0581	581

Food-and-drink promotional texts	CLANESes Word number: 915, 340			TRA-Clanes Word number: 30, 980		
Anchor candidate	**Raw freq**	p_1 %	**Freq per million words**	**Raw freq**	p_2 %	**Freq per million words**
nuestro/our (m. s.)	223	0.0244	244	16	0.0516	516
nuestr*/your (lemma)	295	0.0322	322	5	0.0161	161
tu/your (possessive)	274	0.0299	299	4	0.0129	129
cada/each	378	0.0413	413	29	0.0936	936
gerund	2,779	0.3036	3,036	59	0.1904	1,904

As shown in Table 26, only 28 candidates appear in both translated and non-translated data; 4 do not occur in any food and drink corpora. Only the former have been considered. The data also reveal differences in the frequency of occurrence of the candidates in each corpus, and our objective now is to determine if these differences are statistically significant. The analysis of the differences is carried out through a hypothesis Z test for two independent proportions. In Table 26, if p_1 is the percentage of occurrence of a particular anchor candidate in the original Spanish corpus and p_2 its percentage of occurrence in the translated one, we contrast the null hypothesis (H_0), which states that both percentages do not show significant differences: H_0: $p_1 = p_2$, to the alternative hypothesis (H_1), which contemplates that anchor candidates may behave differently in the two corpora. If they do not show differences, the null hypothesis is accepted; if, on the contrary, they do, the hypothesis is rejected, and then we have an interference anchor. For example, if we hypothesise that the alternative hypothesis (H_1) for *Adj+Adj* is that $p_1 < p_2$, we obtain a p-value of 0.0004, and then we conclude that the null hypothesis (H_0) is rejected. Table 27 presents the results for CLANESes and TRA_Clanes data.

The quantitative results show 13 statistically significant anchors (see Table 28) and 15 that do not fulfil the requirement of a significant difference between original CLANESes and translated TRA_Clanes data. The third step is operationalising this information. Some anchors appear more, i.e., are overused, in the translated texts than in the original texts, while others appear less, i.e., are underused.

Table 27: Accepted and rejected anchor candidates.

CLANESes-TRA_Clanes	**Alternative hypothesis (H_1)**	***p-value***	**Conclusion on null hypothesis**
Anchor candidate			
-mente/-ly adv	$p_1<p_2$	0	Rejected
esa/ that (dem. f. s.)	$p_1>p_2$	0.2191	Accepted
sin /without + N	$p_1<p_2$	0.3364	Accepted
no + N	$p_1<p_2$	0.0652	Accepted
no + adj	$p_1>p_2$	0.4220	Accepted
adj + N	$p_1>p_2$	0.0378	Rejected
sin embargo/however	$p_1<p_2$	0.8697	Accepted
imperfect indicative	$p_1<p_2$	0	Rejected
estar/be + gerund	$p_1<p_2$	0	Rejected
adj + adj + N	$p_1<p_2$	0.0909	Accepted
N+ adj +adj	$p_1<p_2$	0.0001	Rejected
sido/been + past part	$p_1>p_2$	0.1386	Accepted
(other) passives	$p_1<p_2$	0.0082	Rejected
yo/I	$p_1>p_2$	0.6360	Accepted
no + slot + ningún	$p_1>p_2$	0.9132	Accepted
no+slot+ninguna/none (f. s.)	$p_1>p_2$	0.4955	Accepted
infinitive	$p_1<p_2$	0.0043	Rejected
-mente/-ly adv + adj	$p_1<p_2$	0	Rejected
adj + adj+ adj	$p_1<p_2$	0.2512	Accepted
adj + adj	$p_1<p_2$	0.0004	Rejected
adj + y + adj	$p_1<p_2$	0.4733	Accepted
cualquier/any	$p_1<p_2$	0.0063	Rejected
cualquiera	$p_1<p_2$	0.4602	Accepted
nuestro/our m. s.	$p_1<p_2$	0.0030	Rejected
nuestr*/our lemma	$p_1>p_2$	0.1177	Accepted
tu/your possesive	$p_1>p_2$	0.0855	Accepted
cada/each	$p_1<p_2$	0	Rejected
gerund	$p_1>p_2$	0.0003	Rejected

4.4. Operationalising anchors

This section will focus on making quantitative knowledge applicable, meaning anchors must be operationalised somehow. An earlier attempt contemplated three possibilities drafted after the explanatory statement format in translation behaviour by Toury (2004: 21). The first contemplated probability based on frequency: "Value B tends to be translated by <option x> in contexts of the type β and δ. A possible, but less frequent possibility is <option y>" (Rabadán 2008: 114). The second uses the upper and lower limits of the scope of acceptable, tolerated usage as revealed by corpus data. It is formulated as a quantitative prescription: "A number of occurrences of <phenomenon A> that exceeds/ does not reach magnitude α, or falls outside range γ-ε does not fulfil threshold quality conditions". The third is conditional and refers to qualitative features of anchors: "If a particular occurrence of <phenomenon A> means *x, x* being a transferred use in the language in question, it will detract from intelligibility and acceptability" (Rabadán 2010). To qualify as an anchor does not mean that a particular resource should not be used in translation. It just means it has been adopted as a translation solution more frequently or less frequently than in non-translated language. Under no circumstances should this be interpreted as a ban on perfectly good translation solutions (Echeverría Arriagada 2016). Since the first operationalisation format is purely qualitative, and the third has been rendered unnecessary by the addition of metadata representing the contexts of occurrence, we are then concerned with the second type, which could be streamlined as "if the number of occurrences of anchor x falls outside the limits of acceptable, tolerated usage, it does not fulfil the expected quality conditions".

To account for these limits, we need to determine an acceptability band for anchor occurrence that can be applied to any translated text. An acceptability band here can be defined as the permitted variation in the number of tokens for each anchor in a translated text so that it remains within the boundaries of acceptable usage in the target language.

4.5. Computing an acceptability band

Starting from the significant differences in the percentages of occurrence of the anchors in both corpora, CLANESes, and TRA_Clanes, we set out to determine an acceptability band to assist the post-editing of translated texts. CLANESes results are considered correct, whereas those from TRA_Clanes are set as the threshold of acceptability. One of the limits of the acceptability band is the value obtained from CLANESes; the other is calculated by building a confidence interval using the data from this same corpus. We have built a 95% confidence interval for a proportion (percentage of appearance) to obtain the range of occurrence that a particular anchor should show in any new translation to be within the limits of acceptability. This is computed by considering the error made (ε) when statistically estimating an unknown proportion in a population (p), i.e., here, the anchor tokens in the text. We can calculate a one-sided confidence interval for overused anchors by applying,

$$\hat{p} + z\_\alpha\surd((\hat{p}(1-\hat{p}))/n) = \hat{p} + \varepsilon$$

In this statistical expression $\hat{p}$ stands for the percentage (proportion) of anchor cases obtained from CLANESes; n stands for the total number of words in the corpus; z is the value of the standard normal distribution corresponding to a significance level of 5%; and ε stands for the error in estimating the real, or population, proportion p.[3] For example, if we query the corpus, there are 2,418 cases per million of *Adj* + *Adj* (see Table 26), which means that $\hat{p}$ is 0.2418%. In this corpus, n amounts to 915,340 words; the standard normal distribution for a significance level of 5% is 1.645. As this anchor is overused in the translations, the confidence interval is obtained as follows:

$$[0.002418,\ 0.000248 + \surd((0.002418 \cdot (1 - 0.002418))/915{,}340)) = [0.002418,\ 0.002502]$$

In translated language, the upper boundary for the acceptability band of *Adj* + *Adj* is 2,502 cases per million, and the lower boundary stands at 2,418 cases per million.

3 z_α is the value of the Z standard normal distribution, so the probability of any Z value being higher than z_α is equal to 5%. This value equals 1.645.

When the anchor is underused, we calculate the confidence interval as follows:

$$\hat{p} - z\_\alpha\sqrt{((\hat{p}(1-\hat{p}))/n)} = \hat{p} - \varepsilon$$

For example, there are 10,598 cases per million of *Adj* + *N* (see Table 26), which means that $\hat{p}$ is 1.1578%. In this corpus, *n* amounts to 915,340 words, and the standard normal distribution for a significance level of 5% is 1.645. As this anchor is underused, the confidence interval is

$$[0.011578 - \sqrt{((0.011578\cdot(1-0.011578))/915{,}340)}, 0.011578) = [0.011394,\ 0.011578]$$

In translated language, the upper boundary for the acceptability band of *Adj* + *N* is 11,578 cases per million, and the lower boundary stands at 11,394 cases per million. If we replicate this procedure for all under and overused anchors, we will obtain the upper and the lower limits of the acceptability band for each. Table 29 in section 5 shows the acceptability band for the food and drink domain promotional texts.

4.6. Calculating tolerance limits

To further enhance the predictive power of our anchors, we can also obtain what is known as a tolerance limit. This correction is important because it allows us to corroborate that we meet the specification limits, i.e., that we account for the permissible deviation from the ideal value represented by the original data, here CLANESes results. For non-statisticians, the tolerance limit can be defined as an extra extension of each anchor's appearance frequency over the observed TRA_Clanes frequency. This limit is calculated by computing a one-sided confidence interval for the percentage of translated anchor results, i.e., we bracket the real, or population, proportion from above or below to furnish an upper or lower bound to the figures obtained from the corpus.

To obtain the tolerance limits, we calculate the upper and lower limits from the frequency of occurrence of the respective anchor in the TRA_Clanes corpus, according to the abovementioned formulas. Thus, for overused *Adj* + *Adj*, the upper bound is calculated as follows:

$$0.003422 + \sqrt{((0.003422 \cdot (1 - 0.003422))/30{,}980)} = 0.003967$$

Where 0.3422 is the percentage of occurrence of the anchor in TRA_Clanes, and 30,980 is the total number of words in that corpus. The upper limit is set at 3,967 occurrences per million, while the lower limit remains at 2,418 occurrences per million.

For underused *adj* + *N*, whose percentage of occurrence is 1.0297%, the lower limit is set at:

$$0.01297 - \sqrt{((0.01297 \cdot (1 - 0.01297))/30{,}980)} = 0.009353$$

This means that the lower limit for this anchor is set at 9,353 cases per million, while the upper limit remains at 11,578 cases per million. Tolerance limits for all our anchors are shown in Table 30 in Section 5.

Establishing an acceptability band and tolerance limits for the occurrence of our interference anchors can provide the basis for an accessible aid (PEINT) in identifying grammatical problems when post-editing. This diagnostic aid that saves time and -together with additional tools- can help to implement corrections more efficiently will be presented in section 5.

5. Results and applicability

Our analysis results in 13 significant grammatical interference anchors for texts in the food and drink domain, as shown in Table 28. They include grammatical (both morphological and syntactic) categories, such as *-mente*/-ly adverbs, the infinitive, the gerund, conjugated passives, aspectual periphrases (*estar*/be + gerund) and occurrences of the imperfect indicative. Additionally, function words *cada*/each, *nuestro*/our, and *cualquier*/any are also indicative of interference. Bi-grams adj +N, -mente/-ly adv + adj, and adj + adj and tri-gram N+ adj +adj complete this diagnostic dataset. Some items are part of more than one anchor, as with *-mente*/-ly adverbs and *-mente*/-ly adverb + adj. They have been considered separately because both contexts trigger interference in translations into Spanish, as in example (1).

Table 28: Interference anchors for CLANESes and TRA_Clanes.

CLANESes-TRA_Clanes	**Alternative hypothesis (H_1)**	***p-value***	**Conclusion on null hypothesis**
Anchor candidate			
-mente/-ly adv	$p_1<p_2$	0	Rejected
adj + N	$p_1>p_2$	0.0378	Rejected
imperfect indicative	$p_1<p_2$	0	Rejected
estar/be + gerund	$p_1<p_2$	0	Rejected
N+ adj +adj	$p_1<p_2$	0.0001	Rejected
(other) passives	$p_1<p_2$	0.0082	Rejected
infinitive	$p_1<p_2$	0.0043	Rejected
-mente/-ly adv + adj	$p_1<p_2$	0	Rejected
adj + adj	$p_1<p_2$	0.0004	Rejected
cualquier/any	$p_1<p_2$	0.0063	Rejected
nuestro/our m. s.	$p_1<p_2$	0.0030	Rejected
cada/each	$p_1<p_2$	0	Rejected
gerund	$p_1>p_2$	0.0003	Rejected

Our second dataset (Table 29) presents the anchors' band of acceptability, making available the optimal range in the number of instances for each grammatical anchor calculated per million words, i.e. the band for each new target text will be calculated according to these figures. Falling within the limits of the acceptability band will mean that the text's grammatical usage mirrors the correct, entirely acceptable usage in the target language, Spanish, in this case.

Table 29: Acceptability band for anchors in *food and drink* promotional texts.

Food and drink register	**Difference CLANES/ TRA_Clanes**	**%**		**Per million words**	
Anchor	**Sign**	**Lower limit**	**Upper limit**	**Lower limit**	**Upper limit**
-mente/-ly adv	overused	0.3227%	0.3325%	3,227	3,325
adj + N	underused	1.1394%	1.1578%	11,394	11,578
imperfect indicative	overused	0.1005%	0.1060%	1,005	1,060

(*Continued*)

Table 29: (*Continued*)

Food and drink register	Difference CLANES/ TRA_Clanes	%		Per million words	
Anchor	**Sign**	**Lower limit**	**Upper limit**	**Lower limit**	**Upper limit**
estar/be + gerund	overused	0.0005%	0.0009%	5	9
N+ adj +adj	overused	0.1618%	0.1687%	1,618	1,687
(other) passives	overused	0.0200%	0.0224%	200	224
infinitive	overused	1.5731%	1.5945%	15,731	15,945
-mente/-ly adv + adj	overused	0.0621%	0.0663%	621	663
adj + adj	overused	0.2418%	0.2502%	2,418	2,502
cualquier/any	overused	0.0303%	0.0333%	303	333
nuestro/our m. s.	overused	0.0244%	0.0270%	244	270
cada/ each	overused	0.0413%	0.0448%	413	448
gerund	underused	0.2941%	0.3036%	2,941	3,036

The third dataset (Table 30) shows the tolerance limits calculated for all the anchors identified. These figures constitute the upper and lower absolute limits of permissible use and indicate that anything outside the scope of these limits is considered an error. The tolerance limits include the acceptability band and are calculated per million words. The tolerance limits are critical when programming the PEINT add-on (as shown in section 5.1).

Table 30: Tolerance limits for anchors in food and drink promotional texts.

Food and drink register	Difference CLANES/ TRA_Clanes	%		Per million words	
Anchor	**Sign**	**Lower limit**	**Upper limit**	**Lower limit**	**Upper limit**
-mente/-ly adv	overused	0.3227%	0.6828%	3,227	6,828
adj + N	underused	0.9353%	1.1578%	9,353	11,578
imperfect indicative	overused	0.1005%	0.2810%	1,005	2,810
estar/be + gerund	overused	0.0005%	0.0189%	5	189

Food and drink register	**Difference CLANES/ TRA_Clanes**	**%**		**Per million words**	
Anchor	**Sign**	**Lower limit**	**Upper limit**	**Lower limit**	**Upper limit**
N + adj + adj	overused	0.1618%	0.2986%	1,618	2,986
(other) passives	overused	0.0200%	0.0611%	200	611
infinitive	overused	1.5731%	1.9021%	15,731	19,021
-mente/-ly adv + adj	overused	0.0621%	0.1881%	621	1,881
adj + adj	overused	0.2418%	0.3967%	2,418	3,967
cualquier/any	overused	0.0303%	0.0806%	303	806
nuestro/our m. s.	overused	0.0244%	0.0729%	244	729
cada/each	overused	0.0413%	0.1222%	413	1,222
gerund	underused	0.1497%	0.3036%	1,497	3,036

5.1. The PEINT add-on

To harness the findings in practice, we have developed a software application to analyse translated texts, the PEINT add-on. Each anchor's occurrences are identified through an unsupervised recognition task, and the acceptable in-tolerance-range number for each anchor token in the translation is automatically calculated. The user retains the final decision-making and the extent of the post-editing intervention concerning interference.

One of the objectives considered during the development of PEINT was its integration with a text editor so that it would not be necessary to rely on external tools when using the software. Additionally, this strategy allows for the utilisation of the basic features of the editor, such as writing, formatting, autocorrection, and also integration with other plug-ins. The possibilities of creating extensions for Microsoft Word, LibreOffice, and Google Docs were considered. Ultimately, Google Docs was selected because it is a free web-based application, meaning it is free to use and requires no installation. Furthermore, Google Docs enables the development of add-ons or extensions using Google Apps Script, a JavaScript-based language that facilitates the creation of these custom integrations simply and efficiently.

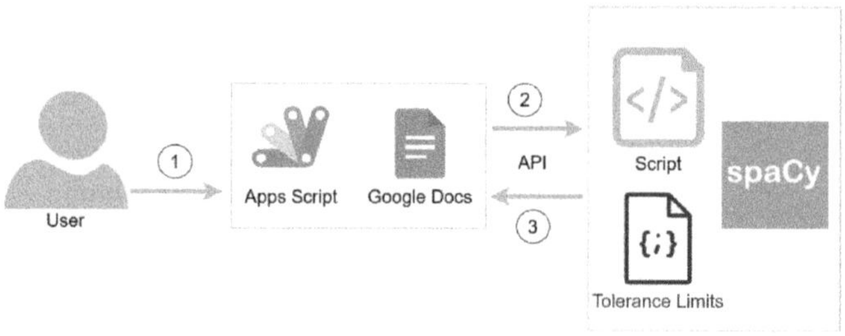

Figure 36: The simple architecture of the PEINT add-on.

The architecture of the application is straightforward, as illustrated in Figure 36. The user interacts with Google Docs and executes the application. Then, Google Apps Script communicates with an API (Application Programming Interface), and the text is analysed. The anchors whose numbers fall outside the tolerance limits are highlighted, generating a brief report. The application's logic is built using SpaCy.

On the one hand, SpaCy's rule-matching engine is employed to identify anchors. On the other hand, the es_core_news_md Spanish model is used for tokenisation and grammatical tagging. Fifteen unique matchers were created, combining these elements, incorporating words, grammatical tags, and regular expressions to recognise each anchor. Figure 37 shows an example of text analysis using the PEINT add-on, and Figure 38 shows the same text re-analysed once the interference issues have been addressed.

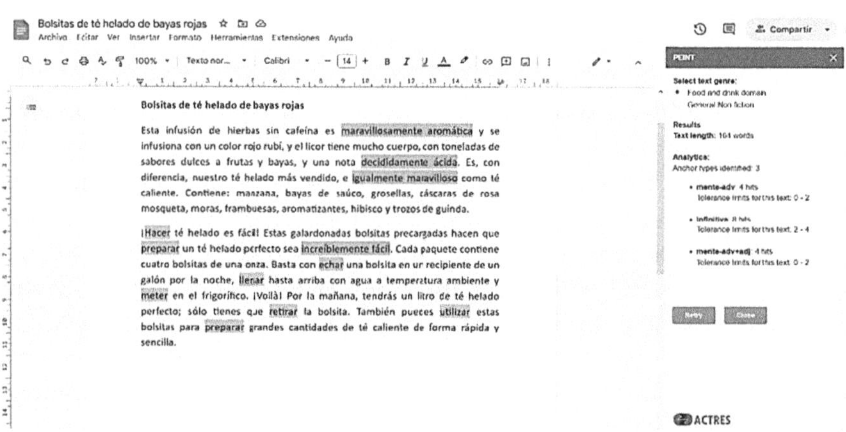

Figure 37: Example of text analysis using the PEINT add-on.

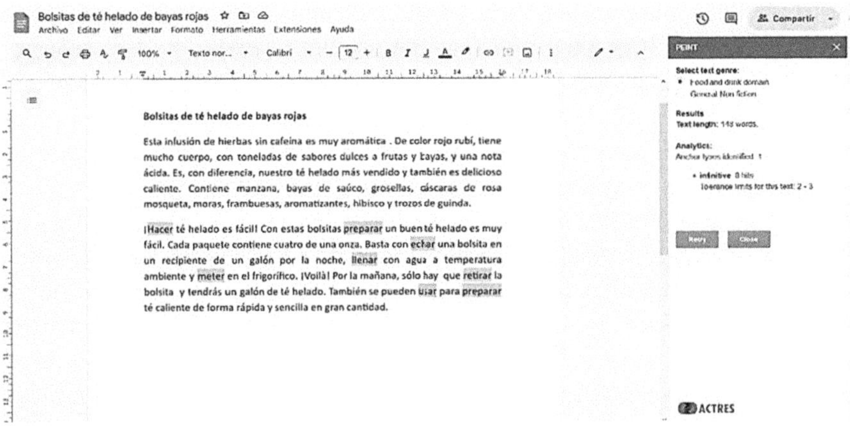

Figure 38: Figure 37 text re-analysed once some of the interference issues had been addressed.

Tests were conducted by running a sample of original Spanish texts through PEINT. The results show that PEINT generally identifies interference, helping to structure the post-editing checklist and saving time. After running an informal test with academics, some of the testers suggested making PEINT do double duty by turning it into a training tool and adding options for alternative translation solutions. It would, however, detract from human decision-making, impose additional normalisation in the target language, and require extensive research into pragmatic meanings and contexts of occurrence at a very granular level to cover all potential cases. Addressing nodes of interference and supplying the post-editor with boundaries will help to reduce inconsistencies in the final document while giving the professionals leverage in their decisions.

6. Conclusions

This proposal may contribute a sound solution for unwanted grammatical interference in the post-editing toolbox for at least three reasons. First, unlike approaches based on previous human post-editing, it uses targeted expert data based on both translated and non-translated language.

Second, when massive amounts of data are not available for training, a suitable solution that may alleviate the problem caused by data scarcity in specific contexts is relying on annotated data, such as those provided by CLANES. Third, offering interference datasets in professional practice may also alleviate the cognitive load involved in identifying errors.

As with any proposal, it has limitations. From the linguists' point of view, the indispensable contrastive work to identify the anchor nodes and to formalise the contexts where there is interference is labour-intensive, even if using computational and statistical aids. Contrast requires richly annotated corpora (e.g., CLANES), as interference may be found in other language levels, such as pragmatic and rhetorical. Identifying and operationalising these contexts would raise acceptability and result in more efficient target texts. Computationally, it is necessary to account for actual source-target language interference and for uses that are errors caused by the MT engine. The fact that this proposal is bound to a language pair and direction makes it possible to replicate the procedure but not to generalise the results to other language combinations, which is needed if willing to reach higher levels of automatisation.

Our proposal addresses the problem of interference in MT outputs and the mixed human-machine text production pipeline in English into Spanish contexts. It also considers the post-editor/translator 'priming' by the MT output and contributes applicable data derived from empirical evidence of natural language usage. The fact that the datasets can be used either integrated with the workflow or as a standalone tool facilitates usage both in highly automated contexts and in those that do not have a cutting-edge technological setup.

If this type of expert data on interference is harvested for other language pairs and directions, it is reasonable to assume that, eventually, interference-cancelling strategies will be deployed directly into unsupervised translation algorithms, thus relieving the need for grammar post-editing. For the time being, however, integrating crucial expert data on cross-linguistic interference in apparently low-key tools offers some answers.

Hugo Sanjurjo-González, Rosa Rabadán and Noelia Ramón

Enhancing template-based text generation using Large Language Models

1. Introduction

According to Reiter and Dale (1997: 57), "text Generation is a subdiscipline of Natural Language Processing used to fulfill specific communicative requirements by automatically generating natural language texts that leverage computational linguistics and artificial intelligence abilities". Li et al. (2024: 1) simplify that definition, and argue that text generation "aims to produce plausible and readable text in human language from input data". Text generation has been considered one of the most challenging tasks of Natural Language Processing (NLP) due to the difficulties in achieving coherence, meaning and quality of the generated text by the machine, as well as considering linguistic structure, grammar, word usage and reasoning (Celikyilmaz et al. 2020).

Traditionally, text generation was mainly based on symbolic approaches that make use of rules according to predefined grammars or statistical analysis (Goyal et al. 2023: 1). Over the years, the ACTRES research group has carried out a variety of corpus-based English-Spanish analyses in the areas of contrastive grammar, rhetoric and phraseology to be used in the development of template-based writing assistants (see Labrador & Ramón, this volume). The aim is to help Spanish users in different professional fields to generate texts in their specific professional fields in English.

Recent advances in deep learning methods and, more concretely, the rise of LLMs (Large Language Models) based on the Transformers architecture (Vaswani et al. 2017) represent a true revolution and incredible progress in the fulfilment of this text generation, as stated by Topal et al. (2021). LLMs have outperformed all previous approaches in text generation. This success has significantly surpassed earlier symbolic, statistical, and deep learning approaches to NLP in terms of both performance and sophistication while also reducing the manual effort required. However, as noted by Maestre et al. (2024), there is still room for improvement. Many tools that rely on symbolic or statistical approaches have become obsolete; nonetheless, they still offer more control over logic and meaning, which can lead to more coherent and contextually relevant texts.

In this chapter, we present an analysis of how various tasks performed by LLMs can contribute to and enhance the classical approach followed by the ACTRES research group over the last few years. The main objective is not to build text generation software using LLM capabilities from scratch but to take advantage of the knowledge and expertise derived from previous corpus-based analysis in combination with the advanced natural language understanding of LLMs in order to optimise the overall process.

We will focus on overcoming the limitations of the template-based approaches, such as the lack of diversity, fluency, and informativeness (Goyal et al. 2023: 3). To achieve this goal, we propose to use LLMs to expand the number of templates available and the vocabulary dynamically. Additionally, we aim to implement spelling and grammar-checking functionalities to facilitate text inclusions beyond the template system, as well as a prompting feature to query information pertinent to the specific textual genre.

The remainder of the paper is organised as follows: Section 2 presents an overview of foundational concepts and recent advancements in text generation. In Section 3, the ACTRES methodology for text generation is explored in two subsections: the methodology (3.1) and the software tool (3.2) employed. Section 4 introduces improvements to these methods by leveraging LLMs. Lastly, Section 5 summarises the findings and outlines future research directions.

2. A brief introduction to text generation technologies

Text generation and Natural Language Generation (NLG) are closely related terms that are often used interchangeably; the former is more related to automatic text creation methods, and the latter focuses on high-quality, human-like, readable text. Generally speaking, an NLG system should be able to reliably generate texts that meet certain manageable constraints that are imposed by the targeted applications and users (Zhang et al. 2023: 2). Those constraints are specific to the task.

The first generation of NLG systems was symbolic and based on rules. Basic systems used template-filling methods, and more sophisticated options used grammars. Template-filling performed very well on small domains and applications. On the other hand, grammar-based systems make some or all of their choices on the basis of the grammar of the language under consideration (Gatt & Krahmer 2018), i.e., rules that specify mappings from input features to syntactic positions and surface forms (Habash et al. 2003). These methods often relied on discourse structures such as the Rhetorical Structure Theory (Mann & Thompson 1987).

Later, the statistical approach performed language processing tasks using information from larger datasets, such as treebanks and linguistically annotated corpora, which offered additional information. These systems perform very effectively when obtaining lexical information such as n-grams or other syntactic patterns, but they cannot extract conceptual knowledge (Habash et al. 2003). Information is often presented in the form of statistics but also as complex rules, dictionary entries or other resources.

The hybrid approach tried to overcome the ambiguity of the linguistically blind statistical hypotheses using linguistically motivated approaches (Habash et al. 2003). Hybrid systems integrate symbolic and statistical techniques to leverage their respective strengths while addressing their weaknesses, particularly by combining rich lexical, grammatical, and conceptual knowledge with statistical data. They aim to reduce ambiguity from statistical hypotheses using linguistically motivated rules and employ statistical methods for final decision-making.

Advances in deep neural networks, such as recurrent neural networks (Hochreiter & Schmidhuber 1997) and generative adversarial networks (Goodfellow et al. 2014), significantly improved the accuracy of various tasks identifying patterns and features that assist in solving several text generation tasks (Goyal et al. 2023: 2). They also enabled machine learning of effective language representations by means of rich word embedding representations.

Up to the present, methods using large-scale pre-trained language models (PTLMs) such as BERT (Devlin et al. 2019), GPT (Radford et al. 2018), or T5 (Raffel et al. 2020), based on the Transformers architecture

(Vaswani et al. 2017), are increasingly being adopted by cutting-edge NLG systems. PTLMs have been trained on vast amounts of corpus data, enabling them to effectively model the distribution of natural language and generate text with an unprecedented level of quality, capturing the linguistic knowledge of vocabulary, syntax, and grammar (Deng et al. 2020).

As Goyal et al. (2023: 3) state, "traditional template-based methods generate reliable texts but lack diversity, fluency, and informativeness," whereas transformer-based models "generate fluent, informative, and controllable text, but the inconsistency with the input information persists." In other words, although LLMs demonstrate incredible performance across a wide range of NLP tasks, they are not perfect. Certain tasks, such as text generation in very specific contexts, may require additional guidelines that LLMs do not inherently possess.

As Kaufer and Ishizaki (2024) assert, Artificial Intelligence should complement human creativity in writing, making the process more effective and inclusive.

3. Text Generation in ACTRES

As stated in Section 2, one of the aims of the ACTRES research group is to develop writing applications addressed to Spanish language non-linguist users in different professional fields and contexts, such as the food and drink industry (Rabadán et al. 2021b; Labrador & Ramón, this volume). This task is addressed by reframing the NLG problem as one of controllable text generation. This refers to the task of generating text according to the given controlled element (Prabhumoye et al. 2020). There are two primary dimensions (Liang et al. 2024: 3):

- Ensuring that the generated text adheres to predefined conditions, such as text structure and thematic focus, and
- maintaining the text's helpfulness, fluency, and diversity as essential quality standards.

Over the years, the research group has developed various text generators based on specific text genres such as online advertisements, dried meat notes, cheese descriptions, wine tasting notes, herbal tea promotional texts, cookie descriptions, culinary recipes and promotional texts for rural accommodation. Demos for these text generators are available at https://actres.unileon.es/demos/generadores/applications.html#generators2Section. All these applications involved constructing a textual representation built upon a rhetorical structure, a set of template-based sentences known as model lines, and a lexicon.

In this section, the linguistic study underlying the textual representation leading to the construction of the generators will be explained first. Next, the software application used as a text generator will be described.

3.1. Constructing the textual representation

A number of steps must be carried out to obtain the textual representation. First, a corpus of the specific text genre in English is compiled. This corpus must be sufficiently large and diverse to allow corpus-based studies. After that, a corpus-based study is carried out using different tools of the ACTRES ecosystem, such as the ACTRES rhetorical tagger, the ACTRES browser, ACM (https://actres.unileon.es/wp/tools/) (Sanjurjo-González 2017), and occasionally other tools like AntConc (Anthony 2024). Next, a conceptual representation of the text domain is established, comprising the following components:

- Text structure: A prototypical rhetorical structure of the specific genre is constructed, comprising moves, steps, and substeps based on Swales' work (1990, 2004). These sections are commonly found in texts of this type, as evidenced by the compiled corpus materials.
- Model lines: They are sentences and patterns that usually appear in the different sections of the document according to the compiled corpus. Sentences are extracted in both languages and analysed to identify similar structures that usually appear in the same context and are grouped under the same category, for instance, presentation suggestions. These sentences are then transformed into templates with several gaps that can be filled using the lexicon in a specific section of the previously stated rhetorical structure.
- Lexicon: It is an English-Spanish glossary that also includes a category corresponding to a gap within the model lines.

Figure 39 shows the relations of these components.

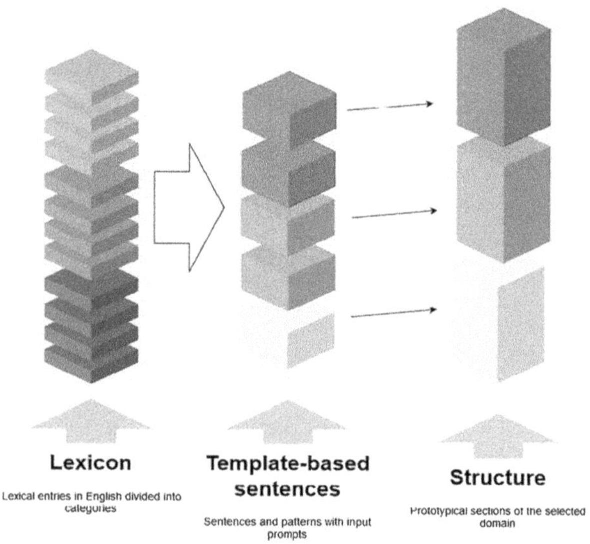

Figure 39: Relations of the components.

At the end of this process, we obtain a framework composed of a hierarchy covering lexical units, phrases, and document sections that are common in English texts in that particular domain. Figure 40 shows an example of a structure (i), a lexicon entry (ii) and a model line (iii).

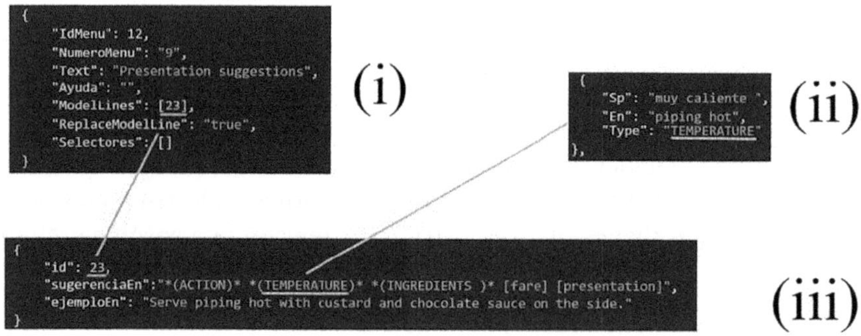

Figure 40: Example of structure, lexicon entry and model line.

3.2. Software application

The proposed architecture is based on a Node.js web application following a model–view–controller design pattern. In this case, all the logic is placed on the client. Text planning structure, sentence planning, and linguistic realisation are stored in a MongoDB database in the form of rules, lexicons, and model lines.

A MEAN (MongoDB Express Angular.JS Node.js) stack framework, characterised by its high flexibility and scalability, is employed. The API REST (Representational State Transfer Application Programming Interface) is the main element of the application, and it allows:

- To get data from the server according to the different services.
- To handle logic to show different views.
- To show information of the controllers taking advantage of the double data binding paradigm of Angular.JS.

Figure 41 shows the generic interface of the application using information from C-BiTeX, a bilingual comparable corpus containing culinary recipes.

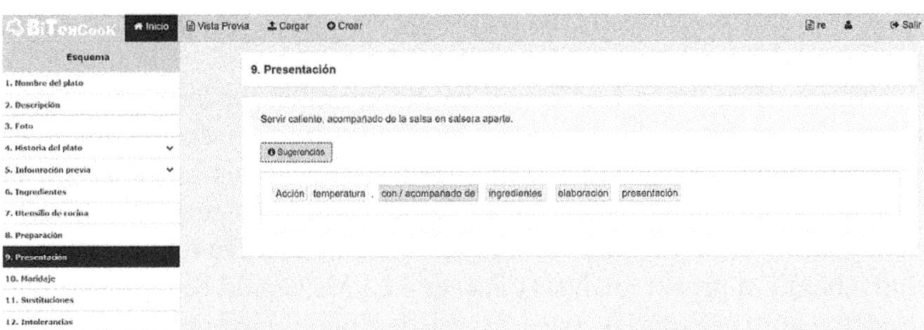

Figure 41: Interface of a developed prototype.

4. Proposed enhancements with LLMs

Proof of concept tests have shown that this template approach using corpus analysis data significantly reduces the amount of manual work compared to writing a document of a particular genre from scratch, increasing the lexical coverage of traditional templates. It is not merely a sentence planner as it provides the prototypical structures of a well-written document of a specific domain. It also adds sophistication as it provides a noticeably larger linguistic diversity.

However, while it is true that the rhetorical structure of the document may be fixed, allowing for the omission or addition of specific options, the flexibility of the system remains limited. The number of model lines is restricted, as is the vocabulary size. Correctness is only ensured if the user adheres to the proposed template sentences. There is a lack of information to corroborate or inquire about specific issues related to the particular genre. For instance, related to cooking recipes, what are the most common food intolerances? It would be very helpful to incorporate verified knowledge that addresses this and other questions instead of relying on sources of information that may not be entirely reliable.

Considering these limitations, this section proposes several areas for improvement that can transform the outdated and restricted system described in Section 3 into a functional and dynamic one. This can be achieved by incorporating some LLM-related activities, making the system more flexible and responsive to user needs. In other words, the use of LLMs can convert restricted and somewhat static text generators into useful and dynamic tools.

Various fine-tuned LLMs will be incorporated for the tasks of paraphrasing, grammar checking, and text generation, as well as for word representation. The chosen LLMs meet the conditions of being useful for the selected tasks, compatible with the required languages, and sufficiently small to be executed on the servers that host the text generators. Undoubtedly, a proper analysis of several LLMs should be carried out to select the most appropriate ones, as well as a fine-tuning process to adjust the model's behaviour to the selected context. This is beyond the scope of this chapter, which aims to highlight some advantages that LLMs can provide in symbolic text generators.

To conduct the experiments, the following text generators will be used:

- BiTeX (Rabadán et al. 2016): Spanish-English text generator composed of a rhetorical structure of 15 sections, 30 model lines and 729 lexicon entries divided into 10 categories.

- FiVi (López-Arroyo & Roberts 2016): Spanish-English text generator composed of a rhetorical structure of 8 main sections and 42 subsections, 92 model lines and 821 lexicon entries divided into 16 categories.

4.1. Paraphrasing model lines

One of the issues identified was the small number of model lines offered by the system. For instance, in FiVi, there are 92 sentences available for 28 inputs of text, resulting in an average of 3.28 sentences per section; in BiTeX, there are 30 sentences available, resulting in an average of 2 sentences per section. In both cases, this amount may be insufficient to provide the required dynamism to the system.

Paraphrasing involves rewriting texts to express the same meaning using different words or sentence structures (Bhagat & Hovy 2013). As a proof of concept, the PEGASUS language model (Zhang et al. 2020) was used. It is a text-to-text generation model according to Hugging Face Natural Language Processing tasks that were fine-tuned for the activity of paraphrase generation for English (https://huggingface.co/tuner007/pegasus_paraphrase). In order to preserve the elements used in the templates, the model was fine-tuned again with a small dataset of about a hundred examples that included the slots to be filled in by the user.

Figure 42 shows the results of this task using one of FiVi's model lines. As is shown, the paraphrasing process includes some of the gaps created in the original sentence-based template. A much more extensive fine-tuning of the model, including more examples of the structures used in the model lines, will undoubtedly improve the paraphrasing process.

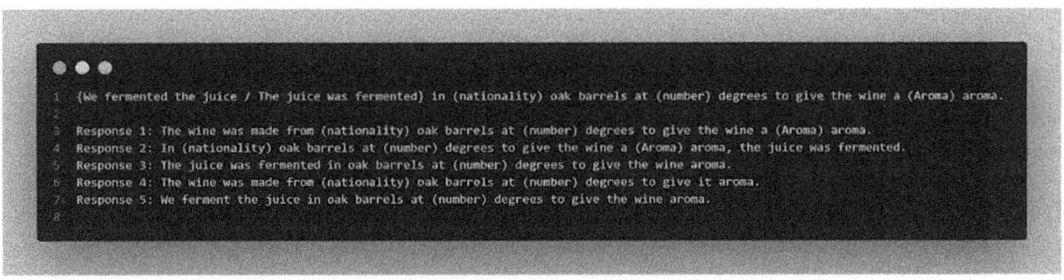
```
{We fermented the juice / The juice was fermented} in (nationality) oak barrels at (number) degrees to give the wine a (Aroma) aroma.

Response 1: The wine was made from (nationality) oak barrels at (number) degrees to give the wine a (Aroma) aroma.
Response 2: In (nationality) oak barrels at (number) degrees to give the wine a (Aroma) aroma, the juice was fermented.
Response 3: The juice was fermented in oak barrels at (number) degrees to give the wine aroma.
Response 4: The wine was made from (nationality) oak barrels at (number) degrees to give it aroma.
Response 5: We ferment the juice in oak barrels at (number) degrees to give the wine aroma.
```

Figure 42: Results of the LLM paraphrasing activity on a model line.

Even considering the potential paraphrasing errors resulting from PEGASUS, it is undoubtedly a valuable tool for increasing the number of available options through its integration into production and by leveraging the model's stochastic nature.

4.2. Spelling and grammar verification

As previously stated, the proposed approach only ensures the correctness of the final text if the user adheres to the template-based sentences provided. As there is a limited number of templates, once more, the dynamism of the system might be limited. One of the possible solutions to ensure the correctness of the user's input is to verify the grammar and spelling of user-entered sentences that do not adhere to the options proposed in the model line. Another text-to-text generation model based on T5 fine-tuned for grammar correction, is employed for this purpose (https://huggingface.co/vennify/t5-base-grammar-correction). In the experiments conducted, it was observed that the model can correct grammatical sentences that are not entirely deficient. Figure 43 illustrates the model's performance in handling simple errors.

Human sentence with errors:

`This sentences has has bads grammar.`

Sentence corrected by the model:

`This sentence has bad grammar`

Human sentence with errors:

`Flavors of concentratd and ripe citrus fruits dominate in the mouth and linger though the finish.`

Sentence corrected by the model:

`Flavors of concentrated and ripe citrus fruits dominate in the mouth and linger through the finish.`

Figure 43: Good results of the spelling and grammar verification on out-of-framework sentences.

However, if the errors are too severe, the model shows little to no improvement, as illustrated in Figure 44.

Human sentence with errors:

```
Flavrs of concentratd d rip citrus frts dominted in the moth and
linger though the finis.
```

Sentence corrected by the model:

```
Flavrs of concentrated d rip citrus frts dominated in the moth
and linger through the finis.
```

Human sentence with errors:

```
Flavors of ripe citrus fruits concentrated and dominates in the
through the finish mouth and linger.
```

Sentence corrected by the model:

```
Flavors of ripe citrus fruits concentrated and dominates in the
through the finish mouth and linger.
```

Figure 44: Poor results of the spelling and grammar verification on out-of-framework sentences.

The model has certain limitations: sentences cannot be entirely random, and they must maintain a basic level of grammar to be corrected. Still, spelling and grammatical verification can serve as a valuable writing aid and enhance the potential of the original proposal.

Another limitation is that this model lacks control conditions for text structure. However, it would be possible to fine-tune the model for checking specific genre grammar. While this is outside the scope of this article, the possibility remains open, and the process is theoretically feasible.

4.3. Question-Answering for genre-specific queries

A third possibility is applying prompting to genre-specific queries. LLMs have introduced the ability to provide personalised assistance with expertise in nearly every subject area through widely known chatbots. Examples of these include ChatGPT, LLaMA, and Gemini, among others (Dam et al. 2024). Despite the occasional issue of hallucinations (Perković et al. 2024) and outdated knowledge, these tools have proven to be valuable when used correctly.

In the case of text generators, one possible application is to utilise the question-answering (QA) capabilities of LLMs to address inquiries related to the specific text genre. QA models can extract answers to specific questions from a given text. Two methods have been applied to develop this feature:

- Using LLM internal knowledge exclusively.
- Using LLM internal knowledge combined with Retrieval Augmented Generation (RAG) allowing the use of external sources of information to answer the question.

In the first method, as an experimental test, the text generation Zephyr-7B-Beta (Rafailov et al. 2024) LLM was used. Although the model was trained in English, it is able to answer questions in Spanish. Figure 45 shows how Zephyr-7B-Beta answers correctly *¿Cómo hacer berenjenas al horno*? (How to make baked eggplants?) using Spanish.

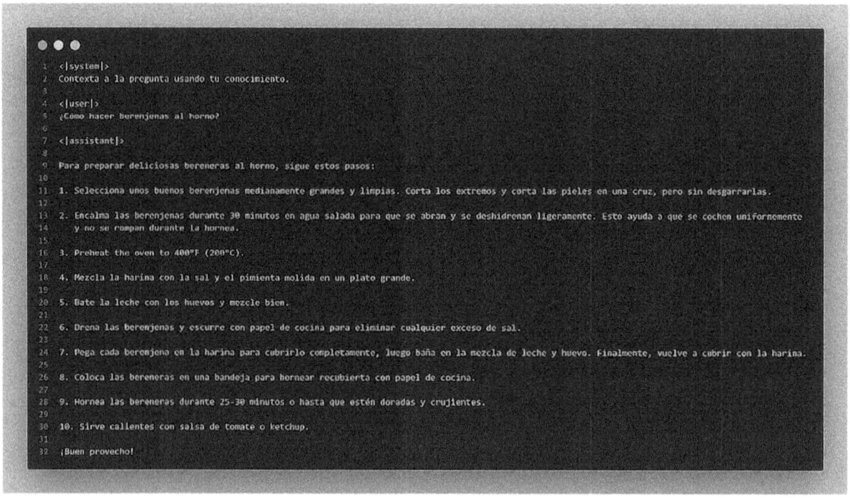

Figure 45: Query using zephyr-7b-beta model without RAG.

In Figure 46, the output from Figure 45 is translated for the reader's convenience.

Figure 47 shows the model's response to the question *¿Cuáles son las intolerancias más frecuentes?* (What are the most common intolerances?). The translation is provided in Figure 48.

```
<|system|>
Answer the question using your knowledge.

<|user|>
How to make baked eggplant?

<|assistant|>

To prepare delicious baked eggplant, follow these steps:

1. Select medium-large and clean eggplants. Cut off the ends and score the skin in a cross, but without tearing it.

2. Soak the eggplants for 30 minutes in salted water so they open and dehydrate slightly. This helps them cook evenly and not break during baking.

3. Preheat the oven to 400°F (200°C).

4. Mix the flour with salt and ground pepper in a large plate.

5. Beat the milk with the eggs and mix well.

6. Drain the eggplants and pat them dry with kitchen paper to remove any excess salt.

7. Coat each eggplant in the flour to cover it completely, then dip it in the milk and egg mixture. Finally, coat again with the flour.

8. Place the eggplants on a baking tray lined with parchment paper.

9. Bake the eggplants for 25-30 minutes or until they are golden and crispy.

10. Serve hot with tomato sauce or ketchup.

Enjoy!
```

Figure 46: Translation of Figure 45 output.

```
<|system|>
Contexta a la pregunta usando tu conocimiento. Usa el siguiente contexto para ayudar:

<|user|>
¿Cuáles son las intolerancias más frecuentes?

<|assistant|>

  Las intolerancias alimentarias son reacciones adversas que se producen después de
  consumir determinados alimentos debido a la falta de enzimas necesarios para
  digerirlos o a la sensibilidad excesiva del organismo hacia ciertos componentes
  alimenticios. Entre las intolerancias alimentarias más frecuentes se encuentran:


  1. Lactosa intolerancia: Esta condición se produce cuando el cuerpo no puede
  digerir la lactosa, un azúcar presente en el leche y otros productos lácteos. Es
  común en adultos que no han consumido leche durante largo tiempo y pierden la
  capacidad de digestar la lactosa.

  2. Intolerancia al gluten: Esta intolerancia se produce debido a la incapacidad
  del cuerpo para digerir el gluten, una proteína presente en los cereales como el
  trigo, el centeno y el cebada. Se conoce también como celiacía y puede causar daño
  intestinal severo si no se maneja correctamente.

  3. Intolerancia al fructosa: Esta intolerancia se produce debido a la incapacidad
  del cuerpo para digerir el fructosa, un azúcar presente en muchos frutos y
  vegetales, así como en algunos productos procesados.

  4. Intolerancia al metilxantina: Esta intolerancia se produce debido a la
  incapacidad del cuerpo para digerir la metilxantina, un compuesto presente en el
  café y el té. Los síntomas incluyen palpitaciones, ansiedad y tremores.

```

Figure 47: Answer to "*¿Cuáles son las intolerancias más frecuentes?*" using LLM.

```
<|system|>
Answer the question using your knowledge. Use the following context to assist:

<|user|>
What are the most common intolerances?

<|assistant|>

Food intolerances are adverse reactions that occur after consuming certain foods due
 to a lack of the enzymes necessary to digest them or due to excessive sensitivity
 of the body towards certain food components. Among the most common food intolerances
 are:

1. Lactose intolerance: This condition occurs when the body cannot digest lactose, a
sugar found in milk and other dairy products. It is common in adults who have not
consumed milk for a long time and lose the ability to digest lactose.

2. Gluten intolerance: This intolerance occurs due to the body's inability to digest
gluten, a protein found in cereals such as wheat, rye, and barley. It is also known as
celiac disease and can cause severe intestinal damage if not properly managed.

3. Fructose intolerance: This intolerance occurs due to the body's inability to digest
fructose, a sugar found in many fruits and vegetables, as well as in some processed
 products.

4. Methylxanthine intolerance: This intolerance occurs due to the body's inability to
digest methylxanthine, a compound found in coffee and tea. Symptoms include
palpitations, anxiety, and tremors.
```

Figure 48: Translation of Figure 47.

The second method uses internal LLM knowledge combined with RAG, i.e., external sources are employed to mitigate hallucinations and curb outdated knowledge. RAG incorporates information from external data sources, serving as supplementary references for the generated output. In other words, RAG can "leverage additional relevant information from external databases to enhance their text generation capabilities" (Fan et al. 2024).

When applying a RAG, all-MiniLM-L6-v2-similarity-es, (https://huggingface.co/jaimevera1107/all-MiniLM-L6-v2-similarity-es) a sentence similarity LLM for Spanish based on all-MiniLM-L6-v2 (Henderson et al. 2019) is used. It is needed to effectively match user queries with relevant documents from external data sources. For text generation, Zephyr-7B-Beta is once again employed.

Two external data sources were compiled to answer the desired questions more effectively:

- A corpus of cooking recipes in Spanish, used for the corpus-based analysis.
- A custom-made corpus focusing on food intolerances created specifically for this purpose.

The same questions were employed to test the RAG system: Spanish versions of *How to make baked eggplants?* and *What are the most common intolerances?* Figures 49 and 50 show the respective results.

```

<|system|>

Contexta a la pregunta usando tu conocimiento. Usa el siguiente contexto para ayudar:
[

Document(metadata={'source': ...}, page_content='solorecetas.com TODAS LAS RECETAS CASERA Receta de berenjenas rellenas al horno'),
Document(metadata={'source': ...}, page_content='Mi abuela Lola ...'),
Document(metadata={'source': ...}, page_content='Cómo hacer cordero asado')
]

<|user|>
¿Cómo hacer berenjenas al horno?

<|assistant|>
Buscando por el contenido del corpus de texto proporcionado, parece que la receta para
hacer berenjenas al horno se encuentra en el archivo con el número de documento 1.
El contenido del mismo es:

solorecetas.com
TODAS LAS RECETAS CASERAS

Receta de berenjenas rellenas al horno [...]
```

Figure 49: Excerpt of answer to *¿Cómo hacer berenjenas al horno?* using RAG.

```

<|system|>
Contexta a la pregunta usando tu conocimiento. Usa el siguiente contexto para ayudar:
[
    Document(metadata={'source': '...'}, page_content='¿Qué son las intolerancias alimentarias?'),
    Document(metadata={'source': '...'}, page_content='Intolerancia a la fructosa'),
    Document(metadata={'source': '...'}, page_content='Intolerancia a la fructosa'),
    Document(metadata={'source': '...'}, page_content='¿Qué es la intolerancia a los alimentos?')
]
<|user|>
¿Cuáles son las intolerancias más frecuentes?

<|assistant|>
Según el contexto proporcionado, se menciona tres tipos de intolerancias alimentarias en particular:
intolerancia a la fructosa (mencionada en los documentos con números 2 y 3),
que puede causar síntomas como dolor abdominal, diarrea, y flatulencia después de consumir alimentos altos en frutosa;
y se sugiere preguntarse qué es la intolerancia a los alimentos en general en el documento con número 4. Sin embargo,
la frecuencia exacta de estas intolerancias varía entre personas y depende de factores genéticos y ambientales.
Se recomienda consultar a un médico o dietista para obtener una diagnóstico y tratamiento personalizados.
```

Figure 50: Excerpt of answer to *¿Cuáles son las intolerancias más frecuentes?* using RAG.

As shown, the system first searches for documents to gather information and then proceeds to write the relevant content: a recipe in the first question and a list of intolerances in the second. These experiments show that text generation is a powerful tool with a wide range of possibilities. Using LLM models alone or in conjunction with RAG can significantly enhance the sophistication of text generators. Nevertheless, managing conditions for text structure and thematic focus have a greater impact than those for spelling and grammar verification. More detailed fine-tuning and careful selection of external knowledge are mandatory.

5. Conclusions and further work

By leveraging the capabilities of LLMs, such as advanced natural language understanding, generation, and contextual reasoning, we explore potential improvements in efficiency, accuracy, and automation within the traditional workflow. Symbolic, statistical, or hybrid text generators can benefit from greater dynamism, preventing the obsolescence of the more consistent and textually reliable symbolic approaches. While this study has demonstrated the effectiveness of integrated LLMs, a more detailed study of the different LLMs available, as well as a much more sophisticated fine-tuning for each of the tasks, is necessary. Several avenues for future research remain open, such as:

- Integrating LLMs in the original software: A proper integration of the tasks proposed in this chapter should be incorporated into the original software.
- Model fine-tuning: The models employed in the experiments should be fine-tuned to the specific characteristics of different textual genres.
- Evaluation of generated documents: Clear and easily applicable protocols for evaluating LLM-generated documents, LLM plus RAG-generated documents and assistance-free documents should be formulated and conducted to measure the performance of the different methods more effectively.
- Exploring new tasks: Search for more tasks in which LLMs can be applied to improve the text generators developed by ACTRES.

To conclude, the integration of LLMs significantly improves all NLP tasks and, in one way or another, facilitates linguistic studies and the development of writing assistance tools. It is expected that LLMs will not only streamline the process of text generation but also provide deeper insights into language patterns and structures for linguistic studies.

References

ACTRES 2024. <https://actres.unileon.es/wp/comparable-corpora>

Ädel, Annelie / Reppen, Randi 2008. The Challenges of Different Settings: An Overview. In Annelie Ädel / Randi, Reppen (eds), *Corpora and Discourse. The Challenges of Different Settings*. Amsterdam: John Benjamins, 1–6.

Adolphs, Svenja 2008. *Corpus and Context. Investigating Pragmatic Functions in Spoken Discourse*. Amsterdam: John Benjamins.

Agarwal, Rajat / Kann, Katharina 2020. Acrostic Poem Generation. In *Proceedings of the 2020 Conference on Empirical Methods in Natural Language Processing (EMNLP)*, 1230–1240. I:10.18653/v1/2020.emnlp-main.94.

Aijmer, Karin / Simon-Vandenbergen, Anne-Marie 2006. *Pragmatic Markers in Contrast*. Oxford: Elsevier.

Aijmer, Karin / Rühlemann, Christoph 2015. *Corpus Pragmatics: A Handbook*. Cambridge: Cambridge University Press.

Al-Aadeli, N. Mhedi 2013. Suggestion and Advice in Three Selected Plays. *Journal of Education and Practice*. 5/4, 14–24.

Andaluz-Pinedo, Olaia / Sanjurjo-González, Hugo 2022. Corpus Tools for Parallel Corpora of Theatre Plays: An Introduction to TAligner and ACM-theatre. *Language Resources & Evaluation*. 56, 651–671.

Anesa, Patrizia 2022. The Legal Translator as a Digital Humanist: On the Use of Digital Corpora in Professional Legal Translation. In Maci, Stefania / Sala, Michele (eds) *Corpus Linguistics and Translation Tools for Digital Humanities: Research Methods and Applications*. London: Bloomsbury Academic, 107–126. <http://dx.doi.org/10.5040/9781350275256.ch-6>

Anthony, Laurence / Lashkia, George V. 2003. Mover: A Machine Learning Tool to Assist in the Reading and Writing of Technical Papers. *IEEE Transactions on Professional Communications*. 46/3, 185–193. <https://doi.org/10.1109/TPC.2003.816789>

Anthony, Laurence 2013. A Critical Look at Software Tools in Corpus Linguistics. *Linguistic Research*. 30/2, 141–161.

Anthony, Laurence 2024. AntConc Version 4.3.1 [Computer Software]. Tokyo, Japan: Waseda University. <https://www.laurenceanthony.net/software>

Archer, Dawn / Wilson, Andrew / Rayson, Paul 2002. Introduction to the USAS Category System. <https://ucrel.lancs.ac.uk/usas/usas_guide.pdf>.

Archer, Dawn / Culpeper, Jonathan / Davies, Matthew 2008. Pragmatic Annotation. In Kytö, Merja *et al* (eds) *Corpus Linguistics: An International Handbook*. Berlin: Mouton de Gruyter, 613–642.

Avner, Ehud A. / Ordan, Noam / Wintner, Shuly 2016. Identifying Translationese at the Word and Sub-Word Level. *Digital Scholarship in the Humanities*. 31/1, 30–54. <https://doi.org/10.1093/llc/fqu047>

Azarova, Larisa / Pustovit, Tetiana / Radomska, Liudmyla / Horchinska, Lyudmyla 2020. Use of Information Technologies in Studying Phraseology in the Course of Ukrainian as a Foreign Language. *Advanced Education*. 7/16, 39–48. <https://doi.org/10.20535/2410-8286.206786>

Aziz, Wilker / Castilho, Sheila / Specia, Lucia 2012. PET: a Tool for Post-editing and Assessing Machine Translation. In *Proceedings of the Eighth International Conference on Language Resources and Evaluation (LREC'12)*. Istanbul, Turkey. European Language Resources Association (ELRA). 3982–3987. <https://aclanthology.org/L12-1587/>

Badar, Hassan / Menacere, Ķarim 2019. Demystifying Phraseology: Implications for Translating Quranic Phraseological Units. *Advances in Language and Literary Studies*, 10/1, 28–40. <https://doi.org/10.7575/aiac.alls.v.10n.1p.28>

Baker, Mona 1996. Corpus-based Translation Studies. The Challenges that Lie Ahead. In Somers, Harold (ed). *Terminology, LSP and Translation: Studies in Language Engineering in Honour of Juan C. Sager*. Amsterdam: John Benjamins, 175–186. <https://doi.org/10.1075/btl.18.17bak>

Baker, Mona 1998. Réexplorer la langue de la traduction: une approche par corpus. *Meta*, 43/4, 480–485. <https://doi.org/10.7202/001951ar>

Baldwin, Timothy / Kim, Su Nam 2010. Multiword Expressions. In Indurkhya, Nitin / Damerau, Fred J. (eds) *Handbook of Natural Language Processing*. New York: Chapman and Hall, 267–292.

Baños, Rocío / Chaume, Frederic 2009. Prefabricated Orality: A Challenge in Audiovisual Translation. In Giorgio Marrano, Michaela *et al*. (eds) *The Translation of Dialects in Multimedia*. Special Issue of InTRAlinea. <https://www.intralinea.org/specials/article/1714>

Bardovi-Harling, Kathleen / Harford, Beverly 1993. Learning the Rules of Academic Talk: A Longitudinal Study of Pragmatic Development. *Studies in Second Language Acquisition*. 15/3, 279–304.

Baroni, Marco / Bernardini, Silvia 2006. A New Approach to the Study of Translationese: Machine-learning the Difference between Original and Translated Text. *Literary and Linguistic Computing*. 21/3, 259–274. <https://doi.org/10.1093/llc/fqi039>

Basturkmen, Helen 2012. A Genre-based Investigation of Discussion Sections of Research Articles in Dentistry and Disciplinary Variation. *Journal of English for Academic Purposes*. 11/2, 134–144. <https://doi.org/10.1016/j.jeap.2011.10.004>

Becerro, Francisco Bautista 2020. Phraseological Variations in Medical-Pharmaceutical Terminology and its Applications for English and German into Spanish Translations. *Scimedicine Journal*. 2/1, 22–29. <https://doi.org/10.28991/scimedj-2020-0201-4>

Benson, Morton / Benson, Evelin / Ilson, Robert 1986. *The BBI Combinatory Dictionary of English: A Guide to Word Combinations*. Amsterdam: John Benjamins.

Bhagat, Rahul / Hovy, Eduard 2013. What is a Paraphrase? *Computational Linguistics*, 39/3, 463–472.

Bhatia, Vijay K. 1993. *Analysing Genre: Language Use in Professional Settings*. London: Longman.

Bhatia, Vijay K. 2004. *Worlds of Written Discourse: A Genre-based View*. London/New York: Continuum.

Bhatia, Vijay K. 2010. Interdiscursivity in Professional Communication. *Discourse & Communication*. 21/1, 32–50. <https://doi.org/10.1177/1750481309351208>

Bhatia, Vijay. K. / Bremner, Stephen 2012. English for Business Communication. *Language Teaching*. 45/4, 410–445. <https://doi.org/10.1017/S0261444812000171>

Biber, Douglas 1993. Representativeness in Corpus Design. In Kytö, Merja / Lüdeling, Anke (eds) *Corpus Linguistics: An International Handbook*. Berlin: Mouton de Gruyter, 613–642.

Biber, Douglas / Johansson, Stig / Leech Geoffrey / Conrad, Susan / Finegan, Edward 1999. *The Longman Grammar of Spoken and Written English*. London: Longman.

Biber, Douglas / Connor, Ulla / Upton, Thomas 2007. *Discourse on the Move. Using Corpus Analysis to Describe Discourse Structure*. Amsterdam: John Benjamins.

Biber, Douglas / Zhang, Meixiu 2018. Expressing Evaluation without Grammatical Stance: Informational Persuasion on the Web. *Corpora*. 13/1, 97–123.

Biel, Łucia 2014. Phraseology in Legal Translation: A Corpus-based Analysis of Textual Mapping in EU Law. In Le, Cheng / King Kui, Sin / Wagner, Anne (eds) *The Ashgate Handbook of Legal Translation*. London: Routledge, 178–192.

Bird, Steven / Klein, Ewan / Loper, Edward 2009. *Natural Language Processing with Python – Analyzing Text with the Natural Language Toolkit*. Sebastopol: O'Reilly Media.

Blagodarna, Olena 2018. Insights Into Post-Editors' Profiles and Post-Editing Practices. *Tradumàtica* 16, 35–51. <https://doi.org/10.5565/rev/tradumatica.198>

Blake, John 2021. *Corpus-Based Study of the Rhetorical Organization and Lexical Realization of Scientific Research Abstracts*. PhD Thesis. England: Aston University. <https://publications.aston.ac.uk/id/eprint/43402/1/BLAKE_JOHN_2021pdfa.pdf>

Blum-Kulka, Shoshana 1986. Shifts of Cohesion and Coherence in Translation. In House, Juliane / Blum-Kulka / Shoshana (eds). *Intercultural Communication: Discourse and Cognition in Translation and Second Language Acquisition*. Tübingen: Narr, 17–35.

Bondi, Marina 2016. CSR Reports in English and Italian: Focus on Generic Structure and Importance Markers. In Garzone, Giuliana E. *et al.* (eds) *Language for Specific Purposes. Research and Translation across Cultures and Media*. Newcastle Upon Tyne: Cambridge Scholars Publishing, 168–199.

Bowker, Lynne / Pearson, Jennifer 2002. *Working with Specialized Language. A Practical Guide to Using Corpora*. London: Routledge.

Bowker, Lynne. 2019. Fit-for-Purpose Translation. In O'Hagan, Minako (ed) *The Routledge Handbook of Translation and Technology*. London: Routledge, 453–468.

Boyd, Adriane / Hana, Jirka / Nicolas, Lionel / Meurers, Detmar / Wisniewski, Katrin / Abel, Andrea / Schöne, Karin / Štindlová, Barbora / Vettori, Chiara 2014. The MERLIN Corpus: Learner Language and the CEFR. In Calzolari, Nicoletta *et al.* (eds) *Proceedings of the Ninth International Conference on Language Resources and Evaluation (LREC'14)*. Reykjavik, Iceland: European Language Resources Association (ELRA), 1281–1288.

Brown, Penelope / Levinson, Stephen C. 1987. *Politeness. Some Universals in Language Usage*. Cambridge: Cambridge University Press.

Brown, Tom B. / Mann, Benjamin / Ryder, Nick / Subbiah, Melanie / Kaplan, Jared / Dhariwal, Prafulla / et al. 2020. Language Models are Few-shot Learners. In *Proceedings of the 34th Conference on Neural Information Processing Systems (NeurIPS 2020)*. 1877–18901. <https://arxiv.org/abs/2005.14165>

Bsharat, Sondos M. / Myrzakhan, Aidar / Shen, Zhiqiang 2023. Principled Instructions Are All You Need for Questioning LLaMA-1/2, GPT-3.5/4. *arXiv:2312.16171*. <http://arxiv.org/abs/2312.16171>

Burchardt, Aljoscha / Erk, Katrin / Frank, Anette / Kowalski, Andrea / Padó, Sebastian / Pinkal, Manfred 2006. The SALSA Corpus: A German Corpus Resource for Lexical Semantics. In Calzolari, Nicoletta *et al.* (eds) *Proceedings of the Fifth International Conference on Language Resources and Evaluation (LREC'06)*. Genoa, Italy: European Language Resources Association (ELRA), 85–94.

Burger, Harald / Dobrovol'skij, Dmitrij / Kühn, Peter / Norrick, Neal 2007. Phraseology: Subject Area, Terminology and Research Topics. In Burger, Harald *et al.* (eds) *Phraseology: An International Handbook of Contemporary Research*. Berlin: Mouton de Gruyter, 10–19.

Cadwell, Patrick / Castilho, Sheila / O'Brien, Sharon / Mitchell, Linda 2016. Human Factors in Machine Translation and Post-Editing among Institutional Translators. *Translation Spaces*, 5/2, 222–243 <https://doi.org/10.1075/ts.5.2.04cad>

Cadwell, Patrick / O'Brien, Sharon / Teixeira, Carlos S. C. 2018. Resistance and Accommodation: Factors for the (Non-) Adoption of Machine Translation among Professional Translators. *Perspectives* 26/3, 301–321.

Calhoun, Sasha / Carletta, Jean / Brenier, Jason M. / Mayo, Neil / Jurafsky, Dan / Steedman, Mark / Beaver, David 2010. The NXT-format Switchboard Corpus: a Rich Resource for Investigating the Syntax, Semantics, Pragmatics and Prosody of Dialogue. *Language Resources and Evaluation*. 44/4, 387–419.

Cappelle, Bert / Depraetere, Ilse / Lesuisse, Mégane 2019. The Necessity Modals Have to, Must, Need to And Should: Using N-Grams to Help Identify Common and Distinct Semantic and Pragmatic Aspects. *Constructions and Frames*. 11/2, 220–243.

Carlsson, Fredrik / Öhman, Joey / Liu, Fangyu / Verlinden, Severine / Nivre, Joakim / Sahlgren, Magnus 2022. Fine-Grained Controllable Text Generation Using Non-Residual Prompting. In *Proceedings of the 60th Annual Meeting of the Association for Computational Linguistics (Volume 1: Long Papers)*. Dublin: Association for Computational Linguistics, 6837–6857. <https://doi.org/10.18653/v1/2022.acllong.47>

Casal, J. Elliot / Kessler, Matt 2023. Rhetorical Move-step Analysis. In Kessler, Matt / Polio, Charlene (eds) *Conducting Genre-based Research in Applied Linguistics*. New York: Routledge, 82–104. <https://doi.org/10.4324/9781003300847-7>

Castilho, Sheila / Doherty, Stephen / Gaspari, Federico / Moorkens, Joos. 2018. Approaches to Human and Machine Translation Quality Assessment. In Moorkens, Joss *et al.* (eds) *Translation Quality Assessment. From Principles to Practice*. Cham: Springer, 9–38.

Castilho, Sheila / Resende, Natalia. 2022. Post-Editese in Literary Translations. *Information*, 13/2, 66. <http://dx.doi.org/10.3390/info13020066>

Celikyilmaz, Asli / Clark, Elizabeth / Gao, Jianfeng. 2020. Evaluation of Text Generation: A Survey. *arXiv preprint* arXiv:2006.14799.

Chen, Mei-Hua / Huang, Shih-Ting / Hsieh, Hung-Ting / Kao, Ting-Hui / Chang, Jason S. 2012. FLOW: A First-Language-oriented Writing Assistant System. In *Proceedings of the 50th Annual Meeting of the Association for Computational Linguistics*, 157–162, Jeju, Republic of Korea, 8–14 July. Association for Computational Linguistics.

Chippada, Bhargav / Saha, Shubajit 2018. Knowledge Amalgam: Generating Jokes and Quotes Together. *arXiv:1806.04387*. <http://arxiv.org/abs/1806.04387>

Chowdhery, Aakanksha / Narang, Sharan / Devlin, Jaob / Bosma, Maarten / Mishra, Gaurav / Roberts, Adam / *et al.* 2023. PaLM: Scaling Language Modeling with Pathways. *Journal of Machine Learning Research*. 24/240, 1–113. <https://jmlr.org/papers/volume24/22-1144/22-1144.pdf>

Chung, Hyung W. / Hou, Le / Longpre, Shayne / Zoph, Barret / Tay, Yi / Fedus, William / *et al.* 2022. Scaling Instruction-Finetuned Language Models. *arXiv/2210.11416*. <https://doi.org/10.48550/arXiv.2210.11416>

Connor, Ulla 2000. Variation in Rhetorical Moves in Grant Proposals of US Humanists and Scientists. *Text and Talk*. 20/1, 1–28. < https://doi.org/10.1515/text.1.2000.20.1.1>

Connor, Ulla / Upton, Thomas A. 2004. The Genre of Grant Proposals: A Corpus Linguistic Analysis. In Connor, Ulla / Upton, Thomas A. (eds) *Discourse in the Professions: Perspectives from Corpus Linguistics*. Amsterdam: John Benjamins, 235–255. <https://doi.org/10.1075/scl.16.10con>

Corpas Pastor, Gloria 2008. *Investigar con corpus en traducción: Los retos de un nuevo paradigma*. Frankfurt: Peter Lang.

Corpas Pastor, Gloria / Seghiri, Míriam 2010. Size Matters: A Quantitative Approach to Corpus Representativeness. In Rabadán, Rosa *et al.* (eds) *Lengua, Traducción, Recepción: En Honor de Julio César Santoyo*. León: Universidad de León, 111–145.

Correia, Gonçalo M. / Martins, Andre 2019. A Simple and Effective Approach to Automatic Post-Editing with Transfer Learning. *ArXiv*. <https://arxiv.org/abs/1906.06253>

Cotos, Elena / Pendar, Nick 2016. Discourse Classification into Rhetorical Functions for AWE Feedback. *CALICO Journal*. 33/1, 92–116. <https://www.jstor.org/stable/calicojournal.33.1.92>

Cotos, Elena 2019. Articulating Societal Benefits in Grant Proposals: Move analysis of Broader Impacts. *English for Specific Purposes*. 54, 15–34. <https://doi.org/10.1016/j.esp.2018.11.002>

Cowie, Anthony P. 1998. Phraseology. In Asher, Ron (ed.) *The Encyclopaedia of Language and Linguistics*. Oxford: Pergamon, 3168–3171.

Cristobalena, Araceli 2014. Text Generator: An Aid for Writing in the Tertiary EST Class. *CORELL: Computer Resources for Language Learning*. 4, 27–41.

Cristobalena, Araceli 2015. A Corpus-based Genre Study of Instruction Manuals for Household Appliances. *Procedia – Social and Behavioral Sciences*. 198, 103–111. <https://doi.org/10.1016/j.sbspro.2015.07.425>

Cristobalena, Araceli 2016. *English-Spanish contrastive analysis of instruction manuals for household appliances*. PhD Thesis. León: Universidad de León. <https://buleria.unileon.es/handle/10612/5728>

Csomay, Eniko / Crawford, William J. 2024. *Doing Corpus Linguistics*. New York: Routledge.

Curry, Niall / Baker, Paul / Brookes, Gavin 2024. Generative AI for Corpus Approaches to Discourse Studies: A Critical Evaluation of ChatGPT. *Applied Corpus Linguistics*. 4/1. <https://doi.org/10.1016/j.acorp.2023.100082>

Da Cunha, Iria / Montané, M. Amor / Hysa, Luis 2017. The arText Prototype: An Automatic System of Writing Specialized Texts. *Proceedings of the EACL 2017 Software Demonstrations*, Valencia, Spain: Association for Computational Linguistics. 57–60. <https://aclanthology.org/E17-3015>

Daems, Joke / De Clercq, Orphée / Macken, Lieve. 2017. Translationese and Post-Editese: How Comparable Is Comparable Quality. *Linguistica Antverpiensia New Series*. 16, 89–103. <http://hdl.handle.net/1854/LU-8516838>

Daems, Joke / Macken, Lieve 2020. Post-Editing Human Translations and Revising Machine Translations. In Koponen, Maarit *et al*. (eds). *Translation Revision and Post-editing. Industry Practices and Cognitive Processes*. London: Routledge, 50–70.

Dai, Andrew M. / Le, Quoc V. 2015. Semi-Supervised Sequence Learning. In *Proceedings of the 29th Conference on Neural Information Processing Systems (NIPS 2015)* Montréal, Canada, 3079–3087.

Dam, Sumit K. / Hong, Chong S. / Qiao, Yu / Zhang, Chaoning 2024. A Complete Survey on LLM-based AI Chatbots. *arXiv preprint arXiv:2406.16937*.

Del Saz Rubio, M. Milagros 2019. A Rhetorical Approach to the Genre of the Abstract within the Field of Food Science and Technology. *Pragmalingüística*. 27, 328–348. <https://doi.org/10.25267/PRAGMALINGUISTICA.2019.I27.17>

Deng, Yuntian / Bakhtin, Anton / Ott, Myle / Szlam, Arthur / Ranzato, Marc'Aurelio 2020. Residual Energy-Based Models for Text Generation. In *International Conference on Learning Representations*. <https://doi.org/10.48550/arXiv.2004.11714>

Depraetere, Ilse 2017. On the Pragmatics of Modal Verbs. *Selected Papers of ISTAL* 22, 14–26.

Deutschmann, Mats 2003. *Apologising in British English*. Umeå: Institutionen för moderna språk, Umeå University.

Devlin, Jacob / Chang, Ming-Wei / Lee, Kenton / Toutanova, Kristina 2019. BERT: Pre-training of Deep Bidirectional Transformers for Language Understanding. In *Proceedings of the 2019 Conference of the North American Chapter of the Association for Computational Linguistics: Human Language Technologies*. Minneapolis, USA. 4171–4186. <https://doi.org/10.18653/v1/N19-1423>

Díez Fernández, María de los Ángeles 2009. *Análisis contrastivo inglés-español de las crónicas futbolísticas en la prensa escrita. De la descripción a las aplicaciones*. PhD Thesis. León: Universidad de León. <https://www.educacion.gob.es/teseo/mostrarRef.do?ref=850494>

Do Campo Bayón, María / Sánchez-Gijón, Pilar 2024. Avoiding 'generatese': the optimization of NLG systems through fit-for-purpose data collections. *DRDHum 2024 Conference*. University of Eastern Finland. <chrome-extension://efaidnbmnnnibpcajpcglclefindmkaj/https://openreview.net/pdf?id=MicqkyVM16>

Do Carmo, Felix / Moorkens, Joss 2021. Differentiating Editing, Post-Editing and Revision. In Koponen, Maarit *et al.* (eds). *Translation Revision and Post-editing. Industry Practices and Cognitive Processes*. London: Routledge, 35–49.

Doval, Irene / Sánchez Nieto / M. Teresa (eds) 2019. *Parallel Corpora for Contrastive and Translation Studies*. Amsterdam: John Benjamins. <https://doi.org/10.1075/scl.90>

Downing, Angela 2006. The English Pragmatic Marker *Surely* and its Functional Counterparts in Spanish. In Aijmer, Karin / Simon-Vandenbergen, Anne-Marie (eds). *Pragmatic Markers in Contrast.* Oxford: Elsevier, 39–58.

Druskat, Susan / Krause, Thomas / Lachenmaier, Clara / Bunzeck, Björn 2023. Hexatomic: An Extensible, OS-Independent Platform for Deep Multi-layer Linguistic Annotation of Corpora. *Journal of Open Source Software.* 8/86, 4825.

EAGLES 1996. Recommendations for Morphosyntactic Categories. <http://www.ilc.cnr.it/EAGLES96/annotate/node9.htm>

Echeverría Arriagada, Carlos I. 2016. La interferencia lingüística de frecuencia. *Boletín de filología.* 51/1, 93–115. <https://dx.doi.org/10.4067/S0718-93032016000100003>

Eisenstein, Jacob 2019. *Introduction to Natural Language Processing.* Cambridge, MA: The MIT Press.

El Adelantado de Segovia, accessed 14/02/2024. <https://www.eladelantado.com/castilla-y-leon/el-972-de-las-3-026-sociedades-de-alimentacion-de-castilla-y-leon-son-pequenas-empresas/>

Evert, Stefan / Hardie, Andrew 2011. Twenty-first Century Corpus Workbench: Updating a Query Architecture for the New Millennium. *In Proceedings of the Corpus Linguistics 2011 Conference.* Birmingham: University of Birmingham. <https://eprints.lancs.ac.uk/id/eprint/62721/>

Fan, Wenqi / Ding, Yujuan / Ning, Liangbo / Wang, Shijie / Li, Hengyun / Yin, Dawei / Chua, Tat-Seng / Li, Qing 2024. A Survey on Rag Meeting LLMs: Towards Retrieval-augmented Large Language Models. In *Proceedings of the 30th ACM SIGKDD Conference on Knowledge Discovery and Data Mining*, 6491–6501. <https://doi.org/10.1145/3637528.3671470>

Flanagan, Marian / Christensen, Tina Paulsen 2014. Testing Post-Editing Guidelines: How Translation Trainees Interpret them and how to Tailor them for Translator Training Purposes. *The Interpreter and Translator Trainer.* 8/2, 257–275. <https://doi.org/10.1080/1750399X.2014.936111>

Flöck, Ilka / Geluykens, Ronald 2015. Speech Acts in Corpus Pragmatics: A Quantitative Contrastive Study of Directives in Spontaneous and Elicited Discourse. In J. Romero-Trillo (ed.) *Yearbook of Corpus Linguistics and Pragmatics 201.* London: Springer, 7–37.

Frawley, William 1984. Prolegomenon to a Theory of Translation. In Frawley, William (ed) *Translation. Literary, Linguistic and Philosophical Perspectives.* Newark: University of Delaware Press, 159–175.

Freitag, Markus / Caswell, Isaac / Roy, Scott 2019. APE at Scale and Its Implications on MT Evaluation Biases. In *Proceedings of the Fourth Conference on Machine Translation*, Florence, Italy: Association for Computational Linguistics, 34–44. <https://aclanthology.org/W19-5204.pdf>

Freitag, Markus / Rei, Ricardo / Mathur, Nitika / Lo, Chi-kiu/ Stewart, Craig / Avramidis, Eleftherios / Kocmi, Tom / Foster, George / Lavie, Alon / Martins, André F. T. 2022. Results of WMT22 Metrics Shared Task: Stop Using BLEU – Neural Metrics Are Better and More Robust. In *Proceedings of the Seventh Conference on Machine Translation (WMT)*. Abu Dhabi, United Arab Emirates: Association for Computational Linguistics, 46–68 <https://aclanthology.org/2022.wmt-1.2.pdf>

Fuertes-Olivera, Pedro / Tarp, Sven 2020. A Window to the Future: Proposal for a Lexicography-Assisted Writing Assistant. *Lexicographica*. 36, 257–86. <https://doi.org/10.1515/lex-2020-0014>

Gao, Tianyu / Fisch, Adam / Chen, Danqi 2021. Making Pre-trained Language Models Better Few-Shot Learners. In *Proceedings of the 59th Annual Meeting of the Association for Computational Linguistics and the 11th International Joint Conference on Natural Language Processing (Volume 1: Long Papers)*. Association for Computational Linguistics, 3816–3830. <https://doi.org/10.18653/v1/2021.acl-long.295>

Garcia McAllister, Paula 2015. Speech Acts: A Synchronic Perspective. In Aijmer, Karin / Rühlemann, Christoph (eds) *Corpus Pragmatics: A Handbook*. Cambridge: Cambridge University Press, 29–51.

Garside, Roger / Leech Geoffrey / McEnery, Tony 1997. *Corpus Annotation. Linguistic Information from Computer Text Corpora*. New York: Addison Wesley Longman.

Gaspari, Federico / Almaghout, Hala / Doherty, Stephen 2015. A Survey of Machine Translation Competences: Insights for Translation Technology Educators and Practitioners. *Perspectives* 23/3, 333–58. <https://doi.org/10.1080/0907676X.2014.979842>

Gatt, Albert / Krahmer, Emiel 2018. Survey of the State of the Art in Natural Language Generation: Core Tasks, Applications and Evaluation. *Journal of Artificial Intelligence Research*. 61, 65–170.

Gee, Leonidas / Zugarini, Andrea / Rigutini, Leonardo / Torroni, Paolo 2022. Fast Vocabulary Transfer for Language Model Compression. In *Proceedings of the 2022 Conference on Empirical Methods in Natural Language Processing: Industry Track*. Abu Dhabi:

Association for Computational Linguistics, 409–416. <https://arxiv.org/html/2402.09977v1>

Gee, Leonidas / Rigutini, Leonardo / Ernandes, Marco / Zugarini, Andrea 2023. Multi-Word Tokenization for Sequence Compression. In *Proceedings of the 2023 Conference on Empirical Methods in Natural Language Processing: Industry Track*. Singapore. Association for Computational Linguistics, 612–621. <https://doi.org/10.18653/v1/2023.emnlp-industry.58>

Gellerstam, Martin 1996. Translations as a Source for Cross-Linguistic Studies. In Aijmer, Karin *et al.* (eds) *Languages in Contrast. Papers from a Symposium on Text-based Cross-linguistic Studies, Lund, 4–5 March 1994*. Lund: Lund University Press, 53–62.

Gerdes, Kim / Kahane, Sylvain / Lacheret, Anne / Pietandrea, Paola / Truong, Arthur 2012. Intonosyntactic Data Structures: The Rhapsodie Treebank of Spoken French. In Ide, Nancy *et al.* (eds) *Proceedings of the Sixth Linguistic Annotation Workshop*. Jeju, Republic of Korea: Association for Computational Linguistics, 85–94. <https://dl.acm.org/doi/proceedings/10.5555/2392747>

Gessler, Luke / Peng, Siyao / Liu, Yang / Zhu, Yilun / Behzad, Shabnam / Zeldes, Amir 2020. AMALGUM – A Free, Balanced, Multilayer English Web Corpus. In Calzolari, Nicoletta *et al.* (eds) *Proceedings of the Twelfth Language Resources and Evaluation Conference*. Marseille, France: European Language Resources Association. <https://doi.org/10.48550/arXiv.2006.10677>

Ginovart Cid, Clara / Colominas Ventura, Carme 2020. The MT Post-Editing Skill Set. In Koponen, Maarit *et al.* (eds). *Translation Revision and Post-editing. Industry Practices and Cognitive Processes*. London: Routledge, 50–70.

Glässer, Rosemary 1994/1995. Relations between Phraseology and Terminology with Special Reference to English. *ALFA*, 7/8, 41–60.

Glide, Margaret 2016. ¿Cuáles son sus recomendaciones? A Comparative Analysis of Spanish and English Advice Given on a Mexican Subreddit. *Indiana University Linguistics Club Working Papers*. 15/1, 181–207.

Godfrey, John. / Holliman, Edward / McDaniel, Jane 1992. SWITCHBOARD: Telephone Speech Corpus for Research and Development. In *IEEE International Conference on Acoustics, Speech, and Signal Processing*, 1, 517–520.

Gokul, Annad 2023. *LLMs and AI: Understanding Its Reach and Impact. Preprints* 2023050195, 1–6. <https://doi.org/10.20944/preprints202305.0195.v1>

Goodfellow, Ian / Pouget-Abadie, Jean / Mirza, Mehdi / Xu, Bing / Warde-Farley, David / Ozair, Sherjil / Courville, Aaron / Bengio, Yoshua 2014. Generative Adversarial Nets. Advances in Neural Information Processing Systems. *arXiv:1406.2661.*

Goyal, Ruplai / Kumar, Parteek / Singh, Vijay P. 2023. A Systematic Survey on Automated Text Generation Tools and Techniques: Application, Evaluation, and Challenges. *Multimedia Tools and Applications*, 82/28, 43089–43144.

Granger, Sylviane / Paquot, Magali 2008. Disentangling the Phraseological Web. In Granger, Sylviane / Meunier, Fanny (eds) *Phraseology. An Interdisciplinary Perspective*. Amsterdam: John Benjamins, 27–49.

Gray, Bethany / Biber, Douglas 2015. Phraseology. In Biber, Douglas / Reppen, Randi (eds) *The Cambridge Handbook of English Corpus Linguistics*. Cambridge: Cambridge University Press, 125–145.

Guerberof Arenas, Anna 2013. What do Professional Translators Think about Post-Editing? *The Journal of Specialised Translation*. 19. <https://jostrans.soap2.ch/issue19/art_guerberof.php>

Guerberof Arenas, Anna 2014. Correlations between Productivity and Quality when Post-editing in a Professional Context. *Machine Translation* 28/3–4, 165–186. <https://doi.org/10.1007/s10590-014-9155-y>

Guerberof, Anna. 2017. Quality is in the Eyes of the Reviewer: A Report on Post Editing Quality Evaluation. In: Jakobsen, Arne Likke/ Mesa-Lao, Bartolomé (eds) *Translation in Transition: Between Cognition, Computing and Technology*. Amsterdam: John Benjamins, 187–205. <https://doi.org/10.1075/btl.133.07gue>

Habash, Nizar / Dorr, Bonnie / Traum, David 2003. Hybrid Natural Language Generation from Lexical Conceptual Structures. *Machine Translation*, 18/2, 81–128.

Hajič, Jan / Hajičová, Eva / Mikulová, Marie / Mírovský, Jirí 2017. Prague dependency treebank. In Ide, Nancy / Pustejovsky, James (eds) *Handbook of Linguistic Annotation*. Dordrecht: Springer, 555–594. <https://doi.org/10.1007/978-94-024-0881-2_21>

Halverson, Sandra L. 2003. The Cognitive Basis of Translation Universals. *Target* 15/ 2, 197–241.

Halverson, Sandra L. 2010. Cognitive Translation Studies: Developments in Theory and Method. In Shreve, Gregory M. / Angelone, Erik (eds) *Translation and Cognition*. Amsterdam: John Benjamins, 349–70

Halverson, Sandra L. 2017. Gravitational Pull in Translation. Testing a Revised Model. In De Sutter, Gert *et al.* (eds) *Empirical Translation*

Studies. New Methodological and Theoretical Traditions. Berlin: Mouton de Gruyter, 9–46. <https://doi.org/10.1515/9783110459586-002>

Hardie, Andrew 2012. CQPweb—Combining Power, Flexibility and Usability in a Corpus Analysis Tool. *International Journal of Corpus Linguistics*. 17/3, 380–409.

Hatim, Basil / Mason, Ian 1990. *Discourse and the Translator*. London/ New York: Longman.

Haverkate, Henk 1984. *Speech Acts, Speaker and Hearers*. Amsterdam: John Benjamins.

Henderson, Matthew / Budzianowski, Paweł / Casanueva, Íñigo / Coope, Sam / Gerz, Daniela / Kumar, Girish / Mrkšić, Nikola / Spithourakis, Georgios / Su, Pei-Hao / Vulić, Ivan / Wen, Tsung-Hsien 2019. A Repository of Conversational Datasets. *arXiv preprint arXiv:1904.06472*. <https://doi.org/10.48550/arXiv.1904.06472>.

Hochreiter, Sepp / Schmidhuber, Jürgen 1997. Long Short-Term *Memory. Neural Computation*, 9/8, 1735–1780. <https://doi.org/10.1162/ neco.1997.9.8.1735>

Höder, Steffen 2012. Annotating Ambiguity. In Durand, Jacques *et al.* (eds) *Multilingual Corpora and Multilingual Corpus Analysis*. Amsterdam: John Benjamins, 245–271.

Honnibal, Matthew / Montani, Ines 2017. spaCy 2: Natural Language Understanding with Bloom Embeddings, Convolutional Neural Networks and Incremental Parsing. <https://sentometrics-research.com/ publication/72/>

Hopkins, Jack / Kiela, Douwe 2017. Automatically Generating Rhythmic Verse with Neural Networks. In *Proceedings of the 5th Annual Meeting Association Computational Linguistics*. 1, 168–78. <https:// aclanthology.org/P17-1016/>

Horacek, Helmut 2000. Building Natural Language Generation Systems. In Reiter, Ehud / Dale, Robert (eds) *Studies in Natural Language Processing*. Cambridge: Cambridge University Press, 277–280. <https://doi.org/10.1016/S0933-3657(00)00114-7>

Hu, Ke/ Cadwell, Patrick 2016. A Comparative Study of Post-editing Guidelines. *Baltic J. Modern Computing*. 4/ 2, 346–353.

Hu, Yingjie / Mai, Gengchen / Cundy, Chris / Choi, Kristy / Lao, Ni / Liu, Wei / et al. 2023. Geo-Knowledge-Guided GPT Models Improve the Extraction of Location Descriptions from Disaster-Related Social Media Messages. *International Journal of Geographical Information Science*. 37/11, 2289–2318. <https://doi.org/10.1080/13658816. 2023.2266495>

Huang, Lei / Yu, Weijiang / Ma, Weitao / Zhong, Weihong / Feng, Zhangyin / Wang, Haotian / et al. 2023. A Survey on Hallucination in Large Language Models: Principles, Taxonomy, Challenges, and Open Questions. *arXiv:2311.05232*. <http://arxiv.org/abs/2311.05232>

Huang, Lihe 2018. Issues on Multimodal Corpus of Chinese Speech Acts: A case in Multimodal Pragmatics. *Digital Scholarship in the Humanities*. 33/2, 316–326.

Hyland, Ken 1998. *Hedging in Scientific Research Articles*. Amsterdam: Benjamins.

Ide, Nancy / Baker, Collin F. / Fellbaum, Christiane / Passonneau, Rebecca J. 2010. The Manually Annotated Sub-Corpus: A Community Resource for and by the People. In Hajič, Jan *et al.* (eds) *Proceedings of the ACL 2010 Conference Short Papers*, 68–73. Uppsala, Sweden: Association for Computational Linguistics. <https://aclanthology.org/P10-2013/>

Ishizaki, Suguru / López-Arroyo, Belén. forthcoming 2026. From Sensory to Narrative. A Corpus-Based Analysis of Wine Tasting Notes in International Contexts. *Journal of General Business and Technical Communication*.

ISO 2017. ISO 18857:2017. Translation services – post-editing of machine translation output: Requirements. <https://www.iso.org/standard/62970.html>

Izquierdo, Marlén 2010. The Combination of Comparable and Translation Corpora and How Translators may Benefit from it. In Gozdz-Roszkowski, Stanislaw (ed.) *Explorations across Languages and Corpora: PALC 2009*. Bern: Peter Lang, 451–480.

Izquierdo, Marlén 2012a. Corpus-based Functionality and Translatability: English-Spanish Progressive Constructions in Contrast and Translation. *Languages in Contrast*, 12/2, 187–210. <https://doi.org/10.1075/lic.12.2.04izq>

Izquierdo, Marlén 2012b. *Estudio contrastivo y de traducción inglés-español. Construcciones de -ing inglesas y sus equivalentes en español*. Published PhD. Editorial Académica Española.

Izquierdo, Marlén 2014. On Describing Similarity and Measuring Equivalence in English-Spanish Translation. *Meta*. 59/1, 140–159 <https://doi.org/10.7202/1026474ar >

Izquierdo, Marlén 2015. Semiperiphrastic Constructions in English: A Contrastive Corpus study. In Oksefjell Ebeling, Signe / Hasselgård, Hilde (eds) *Cross-linguistic Perspectives on Verb Constructions*. Cambridge: Cambridge Scholars, 116–143.

Izquierdo, Marlén / Hofland, Knut / Reigem, Øystein 2008. The ACTRES Parallel Corpus: An English–Spanish Translation Corpus. *Corpora*. 3/1, 31–41. <https://doi.org/10.3366/E1749503208000051>

Izquierdo, Marlén / Pérez Blanco, María 2020. A Multi-level Contrastive Analysis of Promotional Strategies in Specialised Discourse. *English for Specific Purposes*. 58, 43–57. <https://doi.org/10.1016/j.esp.2019.12.002>

Izquierdo, Marlén / Pérez Blanco, María 2023. Interactional Metadiscourse: Building Rapport and Solidarity in Informational-Persuasive Discourse. An English-Spanish Case Study. *Journal of Pragmatics*. *216*, 106–120.

Jackendoff, Ray J. 1997. *The Architecture of the Language Faculty*. Cambridge: MIT Press.

James, Gareth / Witten, Daniela / Hastie, Trevor / Tibshirani, Robert 2013. *An Introduction to Statistical Learning*. New York: Springer.

Jarvis, Scott / Pavlenko, Aneta 2008. *Crosslinguistic Influence in Language and Cognition*. New York: Routledge. <https://doi.org/10.4324/9780203935927>

Jautz, Sabine 2008. Gratitude in British and New Zealand Radio Programmes: Nothing but Gushing? In Schneider, Klaus / Barron, Anne (eds) *Variational Pragmatics: A Focus on Regional Varieties in Pluricentric Languages*. Amsterdam: John Benjamins, 141–178.

Jha, Aditi / Havens, Sam / Dohmann, Jeremy / Trott, Alex / Portes, Jacob 2023. LIMIT: Less Is More for Instruction Tuning Across Evaluation Paradigms. *arXiv:2311.13133*. <https://doi.org/10.48550/arXiv.2311.13133>

Jiang, Xiangying. 2006. Suggestions: What should ESL students know? *System*. 34/1, 36–54.

Jiménez-Crespo, Miguel A. 2010. The Intersection of Localization and Translation: A Corpus Study of Spanish Original and Localized Web Forms. *Translation and Interpreting Studies*. 5/2, 186–207. <https://doi.org/10.1075/tis.5.2.03jim>

Jiménez Yáñez, Ricardo María / Sanjurjo-González, Hugo / Rayson, Paul / Piao, Scott 2018. Building a Spanish exicon for Corpus Analysis. In *Languages at the Crossroads: Training, Accreditation and Context of Use*. Jaén, Spain: Universidad de Jaén, 227–236.

Jin, Guangsa / Li, Chenle L. / Sun, Ya 2020. Exploring the Macrostructure of Research Articles in Economics. *IEEE Transactions on Professional Communication*. 63/3, 227–243. <https://doi.org/10.1109/TPC.2020.3014535>

Joseph, Alwin / Eapen, Naived G. 2024. Conversational Agents and Chatboths. In Pillai, Anitha S. / Tedesco, Roberto (eds.) *Machine Learning and Deep Learning in Natural Language Processing*. Boca Raton: CRC Press, 17–52. <https://doi.org/10.1201/9781003296126>

Jucker, Andreas H. / Taavitsainen, Irma. 2014. Complimenting in the history of American English: A metacommunicative expression analysis. In Taavitsainen, Irma / Jucker, Andreas H. / Tuominen, Jukka (eds) *Diachronic Corpus Pragmatics*. Amsterdam: John Benjamins, 257–276.

Junczys-Dowmunt, Marcin / Grundkiewicz, Roman. 2016. Phrase-based Machine Translation is State-of-the-Art for Automatic Grammatical Error Correction. In *Proceedings of the 2016 Conference on Empirical Methods in Natural Language Processing*. Austin, Texas: Association for Computational Linguistics. 1546–1556. <https://doi.org/10.48550/arXiv.1605.06353>

Junqueira, Luciana 2013. A Genre-Based Investigation of Applied Linguistics Book Reviews in English and Brazilian Portuguese. *Journal of English for Academic Purposes*. 12/3, 203–213. <https://doi.org/10.1016/j.jeap.2013.05.001>

Justeson, John / Katz, Slava 1995. Technical Terminology: Some Linguistic Properties and an Algorithm for Identification in Text. *Natural Language Engineering*. 1/1, 9–27.

Kanoksilapatham, Budsaba 2005. Rhetorical Structure of Biochemistry Research Articles. *English for Specific Purposes*. 24, 269–292. <https://doi.org/10.1016/j.esp.2004.08.003>

Kaufer, David / Ishizaki, Suguru 2024. *The Future of Writing: A Report on the State of Writing at Carnegie Mellon University (Version 5)*. Carnegie Mellon University. <https://www.cmu.edu/dietrich/english/research-and-publications/future_of_writing_kaufer_and_ishizaki_v5.pdf>.

Kilgarriff, Adam / Baisa, Vít / Bušta, Jan / Jakubíček, Miloš / Kovář, Vojtěch / Michelfeit, Jan / Rychlý, Pavel / Suchomel, Vít 2014. *The Sketch Engine: Ten Years On*. Lexicography 1/1, 7–36.

Kim, Minjin / Lu, Xiaofei 2024. Exploring the Potential of Using ChatGPT for Rhetorical Move-step Analysis: The Impact of Prompt Refinement, Few-shot Learning, and Fine-tuning. *English for Academic Purposes*. 71, 101422. <https://doi.org/10.1016/j.jeap.2024.101422>

Kinnunen, Tomi / Leisma, Henri / Machunik, Monika / Kakkonen, Tuomo / Lebrun, Jean-Luc 2012. SWAN-Scientific Writing Assistant: A Tool for Helping Scholars to Write Reader-friendly Manuscripts. *Proceedings of the Demonstrations at the 13th Conference of the*

European Chapter of the Association for Computational Linguistics, 20–24. <https://doi.org/10.13140/2.1.3284.4808>

Klaudy, Kinga 1998. Explicitation. In Baker, Mona / Saldhana, Gabriela (eds) *Encyclopaedia of Translation Studies*. London: Routledge, 80–85.

Kobayashi, Sosuke 2018. Contextual Augmentation: Data Augmentation by Words with Paradigmatic Relations. arXiv preprint *arXiv:1805.06201*. <https://doi.org/10.48550/arXiv.1805.06201>

Koester, Almut. 2010. *Workplace discourse*. Bloosmbury Publishing.

Kohnen, Thomas. 2008. Tracing Directives Through Text And Time: Towards a Methodology of a Corpus-based Diachronic Speech-act Analysis. In Jucker, Andreas H. / Taavitsainen, Irma (eds) *Speech Acts in the History of English*. Amsterdam: John Benjamins, 295–310.

Krause, Thomas / Zeldes, Amir 2016. ANNIS3: A New Architecture for Generic Corpus Query and Visualization. *Digital Scholarship in the Humanities*. 31/1, 118–139.

Krings, Hans P. 2001. *Repairing Texts: Empirical Investigations of Machine Translation Post-editing Processes*. Koby, Geoffrey S. (ed.) Kent, Ohio: Kent State University Press.

Kuhn, Tobias 2014. A Survey and Classification of Controlled Natural Languages. *Computational Linguistics*. 40/1, 121–170.

Kumar, Varun / Choudhary, Ashutosh / Cho, Eunah 2020. Data Augmentation Using Pre-Trained Transformer Models. *arXiv:2003.02245*. <https://doi.org/10.48550/arXiv.2003.02245>

Kupietz, Marc / Banski, Piotr / Diewald, Nils / Trawinski, Beata / Witt, Andreas 2024. EuReCo: Not Building and Yet Using Federated Comparable Corpora for Cross-Linguistic Research. In Zweigenbaum, Pierre *et al* (eds). *Proceedings of the 17th Workshop on Building and Using Comparable Corpora (BUCC) @ LREC-COLING 2024*. Torino, Italia: ELRA and ICCL, 94–103.

Labrador, Belén 2003a. The Role of Corpora in the Study of Paradigmatic Relations. The Case of COBUILDs Bank of English and CREA (Reference Corpus of Contemporary Spanish). *Literary and Linguistic Computing*. 18/3, 315–330.

Labrador, Belén 2003b. Typicality in the Use of English and Spanish Indefinite Quantifiers: A Functional Approach. *Babel*. 49/1, 41–58. <https://doi.org/10.1075/babel.49.1.04lab>

Labrador, Belén 2004. A Methodological Proposal for the Study of Semantic Functions across Languages. *Meta*. 49/2, 360–380. <https://doi.org/10.7202/009357ar>

Labrador, Belén 2007. Contrasting Ways of Expressing Restriction in English and Spanish and Suggesting Translational Options into Spanish. *Languages in Contrast*. 7/1, 29–51. <https://doi.org/10.1075/lic.7.1.03lab>

Labrador, Belén 2011. A Corpus-based Study of the Use of Spanish Demonstratives as Translation Equivalents of English Demonstratives. *Perspectives: Studies in Translatology*. 19/1, 71–87. <https://doi.org/10.1080/0907676X.2010.481047>

Labrador, Belén 2016. Translation as an Aid to ELT: Using an English-Spanish Parallel Corpus (P-ACTRES) to Study English both and its Spanish Counterparts. *Digital Scholarship in the Humanities*. 31/3, 499–512. <https://doi.org/10.1093/llc/fqv009>

Labrador, Belén 2021. Translating Additive Connectors from English into Spanish and vice versa. *Babel*. 67/2, 139–161. <https://doi.org/10.1075/babel.00211.lab>

Labrador, Belén 2023. Run away! Exploring the Iceberg of Core Vocabulary with English-Spanish Parallel Corpora. In: Izquierdo, Marlén / Sanz-Villar, Zuriñe (eds.) *Corpus Use in Cross-linguistic Research. Paving the Way for Teaching, Translation and Professional Communication*. Amsterdam: John Benjamins, 108–123.

Labrador, Belén / Ramón, Noelia / Alaiz-Moretón, Héctor / Sanjurjo-González, Hugo 2014. Rhetorical Structure and Persuasive Language in the Subgenre of Online Advertisements. *English for Specific Purposes*. 34, 38–47. <https://doi.org/10.1016/j.esp.2013.10.002>

Labrador, Belén / Ramón, Noelia 2015. 'Perfectly Smooth, Creamy and Full-flavoured': Online Cheese Descriptions. *Procedia*. 198, 226–232. <https://doi.org/10.1016/j.sbspro.2015.07.440>

Labrador, Belén / Ramón, Noelia 2020. Building a Second-Language Writing Aid for Specific Purposes: Promotional Cheese Descriptions. *English for Specific Purposes*. 60, 40–52. <https://doi.org/10.1016/j.esp.2020.03.003>

Labrador de la Cruz, Belén / Ramón, Noelia 2024. Positive Evaluation in the Translation of Online Promotional Discourse in the Cheese Industry. *IEEE Transactions of Professional Communication,* 63/3, 316–332.

Laviosa-Braithwaithe, Sara 1997. Investigating Simplification in an English Comparable Corpus of Newspaper Articles. In Klaudy, Kinga/ Kohn/ János (eds) *Transferre Necesse Est. Proceedings of the Second International Conference on Current Trends in Studies of Translation and Interpreting*. Budapest: Scholastica, 531–540.

Lee, Ariel N. / Hunter, Cole J. / Ruiz, Nataniel 2023. Platypus: Quick, Cheap, and Powerful Refinement of LLMs. *arXiv:2308.07317.* <https://doi.org/10.48550/arXiv.2308.07317>

Leech, Geoffrey 1993. Corpus Annotation Schemes. *Literary and Linguistic Computing.* 8/4, 275–81.

Leech, Geoffrey 1997. Introducing Corpus Annotation. In Garside, Roger / Leech, Geoffrey / McEnery, Tony (eds) *Corpus Annotation. Linguistic Information from Computer Text Corpora.* London: Longman, 1–18.

Lefer, Marie-Aude / Vogeleer, Svetlana 2013. Interference and Normalization in Genre-controlled Multilingual Corpora. *Belgian Journal of Linguistics*, 27/1, 1–21. <https://doi.org/10.1075/bjl.27.01lef>

Lembersky, Gennadi / Ordan, Noam / Wintner, Shuly 2013. Improving Statistical Machine Translation by Adapting Translation Models to Translationese. *Computational Linguistics* 39/4, 999–1023. <https://doi.org/10.1162/COLI_a_00159>

Lester, Brian / Al-Rfou, Rami / Constant, Noah 2021. The Power of Scale for Parameter-Eicient Prompt Tuning. In *Proceedings of the 2021 Conference on Empirical Methods in Natural Language Processing.* Association for Computational Linguistics, Online and Punta Cana, Dominican Republic, 3045–59. <https://doi.org/10.18653/v1/2021.emnlp-main.243>

Lewis, Mike / Liu, Yinhan / Goyal, Naman / Ghazvininejad, Marjan / Mohamed, Abdelrahman / Levy, Omer / Stoyanov, Veselin / Zettlemoyer, Luke. 2020. BART: Denoising Sequence-to-Sequence Pre-training for Natural Language Generation, Translation, and Comprehension. In Jurafsky, Dan et al (eds) *Proceedings of the 58th Annual Meeting of the Association for Computational Linguistics, Online*, Association for Computational Linguistics, 7871–7880. <https://aclanthology.org/2020.acl-main.703>

Li, Cheng / Wang, Jindong / Zhang, Yixuan / Zhu, Kaijie / Hou, Wenxin / Lian, Jianxun / et al. 2023. Large Language Models Understand and Can be Enhanced by Emotional Stimuli. *arXiv:2307.11760.* <https://doi.org/10.48550/arXiv.2307.11760>

Li, Junyi / Tang, Tianyi / Zhao, Wayne Xin / Nie, Jian-Yun / Wen, Ji-Rong 2022. Pre-Trained Language Models for Text Generation: A Survey. *arXiv:2201.05273.* <https://doi.org/10.48550/arXiv.2201.05273>

Li, Junyi / Tang Tianyi / Zhao,Wayne Xin / Nie, Jian-Yun / Wen, Ji-Rong. 2024. Pre-Trained Language Models for Text Generation: A Survey. *ACM Comput. Surv.* 56/9. <https://doi.org/10.1145/3649449>

Liang, Xun / Wang, Hanyu / Wang, Yezhaohui / Song, Shichao / Yang, Jiawei / Niu, Simin / Hu, Jie / Liu, Dan / Yao, Shunyu / Xiong, Feiyu / Li, Zhiyu 2024. Controllable Text Generation for Large Language Models: A Survey. *arXiv:2408.12599.* <https://doi.org/10.48550/arXiv.2408.12599>

Loi, Chek Kim / Evans, Moyra Sweetnam 2010. Cultural Differences in the Organization of Research Article Introductions from the Field of Educational Psychology: English and Chinese. *Journal of Pragmatics*. 42/10, 2814–2825. <https://doi.org/10.1016/j.pragma.2010.03.010>

López-Arroyo, Belén / Roberts, Roda P. 2014a. English and Spanish Descriptors in Wine Tasting Terminology. *Terminology*. 20/1, 25–49. <https://doi.org/10.1075/term.20.1.02lop>

López-Arroyo, Belén / Roberts, Roda P. 2014b. A Corpus–based Writing Aid for Spanish Language Authors: The Scientific Abstract Generator Prototype. *International Journal of Linguistics and Communication*. 2/2, 13–42.

López-Arroyo, Belén / Roberts, Roda P. 2015a. Unusual Sentence Structure in Wine Tasting Notes: A Contrastive Corpus Based Study. *Languages in Contrast*. 15/2, 162–180. <https://doi.org/10.1075/lic.15.2.01lop>

López-Arroyo, Belén / Roberts, Roda P. 2015b. How Specific Wine Tasting Descriptors Are? *Procedia – Social and Behavioral Sciences*. 198, 287–299. <https://doi.org/10.1016/j.sbspro.2015.07.447>

López-Arroyo, Belén / Roberts, Roda P. 2016. Differences in Wine Tasting Notes in English and Spanish. Babel. 62/3, 370–401. <https://doi.org/10.1075/babel.62.3.02lop>

López-Arroyo, Belén / Moreno-Perez, Leticia 2019. Lexical Chucks in English and Spanish Sales Contracts. *Terminology*. 25/1,32–59.

López-Arroyo, Belén / Sanz-Valdivieso, Lucía 2020. On Describing Olive Oil Tasting Notes in English. *Fachsprache. Journal of Professional and Scientific Communication*. 42/1–2, 27–45. <https://doi.org/10.24989/fs.v42i1-2.1825>

López-Arroyo, Belén / Sanz-Valdivieso, Lucía 2022. The Phraseology of Wine and Olive Oil Tasting Notes: A Corpus Based Semantic Analysis. *Terminology*. 28/1, 37–64. <https://doi.org/10.1075/term.20035.lop>

López-Arroyo, Belén / Sanz-Valdivieso, Lucía 2024. A Hint of the Summery Goodness of Green Grass: A Look at English Descriptors in Tasting Notes. *Revista de Lingüística y Lenguas Aplicadas*. 19, 84–103.

Lorés, Rosa 2004. On RA Abstracts: from Rhetorical Structure to Thematic Organization. *English for Academic Purposes*. 23/3, 280–302. <https://doi.org/10.1016/j.esp.2003.06.001>

Lutzky, Ursula/ Kehoe, Andrew. 2017. "I apologise for my poor blogging": Searching for Apologies in the Birmingham Blog Corpus. *Corpus Pragmatics*. 1, 37–56.

Maestre, María Miró / Martínez-Murillo, Iván / Martin, Tania J. / Navarro-Colorado, Borja / Ferrández, Antonio / Suárez Cueto, Armando / Lloret, Elena 2024. Beyond Generative Artificial Intelligence: Roadmap for Natural Language Generation. *arXiv:2407.10554*. <https://doi.org/10.48550/arXiv.2407.10554>

Mahlow, Cerstin / Dale, Robert 2014. Production Media: Writing as Using Tools in Media Convergent Environments. In Jakobs, Eva-Maria / Perrin, Daniel (eds) *Handbook of Writing and Text Production*. Berlin: De Gruyter Mouton, 209–30.

Maia, Belinda 2003. What are Comparable Corpora? In *Multilingual Corpora: Linguistic Requirements and Technical Perspectives*. Workshop at the Corpus Linguistics Conference, Lancaster, UK. <https://www.coli.uni-saarland.de/conf/muco03/maia.pdf>

Mann, William C. / Thompson, Sandra A. 1987. Rhetorical Structure Theory: Description and Construction of Text Structures. In Kempen, G. (ed.) *Natural Language Generation*. NATO ASI Series (Series E: Applied Sciences). 135, 85–95.

MAPA. Ministerio de Agricultura, Pesca y Alimentación. 2024. *Informe Anual de Comercio Exterior Agroalimentario y Pesquero 2023*. <https://www.mapa.gob.es/es/ministerio/servicios/analisis-y-prospectiva/informecomextanual2023_tcm30-690655.pdf>

Marcellino, William 2023. Public Policy Research Applications of DocuScope's Linguistic Taxonomy. Mining Style and Stance for Sociocultural Insight. In Bron, David W. / Wetzel, Danielle Z. (eds) *Corpora and Rhetorically Informed Text Analysis. The Diverse Applications of DocuScope*. Amsterdam: John Benjamins, 148–66. <https://doi.org/10.1075/scl.109.07mar>

Marco, Josep 2018. Connectives as Indicators of Explicitation in Literary Translation. A Study Based on a Comparable and Parallel Corpus. *Target*. 30/1, 87–111. <https://doi.org/10.1075/target.16042.mar>

Marco, Josep / Tello, Isabel (eds) 2024. *Towards an Empirical Verification of the Gravitational Pull Hypothesis. Evidence from the COVALT Corpus*. Berlin: Peter Lang.

Marcus, Mitchell P. / Santorini, Beatrice / Marcinkiewicz, Mary Ann 1993. Building a Large Annotated Corpus of English: The Penn Treebank. *Computational Linguistics*. 19/2, 313–330.

Martínez-Flor, Alicia 2005. A Theoretical Review of the Speech Act of Suggesting: Towards a Taxonomy for its Use in FLT. *Revista Alicantina de Estudios Ingleses*. 18, 167–187.

Martínez-Flor, Alicia 2010. Suggestions. How Social Norms Affect Pragmatic Behaviour. In Martínez-Flor, Alicia / Usó-Juan, Esther (eds) *Speech Act Performance. Theoretical, Empirical and Methodological Issues*. Amsterdam: John Benjamins, 257–274.

Martínez Vilinsky, Bárbara. 2012. On the Lower Frequency of Occurrence of Spanish Verbal Periphrases in Translated Texts as Evidence for the Unique Items Hypothesis. *Across Languages and Cultures*. 13/2, 197–210. <https://doi.org/10.1556/Acr.13.2012.2.4>

Massardo, Isabella / van der Meer, Jaap / O'Brien, Sharon / Hollowood, Fred / Aranberri, Nora / Drescher, Katrin 2016. Machine Translation Post-editing Guidelines. <https://www.commonspaces.eu/en/oer/taus-post-editing-guidelines/> (consulted 28.10.2024).

McArthur, Tom 1981. *Longman Lexicon of Contemporary English*. London: Longman.

McEnery, Tony / Wilson, Andrew 2001. *Corpus Linguistics. An Introduction*. Edinburgh: Edinburgh University Press.

McEnery, Tony / Hardie, Andrew 2012. *Corpus Linguistics: Method, Theory and Practice*. Cambridge: Cambridge University Press.

Mel'cuk, Igor 1998. Collocations and Lexical Functions. In Cowie, Anthony (ed.) *Phraseology: Theory, Analysis, and Applications*. Oxford: Clarendon Press, 232–53.

Meunier, Fanny / Granger, Sylviane 2009. Introduction. In Meunier, Fanny / Granger, Sylviane (eds) *Phraseology in Foreign Language Learning and Teaching*. Amsterdam: John Benjamins, 15–18. <https://doi.org/10.1017/s0272263109090500>

Milà-Garcia, Alba. 2018. Pragmatic Annotation for a Multi-Layered Analysis of Speech Acts: A Methodological Proposal. *Corpus Pragmatics*. 2, 265–287.

Mitchell, Alexis / Strassel, Stephanie / Huang, Shudong / Zakhary, Ramez 2005. ACE 2004 multilingual training corpus (LDC2005T09) [Data set]. Linguistic Data Consortium. https://doi.org/10.35111/8m4r-v312

Montejo-Ráez, Arturo / Jiménez-Zafra, Salud M. 2022 Current Approaches and Applications in Natural Language Processing. *Applied Sciences*. 12, 4859. <https://doi.org/10.3390/app12104859>

Moorkens, Joos 2018. Eye Tracking as a Measure of Cognitive Effort for Post-editing of Machine Translation. In Walker, Callum/ Federici, Federico M. (eds) *Eye Tracking and Multidisciplinary Studies on Translation*. Amsterdam: John Benjamins, 55–69. <https://doi.org/10.1075/btl.143.04moo>

Moorkens, Joos / O'Brien, Sharon. 2017. Assessing User Interface Needs of Post-editors of Machine Translation. In Kenny, Dorothy (ed.) *Human Issues in Translation Technology*. London: Routledge, 127–148.

Moorkens, Joss / Castilho, Sheila / Gaspari, Federico / Doherty, Stephen 2018. *Translation Quality Assessment. From Principles to Practice*. Cham: Springer. <https://doi.org/10.1007/978-3-319-91241-7>

Moreno-Pérez, Leticia (in press). Phraseology and Natural Language Processing: A Concise Overview. *RESLA*. 38/2.

Moreno-Pérez, Leticia / López-Arroyo, Belén 2023. Wine and Translation: An Analysis of Phraseological Units in English and Spanish Wine Technical Sheets. *Perspectives: Studies in Translation Theory and Practice*. 1–16. <https://doi.org/10.1080/0907676X.2023.2268115>

Moretti, Franco 2005. *Graphs, Maps, Trees: Abstract Models for a Literary History*. London: Verso.

Murtuza, Shariq 2024. Sentinels of the Stream: Unleashing Large Language Models for Dynamic Packet Classification in Software Defined Networks. *ArXiv*, abs/2402.07950. <https://doi.org/10.48550/arXiv.2402.07950>

Nasser, Marwa Adel 2022. A corpus-based study of reviewers' usage of speech acts. *Cogent Arts and Humanities*. 9/1. <https://doi.org/10.1080/23311983.2022.2125155>

Negri, Matteo / Turchi, Marco / Chatterjee, Rajen / Bertoldi, Nicola 2018. eSCAPE: a Large-scale Synthetic Corpus for Automatic Post-editing. *Proceedings of the Eleventh International Conference on Language Resources and Evaluation (LREC 2018)*. Miyazaki, Japan: European Language Resources Association (ELRA), 24–30. <https://doi.org/10.48550/arXiv.1803.07274>

Nesselhauf, Nadja 2004. What are Collocations? In Allerton, David, J. *et al.* (eds) *Phraseological Units: Basic Concepts and their Application*. Berlin: Schwabe, 1–21.

Nickerson, Catherine 2005. English as a Lingua Franca in International Business Contexts. *English for Specific Purposes*. 24/4, 367–380. <https://doi.org/10.1016/j.esp.2005.02.001>

Nikolenko, Olga / Shapovalova, Elena 2021. The Status and Methodological Interpretation of Terminological Phraseological Units in Scientific Technical Texts. In *E3s Web of Conferences* 273, 11005. <https://doi.org/10.1051/e3sconf/202127311005>

Nisioi, Sergiu / Rabinovich, Ella / Dinu, Liviu P. / Wintner, Shuly 2016. A Corpus of Native, Non-native and Translated Texts. In *Proceedings of the Tenth International Conference on Language Resources and Evaluation (LREC'16)*. Portorož, Slovenia: European Language Resources Association (ELRA). 4197–4201. <https://aclanthology.org/L16-1664>

Nitzke, Jean / Gros, Anne-Kathrin. 2021. Preferential Changes in Revision and Post-editing. In Koponen, Maarit *et al.* (eds). *Translation Revision and Post-editing. Industry Practices and Cognitive Processes*. London: Routledge, 21–34.

Noh, Youngbin / Kim, Kuntae / Lee, Minho / Heo, Cheolhun / Jeong, Yongbin / Jeong, Yoosung / Hahm, Younggyun / Oh, Taehwan / Choe, Hyonsu / Park, Seokwon / Kim, Jin-Dong / Choi, Key-Sun 2020. Enhancing Quality of Corpus Annotation: Construction of the Multi-Layer Corpus Annotation and Simplified Validation of the Corpus Annotation. In Le Nguyen, Minh *et al.* (eds). *Proceedings of the 34th Pacific Asia Conference on Language, Information and Computation*, Hanoi: Association for Computational Linguistics, 216–224. <https://aclanthology.org/2020.paclic-1.25>

Nwogu, Kevin N. 1991. Structure of Science Popularizations: A Genre-Analysis Approach to the Schema of Popularized Medical Texts. *English for Specific Purposes*. 10/2, 111–23. <https://doi.org/10.1016/0889-4906(91)90004-G>

O'Brien, Sharon 2011a. Towards Predicting Post-editing Productivity. *Machine Translation*. 25, 197–215 <https://doi.org/10.1007/s10590-011-9096-7>

O'Brien, Sharon 2011b. Introduction to Post-editing: Who, What, How and Where to Next? <https://aclanthology.org/2010.amta-tutorials.1.pdf>

O'Brien, Sharon 2022. How to Deal with Errors in Machine Translation: Post-editing. In Kenny, Dorothy (ed) *Machine Translation for Everyone: Empowering Users in the Age of Artificial Intelligence*. Berlin: Language Science Press, 105–120. <https://doi.org/10.5281/zenodo.6653406>

Odlin, Terence 2005. Crosslinguistic Influence and Conceptual Transfer: What are the Concepts? *Annual Review of Applied Linguistics*. 25, 3–25. <https://doi.org/10.1017/S0267190505000012>

O'Donnell, Michael 2008. The UAM Corpus Tool: Software for Corpus Annotation and Exploration. In Bretones-Callejas, Carmen M. *et al.* (eds) *Applied Linguistics Now: Understanding Language and Mind*. Almería: Universidad de Almería, 1433–1447.

O'Keeffe, Anne / Clancy, Brian/ Adolphs, Svenja 2011. *Introducing Pragmatics in Use*. Abingdon, Oxfordshire: Routledge.

Olohan, Maeve / Baker, Mona 2000. Reporting that in Translated English. Evidence for Subconscious Processes of Explicitation? *Across Languages and Cultures*, 1/2, 141–158. <https://doi.org/10.1556/Acr.1.2000.2.1>

Ortego Antón, María Teresa 2019. *La terminología del sector agroalimentario (español-inglés) en los estudios contrastivos y de traducción especializada basados en corpus: Los embutidos*. Berlín: Peter Lang.

Ortego Antón, María Teresa 2020. Las fichas descriptivas de embutidos en español y en inglés: Un análisis contrastivo de la estructura retórica basado en corpus. *Revista Signos*. 53/102, 170–194. <http://dx.doi.org/10.4067/S0718-09342020000100170>

Ortego Antón, María Teresa 2023. Building Corpus-based Writing Aids from Spanish into English: The Case of GEFEM. In Izquierdo, Marlén / Sanz-Villar, Zuriñe (eds). *Corpus Use in Cross-linguistic Research. Paving the Way for Teaching, Translation and Professional Communication*. Amsterdam: John Benjamins, 216–233.

Ortego Antón, María Teresa 2024a. The Design of TorreznoTRAD: The Semiautomatic Spanish-English Writing and Translation Aid Tool. In Peñuelas Gil, Isabel / Ortego Antón, María Teresa (eds) *Interpreting and Translation for Agri-food Professionals in the Global Marketplace*. Berlin: De Gruyter, 69–84. <https://doi.org/10.1515/9783111101729-004>

Ortego Antón, María Teresa 2024b. Metodología para el diseño de un asistente semiautomático de redacción y de traducción de fichas descriptivas de embutidos del español al inglés. *Cadernos de Tradução*. 44/1, 1–20. <https://doi.org/10.5007/2175-7968.2024.e94647>

Ortego Antón, María Teresa 2024c. Designing a Corpus-based Writing Aid Tool for the Agrifood Industry: The Case of TorreznoTRAD. In Alonso-Almeida, Francisco (ed) *Insights in (Inter)cultural and Cross-cultural Communication*. Valencia: Tirant Lo Blanch, 51–66.

Ortego Antón, María Teresa / Fernández Nistal, Purificación 2020. Estudio contrastivo de la terminología de embutidos en inglés y en español con ParaConc y tlCorpus a partir del corpus paralelo P-GEFEM y del comparable C-GEFEM. In Seghiri, Miriam (ed) *La lingüística de corpus aplicada al desarrollo de la competencia tecnológica en los estudios de traducción e interpretación y la enseñanza de segundas lenguas*. Bern: Peter Lang, 23–48.

Ostyakova, Lidiia / Petukhova, Kseniia / Smilga, Veronika / Zharikova, Dilyara 2023. Linguistic Annotation Generation with ChatGPT: a Synthetic Dataset of Speech Functions for Discourse Annotation of Casual Conversations. In *Proceedings of the International Conference Computational Linguistics and Intellectual Technologies: "Dialogue 2023"*, 1–18. <https://doi.org/10.28995/2075-7182-2023-22-386-403>

Otani, Naoki / Ozaki Satoru / Zhao Xingyuan / Li Yucen / St. Johns Micaelah / Levin, Lori 2020. Pre-Tokenization of Multi-Word Expressions in Cross-Lingual Word Embeddings. In *Proceedings of the 2020 Conference on Empirical Methods in Natural Language Processing (EMNLP)*. Online: Association for Computational Linguistics), 4451–4464. <https://aclanthology.org/2020.emnlp-main.360/>

Otero, Pablo G. / López, Isaac G. 2010. Wikipedia as Multilingual Source of Comparable Corpora. In Rapp, Reinhard *et al.* (eds) *Proceedings of the 3rd Workshop on Building and Using Comparable Corpora*. Malta: LREC, 21–25. <http://www.lrec-conf.org/proceedings/lrec2010/workshops/W12.pdf>

Otter, Daniel W. / Medina, Julian R. / Kalita, Jugal K. 2021. A Survey of the Usages of Deep Learning for Natural Language Processing. In *IEEE Transactions on Neural Networks and Learning Systems*. 32/2, 604–24. <https://doi.org/10.1109/tnnls.2020.2979670>

Ouyang, Long / Wu, Jefrey / Jiang, Xu / Almeida, Diogo / Wainwright, Carroll / Mishkin, Pamela *et al.* 2022. Training Language Models to Follow Instructions with Human Feedback. In Koyejo, Sanmi *et al.* (eds) *Advances in Neural Information Processing Systems*. 35. Curran Associates, Inc., 27730-27744. <https://proceedings.neurips.cc/paper_files/paper/2022/hash/b1efde53be364a73914f58805a001731-Abstract-Conference.html>

Øverås, Linn 1998. In Search of the Third Code: an Investigation of Norms in Literary Translation. *Meta*. 43/4, 571–588. <https://doi.org/10.7202/003775ar>

Parkinson, Jean 2017. The Student Laboratory Report Genre: A Genre Analysis. *English for Specific Purposes*. 45, 1–13. <https://doi.org/10.1016/j.esp.2016.08.001>

Peng, Baolin / Li, Chunyuan / He, Pengcheng / Galley, Michel / Gao, Jianfeng 2023. Instruction Tuning with GPT-4. *arXiv:2304.03277*. <https://doi.org/10.48550/arXiv.2304.03277>

Peñuelas Gil, Isabel / Ortego Antón, María Teresa 2024. La estructura retórica EN-ES de las fichas de torrezno. In Sánchez Carnicer, Jaime / Arce Romeral, Lorena (eds). *Nuevos avances tecnológicos en teoría y práctica de la traducción e interpretación*. Berlin: Peter Lang, 155–176.

Pérez Blanco, María 2013. *La expresión lingüística de la evaluación en el discurso de opinión: análisis léxico-contrastivo inglés-español*. PhD Thesis. León: Universidad de León. <https://buleria.unileon.es/handle/10612/8214>

Pérez Blanco, María / Izquierdo, Marlén 2021. Developing a Corpus-informed Tool for Spanish Professionals Writing Specialized Texts in English. In Lavid-López, Julia *et al.* (eds) *Corpora in Translation and Contrastive Research in the Digital Age*. Amsterdam: John Benjamins, 147–173. <https://doi.org/10.1075/btl.158.06per>

Pérez Blanco, María / Izquierdo, Marlén 2022. Engaging with Customer's Emotions: A Case Study in English-Spanish Online Food Advertising. *Languages in Contrast*. 22/1, 43–76. <https://doi.org/10.1075/lic.19016.per>

Perković, Gabrileja / Drobnjak, Antun / Botički, Ivica 2024. Hallucinations in LLMs: Understanding and Addressing Challenges. In *47th MIPRO ICT and Electronics Convention*, IEEE, 2084–2088. <https://ieeexplore.ieee.org/document/10569238>

Petrov, Slav / Das, Dipanjan / McDonald, Ryan 2011. A Universal Part-of-Speech Tagset. *arXiv:1104.2086*. <https://doi.org/10.48550/arXiv.1104.2086>

Pho, Phuong Dzung 2008. Research Article Abstracts in Applied Linguistics and Educational Technology: A Study of Linguistic Realizations of Rhetorical Structure and Authorial Stance. *Discourse Studies*. 10/2, 231–250. <https://doi.org/10.1177/1461445607087010>

Piao, Scott / Bianchi, Francesca / Dayrell, Carmen / D'Egidio, Angela / Rayson, Paul. 2015. Development of the Multilingual Semantic Annotation System. In *Proceedings of the 2015 Conference of the North American Chapter of the Association for Computational Linguistics: Human Language Technologies*. Denver, Colorado: Association for Computational Linguistics. 1268–1274. <https://doi.org/10.3115/v1/N15-1137>

Pillai, Anitha S. / Tedesco, Roman (eds) 2024. *Machine Learning and Deep Learning in Natural Language Processing*. CRC Press. <https://doi.org/10.1201/9781003296126>

Pizarro Sánchez, Isabel 2017. A Corpus-Based Analysis of Genre-Specific Multi-Word Combinations. Minutes in English and Spanish. In Egan, Thomas / Dirdal, Hildegunn (eds) *Cross-linguistic Correspondences: From Lexis to Genre*. Amsterdam: John Benjamins, 221–252. <https://doi.org/10.1075/slcs.191.09san>

Pizarro Sánchez, Isabel / Pérez Ruiz, Leonor 2024. Rhetorical Structure and Promotional Language in Baked Product Descriptions: An English-Spanish Contrastive Analysis. In Ortego Antón, María Teresa / Peñuelas Gil, Isabel (eds) *Interpreting and Translation for Agri-food Professionals in the Global Marketplace*. Berlin, Boston: De Gruyter, 85–103. <https://doi.org/10.1515/9783111101729-005>

Placencia, Maria Elena. 2012. Online Peer-to-Peer Advice in Spanish Yahoo! Respuestas. In Limberg, Holger / Locher, Miriam A. (eds) *Advice in Discourse*. Amsterdam: John Benjamins, 281–306.

Pollock, Matthew / Blaker, Nicholas M. 2021. *¿Qué me recomiendas? Teaching the Pragmatics of Recommendations.* Special volume on *Teaching of Pragmatics. 21* < https://scholarworks.iu.edu/journals/index.php/iulcwp/article/view/31873/36345>

Posteguillo, Santiago 1999. The Schematic Structure of Computer Science Research Articles. *English for Specific Purposes*. 18/2, 139–160. <https://doi.org/10.1016/S0889-4906(98)00001-5>

Potts, Amanda / Baker, Paul 2012. Does Semantic Tagging Identify Cultural Change in British and American English? *International Journal of Corpus Linguistics*. 17/3, 295–324.

Pourdamghani, Nima / Aldarrab, Nada / Ghazvininejad, Marjan / Knight, Kevin / May, Jonathan 2019. Translating Translationese: A Two-Step Approach to Unsupervised Machine Translation. In *Proceedings of the 57th Annual Meeting of the Association for Computational Linguistics*. Florence: Association for Computational Linguistics. 3057–3062. <https://doi.org/10.48550/arXiv.1906.05683>

Prabhumoye, Shrimai / Black, Alan W. / Salakhutdinov, Ruslan 2020. Exploring Controllable Text Generation Techniques. In *Proceedings of the 28th International Conference on Computational Linguistics*, Barcelona: ACL, 1–14.

Rabadán, Rosa 2006. Modality and Modal Verbs in Contrast. *Languages in Contrast*. 6/2, 261–306. <https://doi.org/10.1075/lic.6.2.04rab>

Rabadán, Rosa 2007. Translating the 'Predictive' and 'Hypothetical' Meanings English-Spanish. *Meta*. 52/3, 484–502. <https://doi.org/10.7202/016734ar>

Rabadán, Rosa 2008. Refining the Idea of 'Applied Extension'. In Pym, Anthony / Shlesinger, Miriam / Simeoni, Daniel (eds) *Beyond Descriptive Translation Studies*. Amsterdam: John Benjamins. 103–117. <https://doi.org/10.1075/btl.75.09rab>

Rabadán, Rosa 2009. The Present Tenses in English and in Spanish: A Corpus-based Approach to Cross-linguistic Meaning and Grammatical

Transfer. In Oleksy, Wieslaw / Stalmaszczyk, Piotr (eds) *Cognitive Approaches to Language and Linguistic Data. Studies in honor of Barbara Lewandowska-Tomaszczyk*. Frankfurt am Main: Peter Lang, 461–478.

Rabadán, Rosa 2010. Applied Translation Studies. In Gambier, Yves / van Doorslaer, Luc (eds) *Handbook of Translation Studies*. Volume 1. Amsterdam: John Benjamins, 7–11. <https://doi.org/10.1075/hts.1.app1>

Rabadán, Rosa 2011. Any into Spanish: A Corpus-Based Analysis of a Translation Problem. *Linguistica Pragensia*. 21/2, 57–69. <https://doi.org/10.2478/v10017-011-0005-y>

Rabadán, Rosa 2015. A Corpus-based Study of Aspect: Still and Already + Verb Phrase Constructions into Spanish. *Nordic Journal of English Studies*. 14/1, 34–61. <https://doi.org/10.35360/njes.339>

Rabadán, Rosa 2016. Proposals in Meeting Minutes. An English-Spanish Corpus-based Study. *Languages in Contrast*. 16/2, 213–238. <https://doi.org/10.1075/lic.16.2.03rab>

Rabadán, Rosa 2019. Working with Parallel Corpora. Usefulness and Usability. In Doval, Irene / Sánchez Nieto / M. Teresa (eds) 2019. Parallel Corpora for Contrastive and Translation Studies. Amsterdam: John Benjamins, 57–78. <https://doi.org/10.1075/scl.90.04rab>

Rabadán, Rosa 2023. Light Verb Constructions in English-Spanish Translations: What Corpora can Tell Us. In Izquierdo, Marlén / Sanz-Villar, Zuriñe (eds.) *Corpus Use in Cross-linguistic Research. Paving the Way for Teaching, Translation and Professional Communication*. Amsterdam: John Benjamins, 34–50. <https://doi.org/10.1075/scl.113.02rab>

Rabadán, Rosa / Labrador, Belén / Ramón, Noelia 2009. Corpus-Based Contrastive Analysis and Translation Universals: A Tool for Translation Quality Assessment English-Spanish? *Babel*. 55/4, 303–328. <https://doi.org/10.1075/babel.55.4.01rab>

Rabadán, Rosa / Díez Fernández, María de los Ángeles / Fernández Díaz, Ramón Ángel / López-Arroyo, Belén 2011. Writing Abstracts: Technological Applications from a Corpus-based Study. In: Talaván, Noa / Martín Monje, Elena / Palazón, Francisco (eds.) *Innovation in the Teaching and Processing of LSPs*. Madrid: UNED, 325–335.

Rabadán, Rosa / Izquierdo, Marlén 2013a. A Corpus-based Analysis of English Affixal Negation Translated into Spanish. In Aijmer, Karin / Altenberg, Bengt (eds.) *Advances in Corpus-based Contrastive Linguistics. Studies in Honour of Stig Johansson*. Amsterdam: John Benjamins, 57–82.

Rabadán, Rosa / Izquierdo, Marlén 2013b. A Corpus-based Study of English Approximate Negators and their Translation into Spanish. *Bergen Language and Linguistics Studies*. 3/1, 43–59. <https://doi.org/10.15845/bells.v3i1.361>

Rabadán, Rosa / Labrador, Belén / Ramón, Noelia / Sanjurjo-González, Hugo / García- Gallego, Ana / Alaiz, Héctor / Fernández, Ramón-Ángel 2014. Semi-Automatic Procedure for Evaluating the Grammatical Quality of Translations of Spanish Texts into English PETRA 1.0© (©00/2014/981) <https://actres.unileon.es/demos/generadores/applications.html#t>

Rabadán, Rosa / Sanjurjo-González, Hugo / Colwell, Veronica 2016. Bi-Texting Your Food: Helping the Gastro Industry Reach the Global Market. In Moreno Ortiz, Antonio / Pérez-Hernández, Chantal (eds.) *CILC2016. 8th International Conference on Corpus Linguistics*. EasyChair: EPiC Series in Language and Linguistics 1, 361–371. <https://doi.org/10.29007/4xtp>

Rabadán, Rosa / Ramón, Noelia / Sanjurjo-González, Hugo 2021a. Pragmatic Annotation of a Domain-restricted English-Spanish Comparable Corpus. *Bergen Language and Linguistics Studies*. 11/1, 209–23. <https://doi.org/10.15845/bells.v11i1.3445>

Rabadán, Rosa / Pizarro, Isabel / Sanjurjo-González, Hugo 2021b. Authoring Support for Spanish Language Writers: A Genre-restricted Case Study. *RESLA*. 34/2, 677–717. <https://doi.org/10.1075/resla.19048.rab>

Rabadán, Rosa / Gutiérrez-Lanza, Camino 2023. Interference, Explicitation, Implicitation and Normalization in Third Code Spanish: Evidence from Discourse Markers. *Across Languages and Cultures*, 24/1, 1–24. <https://doi.org/10.1556/084.2022.00223>

Rabinovich, Ella / Wintner, Shuly 2015 Unsupervised Identification of Translationese. *Transactions of the Association for Computational Linguistics* 3, 419–432. <https://doi.org/10.1162/tacl_a_00148>

Radford, Alec / Narasimhan, Karthik / Salimans, Tim / Sutskever, Ilya 2018. Improving Language Understanding by Generative Pre-training. <https://hayate-lab.com/wp-content/uploads/2023/05/43372bfa750340059ad87ac8e538c53b.pdf>

Radford, Alec / Wu, Jeffrey / Child, Rewon / Luan, David / Amodei, Dario / Sutskever, Ilya 2019. Language Models are Unsupervised Multitask Learners. *OpenAI Blog*. 1/8, 9. <https://d4mucfpksywv.cloudfront.net/better-language-models/language-models.pdf>

Rafailov, Rafael / Sharma, Archit / Mitchell, Eric / Manning, Christopher D. / Ermon, Stefano / Finn, Chelsea 2024. Direct Preference Optimization:

Your Language Model is Secretly a Reward Model. *Advances in Neural Information Processing Systems*. 36, 28954–28967.

Raffel, Colin / Shazeer, Noam / Roberts, Adam / Lee, Katherine / Narang, Sharan / Matena, Michael / Zhou, Yanqi / Li, Wei / Liu, Peter J. 2020. Exploring the Limits of Transfer Learning with a Unified Text-to-text Transformer. *Journal of Machine Learning Research*. 21, 1–67. <https://arxiv.org/abs/1910.10683>.

Ramón, Noelia 2004. Modifying Nouns: An English-Spanish Corpus-Based Contrast of Three Word Pairs. *Journal of English Studies*. 4, 171–184.

Ramón, Noelia. 2006a. Mapping Meaning onto Form: A Corpus-based Contrastive Study of Nominal Modification in English and Spanish. *Languages in Contrast*. 6/2, 307–334. <https://doi.org/10.1075/lic.6.2.05ram>

Ramón, Noelia 2006b. Multiple Modification in English and Spanish NPs. *International Journal of Corpus Linguistics*. 11/4, 463–495 <https://doi.org/10.1075/ijcl.11.4.06ram>

Ramón, Noelia 2009. Translating Epistemic Adverbs from English into Spanish: Evidence from a Parallel Corpus. *Meta*. 54/1, 73–96. <https://doi.org/10.7202/029794ar>

Ramón, Noelia 2015. Comparing Original and Translated Spanish: A Corpus-Based Analysis of Adjective Position. *Babel*. 61/4, 527–551. <https://doi.org/10.1075/babel.61.4.05ram>

Ramón, Noelia 2023. Exploring Near-synonymy through Translation Corpora. A Case Study on 'Begin' and 'Start' in the English-Spanish Parallel Corpus PACTRES. In Izquierdo, Marlén /Sanz-Villar, Zuriñe (eds.) *Corpus Use in Cross-linguistic Research. Paving the Way for Teaching, Translation and Professional Communication*. Amsterdam: John Benjamins, 91–107. <https://doi.org/10.1075/scl.113.05ram>

Ramón, Noelia / Labrador, Belén 2008. Translations of '-ly' Adverbs of Degree in an English-Spanish Parallel Corpus. *Target*. 20/2, 275–296. <https://doi.org/10.1075/target.20.2.05ram>

Ramón, Noelia / Labrador, Belén 2015. The Rhetorical Structure of Technical Brochures: A Proposal for Technical Writing. *Procedia*. 173, 241–245. <https://doi.org/10.1016/j.sbspro.2015.02.059>

Ramón, Noelia / Gutiérrez-Lanza, Camino 2018. Translation Description for Assessment and Post-Editing. *Target* 30/1, 112–136. <https://doi.org/10.1075/target.15098.ram>

Ramón, Noelia / Labrador, Belén 2018. Selling Cheese Online: Key Nouns in Cheese Descriptions. *Terminology*. 24/2, 210–235. <https://doi.org/10.1075/term.00019.ram>

Ramón, Noelia / Rabadán, Rosa June 2024. *English-Spanish Promotional Texts and Essays: Verbal Use as a Register Marker?* Paper presented at the ICAME 45 Pre-conference workshop Interlocking Multilingual Corpora and Register(s): Diversity and Innovation. Vigo.

Rawte, Vipula / Chakraborty, Swagata / Pathak, Agnibh / Sarkar, Anubhav / Tonmoy, S. M. Towhidul Islam / Chadha, Aman / *et al.* 2023. The Troubling Emergence of Hallucination in Large Language Models – An Extensive Definition, Quantification, and Prescriptive Remediations. *arXiv:2310.04988*. <http://arxiv.org/abs/2310.04988>

Rayson, Paul / Archer, Dawn / Piao, Scott S.L. / McEnery, Tony 2004. The UCREL Semantic Analysis System. In *Proceedings of the Workshop Beyond Named Entity Recognition, Semantic Labelling NLP Tasks* (LREC 2004). 7–12.

Reed, Alan. 1977. *CLOC: A Collocation Package*. Association for Literary and Linguistic Computing Bulletin. 5/2, 168–173.

Reiter, Ehud / Dale, Robert. 1997. Building Applied Natural Language Generation Systems. *Natural Language Engineering*. 3(1), 57–87.

Rico Pérez, Celia 2024. Re-thinking Machine Translation Post-editing Guidelines. *Journal of Specialised Translation* 41. 26–47. <https://doi.org/10.26034/cm.jostrans.2024.4696>

Rico, Celia / Ariano, Martín 2014. Defining Language Dependent Post-editing Guidelines: The Case of the Language Pair English-Spanish. In O'Brien, Sharon et al. (eds) *Post-editing of Machine Translation: Processes and Applications*. Newcastle upon Tyne: Cambridge Scholars Publishing, 299–322.

Roberts, Roda P. 1998. Phraseology and Translation. In Bravo Gozalo, José María / Fernández Nistal, Purificación (eds) *La traducción: Orientaciones lingüísticas y culturales*. Valladolid: Secretariado de Publicaciones, 61–77.

Rühlemann, Christoph. 2010. What Can a Corpus Tell us about Pragmatics? In O'Keeffe, Anne / McCarthy, Michael (eds) *The Routledge Handbook of Corpus Linguistics*. London: Routledge, 263–280.

Rühlemann, Christoph / Clancy, Brian. 2018. Corpus Linguistics and Pragmatics. In Ilie, Cornelia / Norrick, Neal (eds) *Pragmatics and its Interfaces*. Amsterdam: John Benjamins, 241–266.

Sag, Ican / Baldwin, Timothy / Bond, Francis / Copestake, Ann / Flickinger, Dan 2002. Multiword Expressions: A Pain in the Neck for NLP. In Gelbukh, Alexander (ed.) *Computational Linguistics and Intelligent Text Processing*. Berlin: Springer, 1–15.

Sakamoto, Akiko. 2019. Why Do Many Translators Resist Post-Editing? A Sociological Analysis Using Bourdieu's Concepts. *Journal of Specialised Translation* 31. 201–216.

Samraj, Betty 2002. Introductions in Research Articles: Variation across Disciplines. *English for Specific Purposes*. 21/1, 1–17. <https://doi.org/10.1016/S0889-4906(00)00023-5>

Sánchez Carnicer, Jaime 2022. *Traducción y discapacidad. Un estudio comparado de la terminología inglés-español en la prensa escrita*. Berlin: Peter Lang.

Sanjurjo-González, Hugo 2017. *Creación de un Framework para el Tratamiento de Corpus lingüísticos* [Development of a Framework for Corpus Linguistic Analysis]. Doctoral dissertation. University of León, Spain. <http://hdl.handle.net/10612/6920>

Sanjurjo-González, Hugo 2018. *Creación de un Framework para el Tratamiento de Corpus lingüísticos* [Development of a Framework for Corpus Linguistic Analysis]. León, Spain: Servicio de Publicaciones de la Universidad de León.

Sanjurjo-González, Hugo 2020. Increasing Accuracy of a Semantic Word-labelling Tool Based on a Small Lexicon. In *Proceedings of the 17th International Conference on Natural Language Processing (ICON)*. Indian Institute of Technology Patna, Patna, India: NLP Association of India (NLPAI), 10–14. <https://aclanthology.org/2020.icon-main.2.pdf>

Sanjurjo-González, Hugo 2021. Improving Accuracy of an Existing Semantic Word-labelling Tool Using Word Embeddings. *Proceedings. of the 16th Iberian Conference on Information Systems and Technologies (CISTI 2021)*. Chaves, Portugal, 1–5. <https://doi.org/10.23919/CISTI52073.2021.9476323>

Sanjurjo-González, Hugo. Forthcoming a. Hybrid Models for Rhetorical Structure Annotation.

Sanjurjo-González, Hugo. Forthcoming b. Annotating Pragmatics: A Novel Approach Using Large Language Models.

Sanjurjo-González, Hugo / Alaiz-Moretón, Héctor / Ramón, Noelia / Labrador, Belén / García, Isaías 2019. Using an Ontology-based Approach to Build Open Assisting Tools in Foreign Language Writing. *Journal of Information Systems Engineering & Management*. 4/2, em0099. <https://doi.org/10.29333/jisem/5931>

Sanjurjo-González, Hugo / Izquierdo, Marlén 2019. P-ACTRES 2.0. A Parallel Corpus for Cross-linguistic Research. In: Doval, Irene / Sánchez Nieto, M. Teresa (eds.) *Parallel Corpora for Contrastive and Translation Studies*. Amsterdam: John Benjamins, 215–232. <https://doi.org/10.1075/scl.90.13san>

Sanjurjo-González, Hugo / Andaluz-Pinedo, Olaia 2021. OpenTagger: A Flexible and User–friendly Linguistic Tagger. *56th Linguistics Colloquium*.<http://web.vu.lt/flf/s.volungeviciene/files/2009/08/Abstracts-56-LingColl-draft.pdf>

Sanz-Valdivieso, Lucía 2024. Technology-Powered Multilingual Professional and Technical Writing: An Integrative Literature Review of Landmark and the Latest Writing Assistance Tools. In López-Arroyo, Belén / Wang, Xiao / Ishizaki, Suguru (eds) *IEEE Transactions on Professional Communication. Special Issue Building Bridges Between Technical and Professional Communication and Translation Studies*. 67/3, 301 – 315. <10.1109/TPC.2024.3419288>

Sanz-Valdivieso, Lucía / López-Arroyo, Belén 2023. Google Translate vs. ChatGPT: Can Non-Language Professionals Trust them for Specialized Translation? In Orăsan, Constantin *et al.* (eds) *International Conference on Human-Informed Translation and Interpreting Technology (HiT-IT 2023)*. Naples, Italy, 97–107. <https://doi.org/10.26615/issn.2683-0078.2023_008>

Savelyeva, Maria / Khomutnikova, Elena / Borovykh, Yulia 2019. Semantic Classification of Object Phraseological Units with Zoonymic Component in English. In *SHS Web of Conferences* 69: 00099. <https://doi.org/10.1051/shsconf/20196900099>

Schmid, Helmut 1995. Treetagger: A Language Independent Part-of-Speech Tagger. *Institut für Maschinelle Sprachverarbeitung*. 43, 28.

Schmid, Helmut 1999. Improvements in Part-of-Speech Tagging with an Application to German. In Amstrong, Susan *et al.* (eds) *Natural Language Processing Using Large Corpora*. Berlin: Springer, 13–27.

Schmidt, Thomas / Wörner, Kai. 2014. EXMARaLDA. In Durand, Jacques *et al.* (eds) *The Oxford Handbook of Corpus Phonology*. Oxford: Oxford Academic.

Schwitter, Rolf 2010. Controlled Natural Languages for Knowledge Representation. *Proceedings of the 23rd International Conference on Computational Linguistics: Poster Volume*, 1113–1121.

Scott, Mike 1996. *WordSmith Tools*. Oxford: Oxford University Press.

Scott, Mike / Johns, Tim 1993. *MicroConcord* [Software].

Searle, John R. 1969. *Speech Acts*. Cambridge: CUP.

Seghiri, Míriam 2006. *Compilación de un Corpus Trilingüe de Seguros Turísticos (Español-Inglés-Italiano): Aspectos de Evaluación, Catalogación, Diseño y Representatividad*. PhD Thesis. Málaga: Universidad de Málaga. < http://hdl.handle.net/10630/2715>

Seghiri, Míriam 2017. Metodología de elaboración de un glosario bilingüe y bidireccional (inglés-español/español–inglés) basado en corpus para la traducción de manuales de instrucciones de televisores. *Babel*. 63/1, 43–64. <https://doi.org/10.1075/babel.63.1.04seg>

Selinker, Larry 1972. Interlanguage. *International Review of Applied Linguistics in Language Teaching*. 10/1–4, 209–232.

Simard, Michel / Ueffing, Nicola / Isabelle, Pierre / Kuhn, Roland 2007. Rule-Based Translation with StatisticalPhrase-Based Post-Editing. In *Proceedings of the Second Workshop on Statistical Machine Translation*. Prague: Association for Computational Linguistics, 203–206. <https://aclanthology.org/W07-0728.pdf>

Sinclair, John 1987. *Looking Up. An Account of the COBUILD Project in Lexical Computing*. London: Collins Cobuild.

Sinclair, John 1996. *Preliminary Recommendations on Corpus Typology*. EAGLES (Expert Advisory Group on Language Engineering Standards) EAG-TCWG-CTYP/P. <https://www.ilc.cnr.it/EAGLES96/corpustyp/corpustyp.html>

Sinclair, John 2000. Lexical Grammar. *Naujoji Metodolojia*. 24, 191–203.

Sinclair, John / Coulthard, Malcolm 1975. *Towards an Analysis of Discourse*. London: OUP.

Soler-Monreal, Carmen / Carbonell-Olivares, María / Gil-Salom, Luz 2011. A Contrastive Study of the Rhetorical Organisation of English and Spanish PhD Thesis Introductions. *English for Specific Purposes*. 30/1, 4–17. <https://doi.org/10.1016/j.esp.2010.04.005>

Sominsky, Ilia / Wintner, Shuly 2019. Automatic Detection ofTranslation Direction. *Proceedings of the International Conference on Recent Advances in Natural Language Processing (RANLP 2019)*. Varna, Bulgaria: INCOMA Ltd., 1131–1140. 10.26615/978-954-452-056-4_130. <https://aclanthology.org/R19-1130>

Statista 2023. *Food & Drink - Worldwide*. <https://www.statista.com/outlook/amo/app/food-drink/worldwide>

Stede, Manfred / Neumann, Arne 2014. Potsdam Commentary Corpus 2.0: Annotation for Discourse Research. In Calzolari, Nicoletta et al. (eds) *Proceedings of the Ninth International Conference on Language Resources and Evaluation (LREC'14)*. Reykjavik, Iceland: European Language Resources Association (ELRA), 925–929.

Stede, Manfred / Umbach, Carla 1998. Dimlex: A Lexicon of Discourse Markers for Text Generation and Understanding. In *Proceedings of the 36th Annual Meeting of the Association for Computational*

Linguistics and 17th International Conference on Computational Linguistics, 2, 1238–1242.

Stenetorp, Pontus / Pyysalo, Sampo / Topić, Goran / Ohta, Tomoko / Ananiadou, Sophia / Tsujii, Jun'ichi 2012. brat: a Web-based Tool for NLP-Assisted Text Annotation. In Segond, Frédérique (ed) *Proceedings of the Demonstrations Session at European Chapter of the Association for Computational Linguistics (EACL 2012)*. Avignon, France: Association for Computational Linguistics, 102–107.

Stenström, Anna-Brita. 2006. The Spanish Discourse Markers *O Sea* and *Pues* and their English Correspondences. In Aijmer, Karin / Simon-Vandenbergen, Anne-Marie (eds) *Pragmatic Markers in Contrast*. Oxford: Elsevier, 155–177.

Stymne, Sara 2017. The Effect of Translationese on Tuning for Statistical Machine Translation. In *Proceedings of the 21st Nordic Conference on Computational Linguistics*. Gothenburg: Association for Computational Linguistics, 241–246. <https://aclanthology.org/W17-0230.pdf>

Suter, Hans-Jürg 1993. *The Wedding Report: A Prototypical Approach to the Study of Text Types*. Amsterdam: John Benjamins.

Sutskever, Ilya / Vinyals, Oriol / Le, Quoc V. 2014. Sequence to Sequence Learning with Neural Networks. In *Proceedings of the 27th International Conference on Neural Information Processing Systems*, 3104–3112. <https://papers.nips.cc/paper_files/paper/2014>

Swales, John M. 1990. *Genre Analysis: English in Academic and Research Settings*. Cambridge: Cambridge University Press.

Swales, John M. 2004. *Research Genres: Explorations and Applications*. Cambridge University Press.

Taulé, Mariona / Martí, M. Antònia / Recasens, Marta 2008. AnCora: Multilevel Annotated Corpora for Catalan and Spanish. In Calzolari, Nicoletta *et al.* (eds) *Proceedings of the Sixth International Conference on Language Resources and Evaluation (LREC'08)*. Marrakech: European Language Resources Association (ELRA). <http://www.lrec-conf.org/proceedings/lrec2008/pdf/35_paper.pdf>

TAUS 2024. MT Post-editing Guidelines. <https://www.taus.net/resources/reports/mt-post-editing-guidelines>

Teich, Elke 2003. *Cross-linguistic Variation in System and Text*. Berlin: Mouton de Gruyter. <https://doi.org/10.1515/9783110896541>

Tezcan, Arda / Hoste, Veronique / Macken, Lieve 2020. Estimating Word-Level Quality of Statistical Machine Translation Output Using Monolingual Information Alone. *Natural Language Engineering*. 26/1, 73–94. <https://doi.org/10.1017/S1351324919000111>

Thompson, Henry S. / Anderson, Anne / Bard, Ellen Gurman / Doherty-Sneddon, Gwyneth / Newlands, Alison / Sotillo, Cathy 1993. The HCRC Map Task Corpus: Natural Dialogue for Speech Recognition. In *Proceedings of the Workshop on Human Language Technology*. 25–30. <https://doi.org/10.3115/1075671.1075677>.

Thompson, Susan 1994. Frameworks and Context: A Genre Based Approach to Analyzing Lecture Introductions. *English for Specific Purposes*. 13/2, 171–186. <https://doi.org/10.1016/0889-4906(94)90014-0>

Tirkkonen-Condit, Sonja 2002. Translationese – a Myth or an Empirical Fact? A Study into the Linguistic Identifiability of Translated Language. *Target*. 14/2, 207–220. <https://doi.org/10.1075/target.14.2.02tir>

Tirkkonen-Condit, Sonja 2004. Unique Items – Over- or Under-represented in Translated Language? In Mauranen, Anna / Kujamäki, Pekka (eds). *Translation Universals. Do They Exist?* Amsterdam: John Benjamins, 177–183. < https://doi.org/10.1075/btl.48.14tir>

Tognini-Bonelli, Elena 2001. *Corpus Linguistics at Work*. Amsterdam/Philadelphia: John Benjamins.

Tolochinsky, Elad / Mosafi, Ohad / Rabinovich, Ella / Wintner, Shuly 2018. The UN Parallel Corpus Annotated for Translation Direction. *arXiv:1805.07697v1*. <https://doi.org/10.48550/arXiv.1805.07697>

Topal, M. Onat / Bas, Anil / van Heerden, Imke 2021. Exploring Transformers in Natural Language Generation: GPT, BERT, and XLNet. *arXiv preprint arXiv:2102.08036*. <https://doi.org/10.48550/arXiv.2102.08036>

Toral, Antonio 2019. Post-editese: An Exacerbated Translationese. In: Proceedings of MTSummit 2019. *arXiv:1907.00900*, 273–281. <https://doi.org/10.48550/arXiv.1907.00900>

Toury, Gideon 1995/2012. *Descriptive Translation Studies and Beyond*. Amsterdam: John Benjamins.

Toury, Gideon 2004. Probabilistic Explanations in Translation Studies: Universals – or a Challenge to the Very Concept? In Hansen, Gyde *et al.* (eds) *Claims, Changes and Challenges in Translation Studies*. Amsterdam: John Benjamins, 15–26. <https://doi.org/10.1075/btl.50.03tou>

Tseng, Ming-Yu 2018. Creating a Theoretical Framework: On the Move Structure of Theoretical Framework Sections in Research Articles Related to Language and Linguistics. *Journal of English for Academic Purposes*. 33, 82–99. <https://doi.org/10.1016/j.jeap.2018.01.002.>

Twitto-Shmuel, Naama / Ordan, Noam / Wintner, Shuly 2015. Statistical Machine Translation with Automatic Identification of Translationese. In *Proceedings of the Tenth Workshop on Statistical Machine Translation*. Lisbon, Portugal. Association for Computational Linguistics, 47–57. <https://doi.org/10.18653/v1/W15-3002>

Uchida, Satoru 2024. Using Early LLMs for Corpus Linguistics: Examining ChatGPT's Potential and Limitations. *Applied Corpus Linguistics*. 4/1. <https://doi.org/10.1016/j.acorp.2024.100089>

University of Pennsylvania 2017. *Linguistic Data Consortium* - University of Pennsylvania. <https://www.ldc.upenn.edu/language-resources>.

Upton, Thomas A. 2002. Understanding Direct Mail Letters as a Genre. *International Journal of Corpus Linguistics*. 7/1, 65–85. <https://doi.org/10.1075/ijcl.7.1.04upt>

Upton, Thomas A. / Connor, Ulla 2001. Using Computerized Corpus Analysis to Investigate the Textlinguistic Discourse Moves of a Genre. *English for Specific Purposes*. 20/4, 313–29.

Upton, Thomas A. / Cohen, Mary Ann 2009. An Approach to Corpus-Based Discourse Analysis: The Move Analysis as Example. *Discourse Studies*. 11/5, 57–77. <https://doi.org/10.1177/1461445609341006>

Vaswani, Ashish / Shazeer, Noam / Parmar, Niki / Uszkoreit, Jakob / Jones, Llion / Gomez, Aidan N. / Kaiser, Łukasz / Polosukhin, Illia 2017. Attention is all you need. In Guyon *et al.* (eds) *Advances in Neural Information Processing Systems*, 30. <https://doi.org/10.48550/arXiv.1706.03762>

Vaughan, Elain / Clancy, Brian. 2013. Small Corpora and Pragmatics. *The Yearbook of Corpus Linguistics and Pragmatics*. 1, 53–73.

Vergaro, Carla 2004. Discourse Strategies of Italian and English Sales Promotion Letters. *English for Specific Purposes*. 23/2, 181–207. <https://doi.org/10.1016/S0889-4906(03)00003-6>

Verschueren, Jef 1999. *Understanding Pragmatics*. London: Arnold.

Villavicencio, Aline / Bond, Francis / Korhonen, Anna / McCarthy, Diana 2005. Editorial: Introduction to the Special Issue on Multiword Expressions: Having a Crack at a Hard Nut. *Computer Speech & Language*. 19/4, 365–377.

Virtanen, Tuija / Halmari, Helena 2005. Persuasion Across Genres. Emerging Perspectives. In H. Halmari, Helena / Virtanen, Tuija (eds) *Persuasion Across Genres: A Linguistic Approach*. Amsterdam: John Benjamins, 3–24.

Volansky, Vered / Ordan, Noam / Wintner, Shuly 2015. On the Features of Translationese. *Digital Scholarship in the Humanities*. 30/1, 98–118. <https://doi.org/10.1093/llc/fqt031>

Walker, Crayton 2011. A Corpus-Based Study of the Linguistic Features and Processes which Influence the Way Collocations are Formed: Some Implications for the Learning of Collocations. *Tesol Quarterly*. 45/2, 291–312. <https://doi.org/10.5054/tq.2011.247710>

Wang, Haifeng / Li, Jiwei / Wu, Hua / Hovy, Eduard / Sun, Yu 2022. Pre-Trained Language Models and their Applications. *Engineering*. 25, 51–65. <https://doi.org/10.1016/j.eng.2022.04.024>

Way, Andy 2018. Quality Expectations of Machine Translation. In: Moorkens, Joos *et al.* (eds) *Translation Quality Assessment: From Principles to Practice*. Cham: Springer, 159–178.

Wei, Jason / Bosma, Maarten / Zhao, Vincent / Guu, Kelvin / Wei Yu, Adams / Lester, Brian / et al. 2022. Finetuned Language Models are Zero-Shot Learners. In *International Conference on Learning Representations*. <https://openreview.net/forum?id=gEZrGCozdqR>

Wei, Jia / Zhou, Qiang / Cai, Yici 2018. Poet-Based Poetry Generation: Controlling Personal Style with Recurrent Neural Networks. In *Proceedings of the International Conference in Computing, Netw. Commun. (ICNC)*. Maui, HI, 156–60. 10.1109/ICCNC.2018.8390270.

Weisser, Martin 2018. *How to Do Corpus Pragmatics on Pragmatically Annotated Data: Speech Acts and Beyond.* Amsterdam: John Benjamins.

Weisser, Martin. 2020. Speech Acts in Corpus Pragmatics. Making the Case for an Extended Taxonomy. *International Journal of Corpus Linguistics*. 25/4, 400–425.

Wilson, Jonathan / Hartley, Anthony / Sharoff, Serge / Stephenson, Philip 2010. Advanced Corpus Solutions for Humanities Researchers. In Otoguro, Ryo *et al.* (eds) *Proceedings of the 24th Pacific Asia Conference on Language, Information and Computation (PACLIC 24)*. Sendai, Japan: Institute of Digital Enhancement of Cognitive Processing, Waseda University, 769–778. <https://aclanthology.org/Y10-1089.pdf>

World Bank 2024. *Global Economic Prospects, June 2024*. Washington, DC: World Bank. <https://openknowledge.worldbank.org/server/api/core/bitstreams/6feb9566-e973-4706-a4e1-b3b82a1a758d/content>

Wu, Minghao / Waheed, Abdul / Zhang, Chiyu / Abdul-Mageed, Muhammad / Aji, Alham F. 2023. LaMini-LM: A Diverse Herd of Distilled

Models from Large-Scale Instructions. *arXiv:2304.14402*. <https://doi.org/10.48550/arXiv.2304.14402>

Yifan, Yao / Jinhao, Duan / Kaidi, Xu / Yuanfang, Cai / Zhibo, Sun / Yue, Zhang 2024. A Survey on Large Language Model (LLM) Security and Privacy: The Good, The Bad, and The Ugly. *High-Confidence Computing*, 4/2. <https://doi.org/10.1016/j.hcc.2024.100211>

Yu, Zhiwei / Tan, Jiwei / Wan, X 2018. A Neural Approach to Pun Generation. In *Proceedings of the 56th Annual Meeting of the Association for Computational Linguistics (Volume 1: Long Papers)*. Melbourne: Association for Computational Linguistics, 1650–60. <https://doi.org/10.18653/v1/P18-1153>

Zeldes, Amir 2017. The GUM Corpus: Creating Multilayer Resources in the Classroom. *Language Resources & Evaluation*. 51, 581–612. <https://doi.org/10.1007/s10579-016-9343-x>

Zeldes, Amir. 2019. *Multilayer Corpus Studies*. London: Routledge.

Zhang, Hanqing / Song, Haolin / Li, Shaoyu / Zhou, Ming / Song, Dawei 2023. A Survey of Controllable Text Generation using Transformer-Based Pre-Trained Language Models. *ACM Computing Surveys*. 56/3, 1–37. <https://doi.org/10.1145/3617680>

Zhang, Jingqing / Zhao, Yao / Saleh, Mohammad / Liu, Peter 2020. Pegasus: Pre-training with Extracted Gap-Sentences for Abstractive Summarization. In *International Conference on Machine Learning*, 11328–11339. <https://proceedings.mlr.press/v119/zhang20ae/zhang20ae.pdf>

Zhang, Zhengyan / Han, Xu / Zhou, Hao / Ke, Pei / Gu, Yuxian / Ye, Deming / *et al.* 2021. CPM: A Large-Scale Generative Chinese Pre-Trained Language Model. *AI Open*. 2, 93–9. <https://doi.org/10.1016/j.aiopen.2021.07.001>

Zhou, H. / Liu, T. / Ma, Q. / Yuan, J. / Liu, P. / You, Y. / Yang, H. 2023. *LoBaSS:* Gauging learnability in supervised fine-tuning data (Version 1). *arXiv*. <https://doi.org/10.48550/ARXIV.2310.13008>

Živković, Branka 2022. British and Montenegrin University Lecture Introductions: A Corpus-based Study of their Rhetorical Structure. *Ibérica*. 43, 103–128. <https://doi.org/10.17398/2340-2784.43.103>

Zou, X. / Yin, D. / Zhong, Q. / Yang, H. / Yang, Z. / Tang, J. 2021. Controllable generation from pre-trained language models via inverse prompting. *Proceedings of the 27th ACM SIGKDD Conference on Knowledge Discovery & Data Mining*, 2450–2460. <https://doi.org/10.1145/3447548.3467418>

Index

Notes on Contributors

Ana García-Gallego is an Associate Professor of Statistics and Operational Research at the University of León, Spain, where she teaches Statistics and quantitative methods. Her main area of research is the application of quantitative methods to the social and health sciences. She has published in international journals and presented papers at different national and international conferences. She has also participated in several research projects. She is a member of the ACTRES research team and of GREIS, a group on nursing research.

Marlén Izquierdo is an Associate Professor at the University of País Vasco (UPV/EHU), Spain, where she teaches Academic English, English Language and Corpus Linguistics. Her research interests involve the fields of Contrastive Linguistics and Translation Studies, Learner Language, and English for Specific and Academic Purposes. She participates actively in international conferences, and her most recent publications have appeared in *Journal of Pragmatics, IEEE Transactions of Professional Communication, Languages in Contrast, ESP,* and *Meta*. She has also authored chapters and served as co-editor in collective volumes (John Benjamins, Peter Lang). She is a member of the ACTRES research team and of the TRALIMA/ITZULIK translation group at the UPV/EHU.

Belén Labrador is an Associate Professor of English at the University of León, Spain. Her main research interests lie in English-Spanish Contrastive Analysis, Translation Studies, Corpus Linguistics, English for Specific Purposes, Teacher Training and Teaching English as a Foreign Language. She has published extensively in these areas in international journals like *IEEE Transactions on Professional Communication, Linguistics and Education, Babel, English for Specific Purposes, International Journal of English Studies, Languages in Contrast, Terminology, Digital*

Scholarship in the Humanities, Target, and *Meta*, among others. She is a member of the ACTRES research group and a coordinator for a Teaching Innovation Group.

Belén López-Arroyo is an Associate Professor in ESP at the University of Valladolid, Spain. She currently teaches legal and business translation and Corpus Linguistics. Her research interests include genre analysis, Multilingual Lexicography and Terminology, Contrastive analysis and Translation. Her work has appeared in *Terminology, Meta, Metaphor and Symbol* or *Journal of General Business and Technical Communication,* among others. She has been a visiting scholar at the University of Ottawa, Canada, and at Carnegie Mellon University in Pittsburgh, Pennsylvania, and she participates in the TAPP and EDGE networks for virtual exchanges. She is a member of the ACTRES research team.

Leticia Moreno-Pérez is an Associate Professor at the University of Valladolid, Spain, where she teaches English for Specific Purposes and Specialised Translation. Her research interests are specialised language, legal and business translation and teaching innovation, as well as business English as lingua franca. She has published several chapters and papers and presented at international conferences in these research areas. She is a member of the ACTRES research group and the TechWrit innovation group at Valladolid. Additionally, she has combined her academic work with professional translation and language training in the business sector for over ten years.

María Teresa Ortego Antón is a Professor in Translation and Interpreting at the University of Valladolid, Spain, where she teaches interpreting, agri-food translation, and translation technology. Her primary research interests lie in translation and interpreting technologies. She has published several articles, book chapters, and monographs. She has presented her research at numerous international conferences and actively contributes to both national and international research projects. She is a member of the ACTRES research team and the director of the CITTAC group at the University of Valladolid.

María Pérez Blanco is an Associate Professor at the Department of Modern Languages at the University of León, Spain. Her main research areas are contrastive and corpus linguistics. Her current interests include modality in political and journalistic opinion discourse, as well as contrastive analysis in grammar, phraseology, and rhetoric of under-researched genres. She has authored articles in *Languages in Contrast, Journal of Pragmatics, ESP* and *RESLA* and book chapters edited by John Benjamins and Peter Lang, among others. She is the co-editor of *Evidentiality and Modality in European Languages* (Peter Lang, 2017). She is a member of the ACTRES research group and the DISCOM-COGFUNC research group on cognitive and functional linguistics at Madrid Complutense University.

Isabel Pizarro Sánchez is an Associate Professor at the Department of English at the University of Valladolid, Spain, where she teaches English for Specific Purposes, specialised translation and corpus linguistics. Her primary research interests lie in corpus linguistics and specialised languages, with a particular focus on genre analysis, contrastive linguistics, terminology and translation across various professional domains. She has published several articles in these areas and authored a monograph on business translation. She is a member of the CITTAC and ACTRES research groups.

Rosa Rabadán is a Professor at the Department of Modern Languages at the University of León, Spain, where she teaches Contrastive Linguistics and translation. She has led the Contrastive Analysis and Translation English-Spanish (ACTRES) research group (1998–2020), being responsible for a significant number of publicly funded projects. Her areas of interest include corpus-based contrastive grammar, Translation Studies, and language technology. Her recent work has shifted towards the production of expert language content for language technology and research transference. Her publications have appeared in *Languages in Contrast, Meta, Babel, Across Languages and Cultures, RESLA, Nordic Journal of English Studies, Linguistica Pragensia,* among others, and scholarly volumes published by John Benjamins, Peter Lang and Bloomsbury.

Noelia Ramón is an Associate Professor of English at the University of León, Spain. She has worked on various aspects of corpus-based contrastive studies and translation with English and Spanish as the working languages. Her recent work has focused on contrastive studies based on promotional discourse in the food and drink industry. She is the current leader of the ACTRES research group, which is engaged in producing expert language data for the development of text-production applications in specialised domains. She has published extensively in international journals such as *Target, Babel, Languages in Contrast, International Journal of Corpus Linguistics, Terminology, English for Specific Purposes,* and *IEEE Transactions on Professional Communication.*

Hugo Sanjurjo-Gónzalez is an Associate Professor at the Department of Information, Electronics, and Communication Technologies at the University of Deusto, Spain, where he teaches Computer Science and Intelligent Systems. His primary research interests lie in computational linguistics and natural language processing, with a particular focus on incorporating Large Language Models (LLMs) to enhance linguistic data processing and analysis. His most recent publications include papers in *Logic Journal of the IGPL, Language Resources and Evaluation, Spanish Journal of Applied Linguistics*, and chapters in collective volumes published by Springer and John Benjamins.

Lucía Sanz-Valdivieso is a graduate student currently working towards her PhD degree in Language Technologies at the University of Valladolid, Spain. Her research interests focus on multilingual language technologies for professional communication. Her other fields of interest include English for Specific Purposes, computational linguistics, English as lingua franca, and terminology. She has authored and co-authored several papers published in *Terminology* and *IEEE Transactions on Professional Communication.*

Linguistic Insights

Studies in Language and Communication

This series aims to promote specialist language studies in the fields of linguistic theory and applied linguistics, by publishing volumes that focus on specific aspects of language use in one or several languages and provide valuable insights into language and communication research. A cross-disciplinary approach is favoured and most European languages are accepted.

The series includes two types of books:

- Monographs – featuring in-depth studies on special aspects of language theory, language analysis or language teaching.
- Collected papers – assembling papers from workshops, conferences or symposia.

Each volume of the series is subjected to a double peer-reviewing process.

Vol. 1 Maurizio Gotti & Marina Dossena (eds)
Modality in Specialized Texts. Selected Papers of the 1st CERLIS Conference.
421 pages. 2001. ISBN 3-906767-10-8 · US-ISBN 0-8204-5340-4

Vol. 2 Giuseppina Cortese & Philip Riley (eds)
Domain-specific English. Textual Practices across Communities and Classrooms.
420 pages. 2002. ISBN 3-906768-98-8 · US-ISBN 0-8204-5884-8

Vol. 3 Maurizio Gotti, Dorothee Heller & Marina Dossena (eds) Conflict and Negotiation in Specialized Texts. Selected Papers of the 2nd CERLIS Conference.
470 pages. 2002. ISBN 3-906769-12-7 · US-ISBN 0-8204-5887-2

Vol. 4 Maurizio Gotti, Marina Dossena, Richard Dury, Roberta Facchinetti & Maria Lima
Variation in Central Modals. A Repertoire of Forms and Types of Usage in Middle English and Early Modern English.
364 pages. 2002. ISBN 3-906769-84-4 · US-ISBN 0-8204-5898-8

Editorial address:

Prof. Maurizio Gotti Università di Bergamo, Dipartimento di Lingue, Letterature e Culture Straniere Piazza Rosate 2, 24129 Bergamo, Italy.
Fax: +39 035 2052789, E-Mail: m.gotti@unibg.it

Vol. 5 Stefania Nuccorini (ed.)
Phrases and Phraseology. Data and Descriptions.
187 pages. 2002. ISBN 3-906770-08-7 · US-ISBN 0-8204-5933-X

Vol. 6 Vijay Bhatia, Christopher N. Candlin & Maurizio Gotti (eds) Legal Discourse in Multilingual and Multicultural Contexts. Arbitration Texts in Europe.
385 pages. 2003. ISBN 3-906770-85-0 · US-ISBN 0-8204-6254-3

Vol. 7 Marina Dossena & Charles Jones (eds)
Insights into Late Modern English. 2nd edition.
378 pages. 2003, 2007. ISBN 978-3-03911-257-9 · US-ISBN 978-0-8204-8927-8

Vol. 8 Maurizio Gotti
Specialized Discourse. Linguistic Features and Changing Conventions.
351 pages. 2003, 2005.ISBN 3-03910-606-6 · US-ISBN 0-8204-7000-7

Vol. 9 Alan Partington, John Morley & Louann Haarman (eds)
Corpora and Discourse.
420 pages. 2004. ISBN 3-03910-026-2 · US-ISBN 0-8204-6262-4

Vol. 10 Martina Möllering
The Acquisition of German Modal Particles. A Corpus-Based Approach.
290 pages. 2004. ISBN 3-03910-043-2 · US-ISBN 0-8204-6273-X

Vol. 11 David Hart (ed.)
English Modality in Context. Diachronic Perspectives.
261 pages. 2003. ISBN 3-03910-046-7 · US-ISBN 0-8204-6852-5

Vol. 12 Wendy Swanson
Modes of Co-reference as an Indicator of Genre.
430 pages. 2003. ISBN 3-03910-052-1 · US-ISBN 0-8204-6855-X

Vol. 13 Gina Poncini
Discursive Strategies in Multicultural Business Meetings.
2nd edition. 338 pages. 2004, 2007.
ISBN 978-3-03911-296-8 · US-ISBN 978-0-8204-8937-7

Vol. 14 Christopher N. Candlin & Maurizio Gotti (eds)
Intercultural Aspects of Specialized Communication.
2nd edition. 369 pages. 2004, 2007.
ISBN 978-3-03911-258-6 · US-ISBN 978-0-8204-8926-1

Vol. 15 Gabriella Del Lungo Camiciotti & Elena Tognini Bonelli (eds)
Academic Discourse. New Insights into Evaluation.
234 pages. 2004. ISBN 3-03910-353-9 · US-ISBN 0-8204-7016-3

Vol. 16 Marina Dossena & Roger Lass (eds)
Methods and Data in English Historical Dialectology.
405 pages. 2004. ISBN 3-03910-362-8 · US-ISBN 0-8204-7018-X

Vol. 17 Judy Noguchi
The Science Review Article. An Opportune Genre in the Construction of Science.
274 pages. 2006. ISBN 3-03910-426-8 · US-ISBN 0-8204-7034-1

Vol. 18 Giuseppina Cortese & Anna Duszak (eds)
Identity, Community, Discourse. English in Intercultural Settings.
495 pages. 2005. ISBN 3-03910-632-5 · US-ISBN 0-8204-7163-1

Vol. 19 Anna Trosborg & Poul Erik Flyvholm Jørgensen (eds)
Business Discourse. Texts and Contexts.
250 pages. 2005. ISBN 3-03910-606-6 · US-ISBN 0-8204-7000-7

Vol. 20 Christopher Williams
Tradition and Change in Legal English. Verbal Constructions in Prescriptive Texts.
2nd revised edition. 216 pages. 2005, 2007. ISBN 978-3-03911-444-3.

Vol. 21 Katarzyna Dziubalska-Kolaczyk & Joanna Przedlacka (eds)
English Pronunciation Models: A Changing Scene.
2nd edition. 476 pages. 2005, 2008. ISBN 978-3-03911-682-9.

Vol. 22 Christián Abello-Contesse, Rubén Chacón-Beltrán,
M. Dolores López-Jiménez & M. Mar Torreblanca-López (eds)
Age in L2 Acquisition and Teaching.
214 pages. 2006. ISBN 3-03910-668-6 · US-ISBN 0-8204-7174-7

Vol. 23 Vijay K. Bhatia, Maurizio Gotti, Jan Engberg & Dorothee Heller (eds)
Vagueness in Normative Texts.
474 pages. 2005. ISBN 3-03910-653-8 · US-ISBN 0-8204-7169-0

Vol. 24 Paul Gillaerts & Maurizio Gotti (eds)
Genre Variation in Business Letters. 2nd printing.
407 pages. 2008. ISBN 978-3-03911-681-2.

Vol. 25 Ana María Hornero, María José Luzón & Silvia Murillo (eds)
Corpus Linguistics. Applications for the Study of English.
2nd printing. 526 pages. 2006, 2008. ISBN 978-3-03911-726-0

Vol. 26 J. Lachlan Mackenzie & María de los Ángeles Gómez-González (eds)
Studies in Functional Discourse Grammar.
259 pages. 2005. ISBN 3-03910-696-1 · US-ISBN 0-8204-7558-0

Vol. 27 Debbie G. E. Ho
Classroom Talk. Exploring the Sociocultural Structure of Formal ESL Learning.
2nd edition. 254 pages. 2006, 2007. ISBN 978-3-03911-434-4

Vol. 28 Javier Pérez-Guerra, Dolores González-Álvarez, Jorge L. Bueno-Alonso &
Esperanza Rama-Martínez (eds)
'Of Varying Language and Opposing Creed'. New Insights into Late Modern English.
455 pages. 2007. ISBN 978-3-03910-788-9

Vol. 29 Francesca Bargiela-Chiappini & Maurizio Gotti (eds)
Asian Business Discourse(s).
350 pages. 2005. ISBN 3-03910-804-2 · US-ISBN 0-8204-7574-2

Vol. 30 Nicholas Brownlees (ed.)
News Discourse in Early Modern Britain. Selected Papers of CHINED 2004.
300 pages. 2006. ISBN 3-03910-805-0 · US-ISBN 0-8204-8025-8

Vol. 31 Roberta Facchinetti & Matti Rissanen (eds)
Corpus-based Studies of Diachronic English.
300 pages. 2006. ISBN 3-03910-851-4 · US-ISBN 0-8204-8040-1

Vol. 32 Marina Dossena & Susan M. Fitzmaurice (eds)
Business and Official Correspondence. Historical Investigations.
209 pages. 2006. ISBN 3-03910-880-8 · US-ISBN 0-8204-8352-4

Vol. 33 Giuliana Garzone & Srikant Sarangi (eds)
Discourse, Ideology and Specialized Communication.
494 pages. 2007. ISBN 978-3-03910-888-6

Vol. 34 Giuliana Garzone & Cornelia Ilie (eds)
The Use of English in Institutional and Business Settings. An Intercultural Perspective.
372 pages. 2007. ISBN 978-3-03910-889-3

Vol. 35 Vijay K. Bhatia & Maurizio Gotti (eds)
Explorations in Specialized Genres.
316 pages. 2006. ISBN 3-03910-995-2 · US-ISBN 0-8204-8372-9

Vol. 36 Heribert Picht (ed.)
Modern Approaches to Terminological Theories and Applications.
432 pages. 2006. ISBN 3-03911-156-6 · US-ISBN 0-8204-8380-X

Vol. 37 Anne Wagner & Sophie Cacciaguidi-Fahy (eds)
Legal Language and the Search for Clarity / Le langage juridique et la quête de clarté.
Practice and Tools / Pratiques et instruments.
487 pages. 2006. ISBN 3-03911-169-8 · US-ISBN 0-8204-8388-5

Vol. 38 Juan Carlos Palmer-Silveira, Miguel F. Ruiz-Garrido & Inmaculada Fortanet-Gómez (eds)
Intercultural and International Business Communication. Theory, Research and Teaching.
2nd edition. 343 pages. 2006, 2008. ISBN 978-3-03911-680-5

Vol. 39 Christiane Dalton-Puffer, Dieter Kastovsky, Nikolaus Ritt & Herbert Schendl (eds)
Syntax, Style and Grammatical Norms. English from 1500–2000.
250 pages. 2006. ISBN 3-03911-181-7 · US-ISBN 0-8204-8394-X

Vol. 40 Marina Dossena & Irma Taavitsainen (eds)
Diachronic Perspectives on Domain-Specific English.
280 pages. 2006. ISBN 3-03910-176-0 · US-ISBN 0-8204-8391-5

Vol. 41 John Flowerdew & Maurizio Gotti (eds)
Studies in Specialized Discourse.
293 pages. 2006. ISBN 3-03911-178-7

Vol. 42 Ken Hyland & Marina Bondi (eds)
Academic Discourse Across Disciplines.
320 pages. 2006. ISBN 3-03911-183-3 · US-ISBN 0-8204-8396-6

Vol. 43 Paul Gillaerts & Philip Shaw (eds)
The Map and the Landscape. Norms and Practices in Genre.
256 pages. 2006. ISBN 3-03911-182-5 · US-ISBN 0-8204-8395-4

Vol. 44 Maurizio Gotti & Davide Giannoni (eds)
New Trends in Specialized Discourse Analysis.
301 pages. 2006. ISBN 3-03911-184-1 · US-ISBN 0-8204-8381-8

Vol. 45 Maurizio Gotti & Françoise Salager-Meyer (eds)
Advances in Medical Discourse Analysis. Oral and Written Contexts.
492 pages. 2006. ISBN 3-03911-185-X · US-ISBN 0-8204-8382-6

Vol. 46 Maurizio Gotti & Susan Šarcević (eds)
Insights into Specialized Translation.
396 pages. 2006. ISBN 3-03911-186-8 · US-ISBN 0-8204-8383-4

Vol. 47 Khurshid Ahmad & Margaret Rogers (eds)
Evidence-based LSP. Translation, Text and Terminology.
584 pages. 2007. ISBN 978-3-03911-187-9

Vol. 48 Hao Sun & Dániel Z. Kádár (eds)
It's the Dragon's Turn. Chinese Institutional Discourses.
262 pages. 2008. ISBN 978-3-03911-175-6

Vol. 49 Cristina Suárez-Gómez
Relativization in Early English (950-1250). the Position of Relative Clauses.
149 pages. 2006. ISBN 3-03911-203-1 · US-ISBN 0-8204-8904-2

Vol. 50 Maria Vittoria Calvi & Luisa Chierichetti (eds)
Nuevas tendencias en el discurso de especialidad.
319 pages. 2006. ISBN 978-3-03911-261-6

Vol. 51 Mari Carmen Campoy & María José Luzón (eds)
Spoken Corpora in Applied Linguistics.
274 pages. 2008. ISBN 978-3-03911-275-3

Vol. 52 Konrad Ehlich & Dorothee Heller (Hrsg.)
Die Wissenschaft und ihre Sprachen.
323 pages. 2006. ISBN 978-3-03911-272-2

Vol. 53 Jingyu Zhang
The Semantic Salience Hierarchy Model. The L2 Acquisition of Psych Predicates
273 pages. 2007. ISBN 978-3-03911-300-2

Vol. 54 Norman Fairclough, Giuseppina Cortese & Patrizia Ardizzone (eds)
Discourse and Contemporary Social Change.
555 pages. 2007. ISBN 978-3-03911-276-0

Vol. 55 Jan Engberg, Marianne Grove Ditlevsen, Peter Kastberg & Martin Stegu (eds)
New Directions in LSP Teaching.
331 pages. 2007. ISBN 978-3-03911-433-7

Vol. 56 Dorothee Heller & Konrad Ehlich (Hrsg.)
Studien zur Rechtskommunikation.
322 pages. 2007. ISBN 978-3-03911-436-8

Vol. 57 Teruhiro Ishiguro & Kang-kwong Luke (eds)
Grammar in Cross-Linguistic Perspective.
The Syntax, Semantics, and Pragmatics of Japanese and Chinese.
304 pages. 2012. ISBN 978-3-03911-445-0

Vol. 58 Carmen Frehner Email – SMS – MMS
294 pages. 2008. ISBN 978-3-03911-451-1

Vol. 59 Isabel Balteiro
The Directionality of Conversion in English. A Dia-Synchronic Study.
276 pages. 2007. ISBN 978-3-03911-241-8

Vol. 60 Maria Milagros Del Saz Rubio
English Discourse Markers of Reformulation.
237 pages. 2007. ISBN 978-3-03911-196-1

Vol. 61 Sally Burgess & Pedro Martín-Martín (eds)
English as an Additional Language in Research Publication and Communication.
259 pages. 2008. ISBN 978-3-03911-462-7

Vol. 62 Sandrine Onillon
Pratiques et représentations de l'écrit.
458 pages. 2008. ISBN 978-3-03911-464-1

Vol. 63 Hugo Bowles & Paul Seedhouse (eds)
Conversation Analysis and Language for Specific Purposes.
2nd edition. 337 pages. 2007, 2009. ISBN 978-3-0343-0045-2

Vol. 64 Vijay K. Bhatia, Christopher N. Candlin & Paola Evangelisti Allori (eds)
Language, Culture and the Law.
The Formulation of Legal Concepts across Systems and Cultures.
342 pages. 2008. ISBN 978-3-03911-470-2

Vol. 65 Jonathan Culpeper & Dániel Z. Kádár (eds)
Historical (Im)politeness.
300 pages. 2010. ISBN 978-3-03911-496-2

Vol. 66 Linda Lombardo (ed.)
Using Corpora to Learn about Language and Discourse.
237 pages. 2009. ISBN 978-3-03911-522-8

Vol. 67 Natsumi Wakamoto
Extroversion/Introversion in Foreign Language Learning. Interactions with Learner Strategy Use.
159 pages. 2009. ISBN 978-3-03911-596-9

Vol. 68 Eva Alcón-Soler (ed.)
Learning How to Request in an Instructed Language Learning Context.
260 pages. 2008. ISBN 978-3-03911-601-0

Vol. 69 Domenico Pezzini
The Translation of Religious Texts in the Middle Ages.
428 pages. 2008. ISBN 978-3-03911-600-3

Vol. 70 Tomoko Tode
Effects of Frequency in Classroom Second Language Learning. Quasi-experiment and stimulated-recall analysis.
195 pages. 2008. ISBN 978-3-03911-602-7

Vol. 71 Egor Tsedryk
Fusion symétrique et alternances ditransitives.
211 pages. 2009. ISBN 978-3-03911-609-6

Vol. 72 Cynthia J. Kellett Bidoli & Elana Ochse (eds)
English in International Deaf Communication.
444 pages. 2008. ISBN 978-3-03911-610-2

Vol. 73 Joan C. Beal, Carmela Nocera & Massimo Sturiale (eds)
Perspectives on Prescriptivism.
269 pages. 2008. ISBN 978-3-03911-632-4

Vol. 74 Carol Taylor Torsello, Katherine Ackerley & Erik Castello (eds)
Corpora for University Language Teachers.
308 pages. 2008. ISBN 978-3-03911-639-3

Vol. 75 María Luisa Pérez Cañado (ed.)
English Language Teaching in the European Credit Transfer System. Facing the Challenge.
251 pages. 2009. ISBN 978-3-03911-654-6

Vol. 76 Marina Dossena & Ingrid Tieken-Boon van Ostade (eds)
Studies in Late Modern English Correspondence. Methodology and Data.
291 pages. 2008. ISBN 978-3-03911-658-4

Vol. 77 Ingrid Tieken-Boon van Ostade & Wim van der Wurff (eds)
Current Issues in Late Modern English.
436 pages. 2009. ISBN 978-3-03911-660-7

Vol. 78 Marta Navarro Coy (ed.)
Practical Approaches to Foreign Language Teaching and Learning.
297 pages. 2009. ISBN 978-3-03911-661-4

Vol. 79 Qing Ma
Second Language Vocabulary Acquisition.
333 pages. 2009. ISBN 978-3-03911-666-9

Vol. 80 Martin Solly, Michelangelo Conoscenti & Sandra Campagna (eds)
Verbal/Visual Narrative Texts in Higher Education.
384 pages. 2008. ISBN 978-3-03911-672-0

Vol. 81 Meiko Matsumoto
From Simple Verbs to Periphrastic Expressions:
The Historical Development of Composite Predicates, Phrasal Verbs, and Related Constructions in English.
235 pages. 2008. ISBN 978-3-03911-675-1

Vol. 82 Melinda Dooly
Doing Diversity. Teachers' Construction of Their Classroom Reality.
180 pages. 2009. ISBN 978-3-03911-687-4

Vol. 83 Victoria Guillén-Nieto, Carmen Marimón-Llorca & Chelo Vargas-Sierra (eds)
Intercultural Business Communication and Simulation and Gaming Methodology.
392 pages. 2009. ISBN 978-3-03911-688-1

Vol. 84 Maria Grazia Guido
English as a Lingua Franca in Cross-cultural Immigration Domains.
285 pages. 2008. ISBN 978-3-03911-689-8

Vol. 85 Erik Castello
Text Complexity and Reading Comprehension Tests.
352 pages. 2008. ISBN 978-3-03911-717-8

Vol. 86 Maria-Lluisa Gea-Valor, Isabel García-Izquierdo & Maria-José Esteve (eds)
Linguistic and Translation Studies in Scientific Communication.
317 pages. 2010. ISBN 978-3-0343-0069-8

Vol. 87 Carmen Navarro, Rosa Ma Rodríguez Abella, Francesca Dalle Pezze & Renzo Miotti (eds)
La comunicación especializada.
355 pages. 2008. ISBN 978-3-03911-733-8

Vol. 88 Kiriko Sato
The Development from Case-Forms to Prepositional Constructions in Old English Prose.
231 pages. 2009. ISBN 978-3-03911-763-5

Vol. 89 Dorothee Heller (Hrsg.)
Formulierungsmuster in deutscher und italienischer Fachkommunikation. Intra- und interlinguale Perspektiven.
315 pages. 2008. ISBN 978-3-03911-778-9

Vol. 90 Henning Bergenholtz, Sandro Nielsen & Sven Tarp (eds)
Lexicography at a Crossroads. Dictionaries and Encyclopedias Today, Lexicographical Tools Tomorrow.
372 pages. 2009. ISBN 978-3-03911-799-4

Vol. 91 Manouchehr Moshtagh Khorasani
The Development of Controversies. From the Early Modern Period to Online Discussion Forums.
317 pages. 2009. ISBN 978-3-3911-711-6

Vol. 92 María Luisa Carrió-Pastor (ed.)
Content and Language Integrated Learning. Cultural Diversity.
178 pages. 2009. ISBN 978-3-3911-818-2

Vol. 93 Roger Berry
Terminology in English Language Teaching. Nature and Use.
262 pages. 2010. ISBN 978-3-0343-0013-1

Vol. 94 Roberto Cagliero & Jennifer Jenkins (eds)
Discourses, Communities, and Global Englishes
240 pages. 2010. ISBN 978-3-0343-0012-4

Vol. 95 Facchinetti Roberta, Crystal David, Seidlhofer Barbara (eds)
From International to Local English – And Back Again.
268 pages. 2010. ISBN 978-3-0343-0011-7

Vol. 96 Cesare Gagliardi & Alan Maley (eds)
EIL, ELF, Global English. Teaching and Learning Issues
376 pages. 2010. ISBN 978-3-0343-0010-0

Vol. 97 Sylvie Hancil (ed.)
The Role of Prosody in Affective Speech.
403 pages. 2009. ISBN 978-3-03911-696-6

Vol. 98 Marina Dossena & Roger Lass (eds)
Studies in English and European Historical Dialectology.
257 pages. 2009. ISBN 978-3-0343-0024-7

Vol. 99 Christine Béal
Les interactions quotidiennes en français et en anglais.
De l'approche comparative à l'analyse des situations interculturelles.
424 pages. 2010. ISBN 978-3-0343-0027-8

Vol. 100 Maurizio Gotti (ed.)
Commonality and Individuality in Academic Discourse.
398 pages. 2009. ISBN 978-3-0343-0023-0

Vol. 101 Javier E. Díaz Vera & Rosario Caballero (eds)
Textual Healing. Studies in Medieval English Medical, Scientific and Technical Texts.
213 pages. 2009. ISBN 978-3-03911-822-9

Vol. 102 Nuria Edo Marzá
The Specialised Lexicographical Approach. A Step further in Dictionary-making.
316 pages. 2009. ISBN 978-3-0343-0043-8

Vol. 103 Carlos Prado-Alonso, Lidia Gómez-García, Iria Pastor-Gómez & David Tizón-Couto (eds)
New Trends and Methodologies in Applied English Language Research. Diachronic, Diatopic and Contrastive Studies.
348 pages. 2009. ISBN 978-3-0343-0046-9

Vol. 104 Françoise Salager-Meyer & Beverly A. Lewin
Crossed Words. Criticism in Scholarly Writing?
371 pages. 2011. ISBN 978-3-0343-0049-0.

Vol. 105 Javier Ruano-García
Early Modern Northern English Lexis. A Literary Corpus-Based Study.
611 pages. 2010. ISBN 978-3-0343-0058-2

Vol. 106 Rafael Monroy-Casas
Systems for the Phonetic Transcription of English. Theory and Texts.
280 pages. 2011. ISBN 978-3-0343-0059-9

Vol. 107 Nicola T. Owtram
The Pragmatics of Academic Writing.
A Relevance Approach to the Analysis of Research Article Introductions.
311 pages. 2009. ISBN 978-3-0343-0060-5

Vol. 108 Yolanda Ruiz de Zarobe, Juan Manuel Sierra & Francisco Gallardo del Puerto (eds)
Content and Foreign Language Integrated Learning. Contributions to Multilingualism in European Contexts
343 pages. 2011. ISBN 978-3-0343-0074-2

Vol. 109 Ángeles Linde López & Rosalía Crespo Jiménez (eds)
Professional English in the European context. The EHEA challenge.
374 pages. 2010. ISBN 978-3-0343-0088-9

Vol. 110 Rosalía Rodríguez-Vázquez
The Rhythm of Speech, Verse and Vocal Music. A New Theory.
394 pages. 2010. ISBN 978-3-0343-0309-5

Vol. 111 Anastasios Tsangalidis & Roberta Facchinetti (eds)
Studies on English Modality. In Honour of Frank Palmer.
392 pages. 2009. ISBN 978-3-0343-0310-1

Vol. 112 Jing Huang
Autonomy, Agency and Identity in Foreign Language Learning and Teaching.
400 pages. 2013. ISBN 978-3-0343-0370-5

Vol. 113 Mihhail Lotman & Maria-Kristiina Lotman (eds)
Frontiers in Comparative Prosody. In memoriam: Mikhail Gasparov.
426 pages. 2011. ISBN 978-3-0343-0373-6

Vol. 114 Merja Kytö, John Scahill & Harumi Tanabe (eds)
Language Change and Variation from Old English to Late Modern English. A Festschrift for Minoji Akimoto
422 pages. 2010. ISBN 978-3-0343-0372-9

Vol. 115 Giuliana Garzone & Paola Catenaccio (eds)
Identities across Media and Modes. Discursive Perspectives.
379 pages. 2009. ISBN 978-3-0343-0386-6

Vol. 116 Elena Landone
Los marcadores del discurso y cortesía verbal en español.
390 pages. 2010. ISBN 978-3-0343-0413-9

Vol. 117 Maurizio Gotti & Christopher Williams (eds)
Legal Discourse across Languages and Cultures.
339 pages. 2010. ISBN 978-3-0343-0425-2

Vol. 118 David Hirsh
Academic Vocabulary in Context.
217 pages. 2010. ISBN 978-3-0343-0426-9

Vol. 119 Yvonne Dröschel
Lingua Franca English. The Role of Simplification and Transfer.
358 pages. 2011. ISBN 978-3-0343-0432-0

Vol. 120 Tengku Sepora Tengku Mahadi, Helia Vaezian & Mahmoud Akbari
Corpora in Translation. A Practical Guide.
135 pages. 2010. ISBN 978-3-0343-0434-4

Vol. 121 Davide Simone Giannoni & Celina Frade (eds)
Researching Language and the Law. Textual Features and Translation Issues.
278 pages. 2010. ISBN 978-3-0343-0443-6

Vol. 122 Daniel Madrid & Stephen Hughes (eds)
Studies in Bilingual Education.
472 pages. 2011. ISBN 978-3-0343-0474-0

Vol. 123 Vijay K. Bhatia, Christopher N. Candlin & Maurizio Gotti (eds)
The Discourses of Dispute Resolution.
290 pages. 2010. ISBN 978-3-0343-0476-4

Vol. 124 Davide Simone Giannoni
Mapping Academic Values in the Disciplines. A Corpus-Based Approach.
288 pages. 2010. ISBN 978-3-0343-0488-7

Vol. 125 Giuliana Garzone & James Archibald (eds)
Discourse, Identities and Roles in Specialized Communication.
419 pages. 2010. ISBN 978-3-0343-0494-8

Vol. 126 Iria Pastor-Gómez
The Status and Development of N+N Sequences in Contemporary English Noun Phrases.
216 pages. 2011. ISBN 978-3-0343-0534-1

Vol. 127 Carlos Prado-Alonso
Full-verb Inversion in Written and Spoken English.
261 pages. 2011. ISBN 978-3-0343-0535-8

Vol. 128 Tony Harris & María Moreno Jaén (eds)
Corpus Linguistics in Language Teaching.
214 pages. 2010. ISBN 978-3-0343-0524-2

Vol. 129 Tetsuji Oda & Hiroyuki Eto (eds)
Multiple Perspectives on English Philology and History of Linguistics. A Festschrift for Shoichi Watanabe on his 80th Birthday.
378 pages. 2010. ISBN 978-3-0343-0480-1

Vol. 130 Luisa Chierichetti & Giovanni Garofalo (eds)
Lengua y Derecho. líneas de investigación interdisciplinaria.
283 pages. 2010. 978-3-0343-0463-4

Vol. 131 Paola Evangelisti Allori & Giuliana Garzone (eds)
Discourse, Identities and Genres in Corporate Communication. Sponsorship, Advertising and Organizational Communication.
324 pages. 2011. 978-3-0343-0591-4

Vol. 132 Leyre Ruiz de Zarobe & Yolanda Ruiz de Zarobe (eds)
Speech Acts and Politeness across Languages and Cultures.
402 pages. 2012. 978-3-0343-0611-9

Vol. 133 Thomas Christiansen
Cohesion. A Discourse Perspective.
387 pages. 2011. 978-3-0343-0619-5

Vol. 134 Giuliana Garzone & Maurizio Gotti
Discourse, Communication and the Enterprise. Genres and Trends.
451 pages. 2011. ISBN 978-3-0343-0620-1

Vol. 135 Zsuzsa Hoffmann
Ways of the World's Words.
Language Contact in the Age of Globalization.
334 pages 2011. ISBN 978-3-0343-0673-7

Vol. 136 Cecilia Varcasia (ed.) Becoming Multilingual.
Language Learning and Language Policy between Attitudes and Identities.
213 pages. 2011. ISBN 978-3-0343-0687-5

Vol. 137 Susy Macqueen
The Emergence of Patterns in Second Language Writing. A Sociocognitive Exploration of Lexical Trails.
325 pages. 2012. ISBN 978-3-0343-1010-9

Vol. 138 Maria Vittoria Calvi & Giovanna Mapelli (eds)
La lengua del turismo. Géneros discursivos y terminología.
365 pages. 2011. ISBN 978-3-0343-1011-6

Vol. 139 Ken Lau
Learning to Become a Professional in a Textually-Mediated World. A Text-Oriented Study of Placement Practices.
261 pages. 2012. ISBN 978-3-0343-1016-1

Vol. 140 Sandra Campagna, Giuliana Garzone, Cornelia Ilie & Elizabeth Rowley-Jolivet (eds)
Evolving Genres in Web-mediated Communication.
337 pages. 2012. ISBN 978-3-0343-1013-0

Vol. 141 Edith Esch & Martin Solly (eds)
The Sociolinguistics of Language Education in International Contexts.
263 pages. 2012. ISBN 978-3-0343-1009-3

Vol. 142 Forthcoming.

Vol. 143 David Tizón-Couto
Left Dislocation in English. A Functional-Discoursal Approach.
416 pages. 2012. ISBN 978-3-0343-1037-6

Vol. 144 Margrethe Petersen & Jan Engberg (eds)
Current Trends in LSP Research. Aims and Methods.
323 pages. 2011. ISBN 978-3-0343-1054-3

Vol. 145 David Tizón-Couto, Beatriz Tizón-Couto, Iria Pastor-Gómez & Paula Rodríguez-Puente (eds)
New Trends and Methodologies in Applied English Language Research II.
Studies in Language Variation, Meaning and Learning.
283 pages. 2012. ISBN 978-3-0343-1061-1

Vol. 146 Rita Salvi & Hiromasa Tanaka (eds)
Intercultural Interactions in Business and Management.
306 pages. 2011. ISBN 978-3-0343-1039-0

Vol. 147 Francesco Straniero Sergio & Caterina Falbo (eds)
Breaking Ground in Corpus-based Interpreting Studies.
254 pages. 2012. ISBN 978-3-0343-1071-0

Vol. 148 Forthcoming.

Vol. 149 Vijay K. Bhatia & Paola Evangelisti Allori (eds)
Discourse and Identity in the Professions. Legal, Corporate and Institutional Citizenship.
352 pages. 2011. ISBN 978-3-0343-1079-6

Vol. 150 Maurizio Gotti (ed.)
Academic Identity Traits. A Corpus-Based Investigation.
363 pages. 2012. ISBN 978-3-0343-1141-0

Vol. 151 Priscilla Heynderickx, Sylvain Dieltjens, Geert Jacobs, Paul Gillaerts & Elizabeth de Groot (eds)
The Language Factor in International Business.
New Perspectives on Research, Teaching and Practice.
320 pages. 2012. ISBN 978-3-0343-1090-1

Vol. 152 Paul Gillaerts, Elizabeth de Groot, Sylvain Dieltjens, Priscilla Heynderickx & Geert Jacobs (eds)
Researching Discourse in Business Genres. Cases and Corpora.
215 pages. 2012. ISBN 978-3-0343-1092-5

Vol. 153 Yongyan Zheng
Dynamic Vocabulary Development in a Foreign Language.
262 pages. 2012. ISBN 978-3-0343-1106-9

Vol. 154 Carmen Argondizzo (ed.)
Creativity and Innovation in Language Education.
357 pages. 2012. ISBN 978-3-0343-1080-2

Vol. 155 David Hirsh (ed.)
Current Perspectives in Second Language Vocabulary Research.
180 pages. 2012. ISBN 978-3-0343-1108-3

Vol. 156 Seiji Shinkawa
Unhistorical Gender Assignment in Lahamon's *Brut*. A Case Study of a Late Stage in the Development of Grammatical Gender toward its Ultimate Loss.
186 pages. 2012. ISBN 978-3-0343-1124-3

Vol. 157 Yeonkwon Jung
Basics of Organizational Writing: A Critical Reading Approach.
151 pages. 2014. ISBN 978-3-0343-1137-3.

Vol. 158 Bárbara Eizaga Rebollar (ed.)
Studies in Linguistics and Cognition.
301 pages. 2012. ISBN 978-3-0343-1138-0

Vol. 159 Giuliana Garzone, Paola Catenaccio, Chiara Degano (eds)
Genre Change in the Contemporary World. Short-term Diachronic Perspectives.
329 pages. 2012. ISBN 978-3-0343-1214-1

Vol. 160 Carol Berkenkotter, Vijay K. Bhatia & Maurizio Gotti (eds)
Insights into Academic Genres.
468 pages. 2012. ISBN 978-3-0343-1211-0

Vol. 161 Beatriz Tizón-Couto
Clausal Complements in Native and Learner Spoken English. A corpus-based study with Lindsei and Vicolse.
357 pages. 2013. ISBN 978-3-0343-1184-7

Vol. 162 Patrizia Anesa
Jury Trials and the Popularization of Legal Language. A Discourse Analytical Approach.
247 pages. 2012. ISBN 978-3-0343-1231-8

Vol. 163 David Hirsh
Endangered Languages, Knowledge Systems and Belief Systems.
153 pages. 2013. ISBN 978-3-0343-1232-5

Vol. 164 Eugenia Sainz (ed.)
De la estructura de la frase al tejido del discurso. Estudios contrastivos español/italiano.
305 pages. 2014. ISBN 978-3-0343-1253-0

Vol. 165 Julia Bamford, Franca Poppi & Davide Mazzi (eds)
Space, Place and the Discursive Construction of Identity.
367 pages. 2014. ISBN 978-3-0343-1249-3

Vol. 166 Rita Salvi & Janet Bowker (eds)
Space, Time and the Construction of Identity.
Discursive Indexicality in Cultural, Institutional and Professional Fields.
324 pages. 2013. ISBN 978-3-0343-1254-7

Vol. 167 Shunji Yamazaki & Robert Sigley (eds)
Approaching Language Variation through Corpora. A Festschrift in Honour of Toshio Saito.
421 pages. 2013. ISBN 978-3-0343-1264-6

Vol. 168 Franca Poppi
Global Interactions in English as a Lingua Franca. How written communication is changing under the influence of electronic media and new contexts of use.
249 pages. 2012. ISBN 978-3-0343-1276-9

Vol. 169 Miguel A. Aijón Oliva & María José Serrano
Style in syntax. Investigating variation in Spanish pronoun subjects.
239 pages. 2013. ISBN 978-3-0343-1244-8

Vol. 170 Inés Olza, Óscar Loureda & Manuel Casado-Velarde (eds)
Language Use in the Public Sphere. Methodological Perspectives and Empirical Applications
564 pages. 2014. ISBN 978-3-0343-1286-8

Vol. 171 Aleksandra Matulewska
Legilinguistic Translatology. A Parametric Approach to Legal Translation.
279 pages. 2013. ISBN 978-3-0343-1287-5

Vol. 172 Maurizio Gotti & Carmen Sancho Guinda (eds)
Narratives in Academic and Professional Genres.
513 pages. 2013. ISBN 978-3-0343-1371-1

Vol. 173 Madalina Chitez
Learner corpus profiles. The case of Romanian Learner English.
244 pages. 2014. ISBN 978-3-0343-1410-7

Vol. 174 Chihiro Inoue
Task Equivalence in Speaking Tests.
251 pages. 2013. ISBN 978-3-0343-1417-6

Vol. 175 Gabriel Quiroz & Pedro Patiño (eds.)
LSP in Colombia: advances and challenges.
339 pages. 2014. ISBN 978-3-0343-1434-3

Vol. 176 Catherine Resche
Economic Terms and Beyond: Capitalising on the Wealth of Notions.
How Researchers in Specialised Varieties of English Can Benefit from Focusing on Terms.
332 pages. 2013. ISBN 978-3-0343-1435-0

Vol. 177 Wei Wang
Media representation of migrant workers in China. Identities and stances
198 pages. 2018. 978-3-0343-1436-7

Vol. 178 Cécile Desoutter & Caroline Mellet (dir.)
Le discours rapporté: approches linguistiques et perspectives didactiques.
270 pages. 2013. ISBN 978-3-0343-1292-9

Vol. 179 Ana Díaz-Negrillo & Francisco Javier Díaz-Pérez (eds)
Specialisation and Variation in Language Corpora.
341 pages. 2014. ISBN 978-3-0343-1316-2

Vol. 180 Pilar Alonso
A Multi-dimensional Approach to Discourse Coherence. From Standardness to Creativity.
247 pages. 2014. ISBN 978-3-0343-1325-4

Vol. 181 Alejandro Alcaraz-Sintes & Salvador Valera-Hernández (eds)
Diachrony and Synchrony in English Corpus Linguistics.
393 pages. 2014. ISBN 978-3-0343-1326-1

Vol. 182 Runhan Zhang
Investigating Linguistic Knowledge of a Second Language.
207 pages. 2015. ISBN 978-3-0343-1330-8

Vol. 183 Hajar Abdul Rahim & Shakila Abdul Manan (eds.)
English in Malaysia. Postcolonial and Beyond.
267 pages. 2014. ISBN 978-3-0343-1341-4

Vol. 184 Virginie Fasel Lauzon
Comprendre et apprendre dans l'interaction. Les séquences d'explication en classe de français langue seconde.
292 pages. 2014. ISBN 978-3-0343-1451-0

Vol. 185 Forthcoming.

Vol. 186 Wei Ren
L2 Pragmatic Development in Study Abroad Contexts
256 pages. 2015. ISBN 978-3-0343-1358-2

Vol. 187 Marina Bondi & Rosa Lorés Sanz (eds)
Abstracts in Academic Discourse. Variation and Change.
361 pages. 2014. ISBN 978-3-0343-1483-1

Vol. 188 Giuditta Caliendo
Rethinking Community. Discourse, Identity and Citizenship in the European Union.
240 pages. 2017. ISBN 978-3-0343-1561-6

Vol. 189 Paola Evangelisti Allori (ed.)
Identities in and across Cultures.
315 pages. 2014. ISBN 978-3-0343-1458-9

Vol. 190 Erik Castello, Katherine Ackerley & Francesca Coccetta (eds).
Studies in Learner Corpus Linguistics. Research and Applications for Foreign Language Teaching and Assessment.
358 pages. 2015. ISBN 978-3-0343-1506-7

Vol. 191 Ruth Breeze, Maurizio Gotti & Carmen Sancho Guinda (eds)
Interpersonality in Legal Genres.
389 pages. 2014. ISBN 978-3-0343-1524-1

Vol. 192 Paola Evangelisti Allori, John Bateman & Vijay K. Bhatia (eds)
Evolution in Genre. Emergence, Variation, Multimodality.
364 pages. 2014. ISBN 978-3-0343-1533-3

Vol. 193 Jiyeon Kook
Agency in Arzt-Patient-Gesprächen. Zur interaktionistischen Konzeptualisierung von Agency
271 pages. 2015. ISBN 978-3-0343-1666-8

Vol. 194 Susana Nicolás Román & Juan José Torres Núñez (eds)
Drama and CLIL. A new challenge for the teaching approaches in bilingual education.
170 pages. 2015. ISBN 978-3-0343-1629-3

Vol. 195 Alessandra Molino & Serenella Zanotti (eds)
Observing Norm, Observing Usage. Lexis in Dictionaries and in the Media.
430 pages. 2015. ISBN 978-3-0343-1584-5

Vol. 196 Begoña Soneira
A Lexical Description of English for Architecture. A Corpus-based Approach.
267 pages. 2015. ISBN 978-3-0343-1602-6

Vol. 197 M Luisa Roca-Varela
False Friends in Learner Corpora. A corpus-based study of English false friends in the written and spoken production of Spanish learners.
348 pages. 2015. ISBN 978-3-0343-1620-0

Vol. 198 Rahma Al-Mahrooqi & Christopher Denman
Bridging the Gap between Education and Employment. English Language Instruction in EFL Contexts.
416 pages. 2015. ISBN 978-3-0343-1681-1

Vol. 199 Rita Salvi & Janet Bowker (eds)
The Dissemination of Contemporary Knowledge in English. Genres, discourse strategies and professional practices.
171 pages. 2015. ISBN 978-3-0343-1679-8

Vol. 200 Maurizio Gotti & Davide S. Giannoni (eds)
Corpus Analysis for Descriptive and Pedagogical Purposes. ESP Perspectives.
432 pages. 2014. ISBN 978-3-0343-1516-6

Vol. 201 Ida Ruffolo
The Perception of Nature in Travel Promotion Texts. A Corpus-based Discourse Analysis.
148 pages. 2015. ISBN 978-3-0343-1521-0

Vol. 202 Ives Trevian
English suffixes. Stress-assignment properties, productivity, selection and combinatorial processes.
471 pages. 2015. ISBN 978-3-0343-1576-0

Vol. 203 Maurizio Gotti, Stefania Maci & Michele Sala (eds)
Insights into Medical Communication.
422 pages. 2015. ISBN 978-3-0343-1694-1

Vol. 204 Carmen Argondizzo (ed.)
European Projects in University Language Centres. Creativity, Dynamics, Best Practice.
371 pages. 2015. ISBN 978-3-0343-1696-5

Vol. 205 Aura Luz Duffé Montalván (ed.)
Estudios sobre el léxico. Puntos y contrapuntos.
502 pages. 2016. ISBN 978-3-0343-2011-5

Vol. 206 Maria Pavesi, Maicol Formentelli & Elisa Ghia (eds)
The Languages of Dubbing. Mainstream Audiovisual Translation in Italy.
275 pages. 2014. ISBN 978-3-0343-1646-0

Vol. 207 Ruth Breeze & Inés Olza (eds)
Evaluation in media discourse. European perspectives.
268 pages. 2017. ISBN 978-3-0343-2014-6

Vol. 208 Vijay K. Bhatia & Maurizio Gotti (eds)
Arbitration Discourse in Asia.
331 pages. 2015. ISBN 978-3-0343-2032-0

Vol. 209 Sofía Bemposta-Rivas, Carla Bouzada-Jabois, Yolanda Fernández-Pena, Tamara Bouso, Yolanda J. Calvo-Benzies, Iván Tamaredo (eds)
New trends and methodologies in applied English language research III. Synchronic and diachronic studies on discourse, lexis and grammar processing.
280 pages. 2017. ISBN 978-3-0343-2039-9

Vol. 210 Francisco Alonso Almeida, Laura Cruz García & Víctor González Ruiz (eds)
Corpus-based studies on language varieties.
285 pages. 2016. ISBN 978-3-0343-2044-3

Vol. 211 Juan Pedro Rica Peromingo
Aspectos lingüísticos y técnicos de la traducción audiovisual (TAV).
177 pages. 2016. ISBN 978-3-0343-2055-9

Vol. 212 Maria Vender
Disentangling Dyslexia. VenderPhonological and Processing Deficit in Developmental Dyslexia.
338 pages. 2017. ISBN 978-3-0343-2064-1

Vol. 213 Zhilong Xie
Bilingual Advantages. Contributions of Different Bilingual Experiences to Cognitive Control Differences Among Young-adult Bilinguals.
221 pages. 2016. ISBN 978-3-0343-2081-8

Vol. 214 Larissa D'Angelo
Academic posters. A textual and visual metadiscourse analysis.
367 pages. 2016. ISBN 978-3-0343-2083-2

Vol. 215 Evelyne Berger
Prendre la parole en L2. Regard sur la compétence d'interaction en classe de langue.
246 pages. 2016. ISBN 978-3-0343-2084-9

Vol. 216 David Lasagabaster and Aintzane Doiz (eds)
CLIL experiences in secondary and tertiary education: In search of good practices.
262 pages. 2016. ISBN 978-3-0343-2104-4

Vol. 217 Elena Kkese
Identifying Plosives in L2 English: The Case of L1 Cypriot Greek Speakers.
317 pages. 2016. ISBN 978-3-0343-2060-3

Vol. 218 Sandra Campagna, Elana Ochse, Virginia Pulcini & Martin Solly (eds)
Languaging in and across Communities: New Voices, New Identities. Studies in Honour of Giuseppina Cortese.
507 pages. 2016. ISBN 978-3-0343-2073-3

Vol. 219 Adriana Orlandi & Laura Giacomini (ed.)
Defining collocation for lexicographic purposes. From linguistic theory to lexicographic practice.
328 pages. 2016. ISBN 978-3-0343-2054-2

Vol. 220 Pietro Luigi Iaia
Analysing English as a Lingua Franca in Video Games. Linguistic Features, Experiential and Functional Dimensions of Online and Scripted Interactions.
139 pages. 2016. ISBN 978-3-0343-2138-9

Vol. 221 Dimitrinka G. Níkleva (ed.)
La formación de los docentes de español para inmigrantes en distintos contextos educativos.
390 pages. 2017. ISBN 978-3-0343-2135-8

Vol. 222 Katherine Ackerley, Marta Guarda & Francesca Helm (eds)
Sharing Perspectives on English-Medium Instruction.
308 pages. 2017. ISBN 978-3-0343-2537-0

Vol. 223 Juana I. Marín-Arrese, Julia Lavid-López, Marta Carretero, Elena Domínguez Romero, Ma Victoria Martín de la Rosa & María Pérez Blanco (eds)
Evidentiality and Modality in European Languages. Discourse-pragmatic perspectives.
427 pages. 2017. ISBN 978-3-0343-2437-3

Vol. 224 Gilles Col
Construction du sens : un modèle instructionnel pour la sémantique.
292 pages. 2017. ISBN 978-3-0343-2572-1

Vol. 225 Ana Chiquito & Gabriel Quiroz (eds)
Pobreza, Lenguaje y Medios en América Latina.
362 pages. 2017. ISBN 978-3-0343-2142-6

Vol. 226 Xu Zhang
English Quasi-Numeral Classifiers. A Corpus-Based Cognitive-Typological Study.
360 pages. 2017. ISBN 978-3-0343-2818-0

Vol. 227 María Ángeles Orts, Ruth Breeze & Maurizio Gotti (eds)
Power, Persuasion and Manipulation in Specialised Genres. Providing Keys to the Rhetoric of Professional Communities.
368 pages. 2017. ISBN 978-3-0343-3010-7

Vol. 228 Maurizio Gotti, Stefania Maci & Michele Sala (eds)
Ways of Seeing, Ways of Being: Representing the Voices of Tourism.
453 pages. 2017. ISBN 978-3-0343-3031-2

Vol. 229 Dino Selvaggi
Plurilingual Code-Switching between Standard and Local Varieties.
A Socio-Psycholinguistic Approach
371 pages. 2018. ISBN 978-3-0343-2663-6

Vol. 230 Anca-Cristina Sterie
Interprofessional interactions at the hospital. Nurses' requests and reports of problems in calls with physicians.
371 pages. 2017. ISBN 978-3-0343-2734-3

Vol. 231 Xiaodong Zhang
Understanding Chinese EFL Teachers' Beliefs and Practices in the Textbook-Based Classroom.
189 pages. 2017. ISBN 978-3-0343-3053-4

Vol. 232 Manuela Caterina Moroni & Federica Ricci Garotti (Hrsg.)
Brücken schlagen zwischen Sprachwissenschaft und DaF-Didaktik.
345 pages. 2017. ISBN 978-3-0343-2667-4

Vol. 233 Dimitrinka Georgieva Níkleva
Necesidades y tendencias en la formación del profesorado de español como lengua extranjera
401 pages. 2017. ISBN 978-3-0343-2946-0

Vol. 234 Juan Santana-Lario & Salvador Valera (Hrsg.)
Competing patterns in English affixation.
272 pages. 2017. ISBN 978-3-0343-2701-5

Vol. 235 Francisco Salgado-Robles
Desarrollo de la competencia sociolingüística por aprendices de español en un contexto de inmersión en el extranjero
241 pages. 2018. ISBN 978-3-0343-2323-9

Vol. 236 Maria Chiara Janner
Sguardi linguistici sulla marca. Analisi morfosintattica dei nomi commerciali in italiano
345 pages. 2017. ISBN 978-3-0343-2667-4

Vol. 237 Bárbara Herrero Muñoz-Cobo & Otman El Azami Zalachi
La primavera del árabe marroquí.
192 pages. 2017. ISBN 978-3-0343-3104-3

Vol. 238 Consuelo Pascual Escagedo
El papel del oyente en la construcción de la conversación espontánea de estudiantes italianos en su interlengua y en su lengua materna
295 pages. 2017. ISBN 978-3-0343-3186-9

Vol. 239 Stefania M. Maci
The MS Digby 133 Mary Magdalene. Beyond scribal practices: language, discourse, values and attitudes.
336 pages. 2017. ISBN 978-3-0343-3256-9

Vol. 240 Eliecer Crespo-Fernández
Taboo in Discourse. Studies on Attenuation and Offence in Communication.
326 pages. 2018. ISBN 978-3-0343-3018-3

Vol. 241 Jana Altmanova, Maria Centrella, Katherine E. Russo (eds)
Terminology & Discourse / Terminologie et discours.
424 pages. 2018. ISBN 978-3-0343-2417-5

Vol. 242 Xavier Blanco et Inès Sfar (dir.)
Lexicologie(s) : approches croisées en sémantique lexicale.
442 pages. 2018. ISBN 978-3-0343-3056-5

Vol. 243 Yunfeng Ge
Resolution of Conflict of Interest in Chinese Civil Court Hearings. A Perspective of Discourse Information Theory.
302 pages. 2018. ISBN 978-3-0343-3313-9

Vol. 244 Carla Vergaro
Illocutionary Shell Nouns in English
322 pages. 2018. ISBN 978-3-0343-3069-5

Vol. 245 Paolo Frassi
L'adjectif en français et sa définition lexicographique.
270 pages. 2018. ISBN 978-3-0343-3394-8

Vol. 246 Suwilai Premsrirat and David Hirsh (eds)
Language Revitalization. Insights from Thailand
328 pages. 2018. ISBN 978-3-0343-3497-6

Vol. 247 Wei Wang
Researching Learning and Learners in Genre-based Academic Writing Instruction
282 pages. 2018. ISBN 978-3-0343-3297-2

Vol. 248 Isusi Alabarte, Alberto & Lahuerta Martínez, Ana Cristina (eds)
La comprensión lectora de lengua extranjera Estudio de los factores de familiaridad, interés, género y métodos de evaluación
336 pages. 2018. ISBN 978-3-0343-3493-8

Vol. 249 Mercedes Eurrutia Cavero
Approche didactique du langage techno-scientifique Terminologie et discours
374 pages. 2018. ISBN 978-3-0343-3512-6

Vol. 250 Aurora Ruiz Mezcua (ed.)
Approaches to Telephone Interpretation Research, Innovation, Teaching and Transference
268 pages. 2018. ISBN 978-3-0343-3330-6

Vol. 251 Morini Massimiliano A Day in the News
A Stylistic Analysis of Newsspeak
188 pages. 2018. ISBN 978-3-0343-3507-2

Vol. 252 Ignacio Guillén-Galve & Ignacio Vázquez-Orta (eds.)
English as a Lingua Franca and Intercultural Communication Implications and Applications in the Field of English Language Teaching
414 pages. 2018. ISBN 978-3-0343-2763-3

Vol. 253 Bianca Del Villano
Using the Devil with Courtesy
Shakespeare and the Language of (Im)Politeness
216 pages. 2018. ISBN 978-3-0343-2315-4

Vol. 254 David Hirsh (ed.)
Explorations in Second Language Vocabulary Research
252 pages. 2018. ISBN 978-3-0343-2940-8

Vol. 255 Tania Baumann (ed.)
Reiseführer - Sprach- und Kulturmittlung im Tourismus / Le guide turistiche - mediazione linguistica e culturale in ambito turistico
270 pages. 2018. ISBN 978-3-0343-3402-0

Vol. 256 Ariadna Sánchez-Hernández & Ana Herraiz-Martínez (eds)
Learning second language pragmatics beyond traditional contexts
376 pages. 2018. ISBN 978-3-0343-3437-2

Vol. 257 Albert Bastardas-Boada, Emili Boix-Fuster, Rosa Maria Torrens (eds)
Family Multilingualism in Medium-Sized Linguistic Communities
336 pages. 2019. ISBN 978-3-0343-2536-3

Vol. 258 Yuyang Cai
Examining the Interaction among Components of English for Specific Purposes Ability in Reading. The Triple-Decker Model
296 pages. 2020. 978-3-0343-2913-2

Vol. 259 Catia Nannoni
Participe présent et gérondif dans la presse française contemporaine
176 pages. 2019. ISBN 978-3-0343-3631-4

Vol. 260 Nieves Rodríguez Pérez & Bárbara Heinsch (eds.)
Contextos multilingües. Mediadores interculturales, formación del profesorado de lenguas extranjeras
289 pages. 2019. ISBN 978-3-0343-3768-7

Vol. 261 Giuliana Elena Garzone, Mara Logaldo, Francesca Santulli (eds.)
Investigating Conflict Discourses in the Periodical Press
244 pages. 2020. ISBN 978-3-0343-3668-0

Vol. 262 Laura Nadal
Lingüística experimental y contraargumentación
233 pages. 2019. ISBN 978-3-0343-3791-5

Vol. 263 Claudia Claridge & Merja Kytö (eds.)
Punctuation in Context – Past and Present Perspectives
288 pages. 2019. ISBN 978-3-0343-3790-8

Vol. 264 Maurizio Gotti, Stefania Maci, Michele Sala (eds.)
Scholarly Pathways
530 pages. 2020. ISBN 978-3-0343-3860-8

Vol. 265 Ruth Breeze, Ana M. Fernández Vallejo (eds.)
Politics and populism across modes and media
350 pages. 2020. ISBN 978-3-0343-3707-6

Vol. 266 Jean Marguerite Jimenez
Understanding the Effects of Immediate Electronic Corrective Feedback on Second Language Development
252 pages. 2020. ISBN 978-3-0343-3815-8

Vol. 267 Sergio Rodríguez-Tapia, Adela González-Fernández (eds)
Lenguas y turismo: estudios en torno al discurso, la didáctica y la divulgación
380 pages. 2020. ISBN 978-3-0343-3881-3

Vol. 268 Ana Bocanegra-Valle (ed.)
Applied Linguistics and Knowledge Transfer. Employability, Internationalisation and Social Challenges
344 pages. 2020. ISBN 978-3-0343-3714-4

Vol. 269 Beatrice Garzelli
La traducción audiovisual español-italiano.Películas y cortos entre humor y habla soez
202 pages. 2020. ISBN 978-3-0343-4013-7

Vol. 270 Iván Tamaredo
Complexity, Efficiency, and Language Contact. Pronoun Omission in World Englishes
292 pages. 2020. ISBN 978-3-0343-3902-5

Vol. 271 Silvia Domenica Zollo,
Origine et histoire du vocabulaire des arts de la table. Analyse lexicale et exploitation de corpus textuels
239 pages. 2020. ISBN 978-3-0343-3890-5

Vol. 272 Paola Paissa, Michelangelo Conoscenti, Ruggero Druetta, Martin Solly (eds.)
Metaphor and Conflict / Métaphore et conflit
385 pages. 2021. 978-3-0343-4068-7

Vol. 273 María Martínez-Atienza de Dios,
Entre el léxico y la sintaxis: las fases de los eventos
178 pages. 2021. 978-3-0343-4173-8

Vol. 274 Noelia Castro-Chao,
Argument Structure in Flux. The Development of Impersonal Constructions in Middle and Early Modern English, with Special Reference to Verbs of Desire.
300 pages. 2021. 978-3-0343-4189-9

Vol. 275 Gabriella Carobbio, Cécile Desoutter, Aurora Fragonara (eds.)
Macht, Ratio und Emotion: Diskurse im digitalen Zeitalter / Pouvoir, raison et émotion: les discours à l'ère du numérique
246 pages. 2020. 978-3-0343-4184-4

Vol. 276 Miguel Fuster-Márquez, José Santaemilia, Carmen Gregori-Signes, Paula Rodríguez-Abru-ñeiras (eds.)
Exploring discourse and ideology through corpora
293 pages. 2021. 978-3-0343-3969-8

Vol. 277 Tamara Bouso
Changes in Argument Structure The Transitivizing Reaction Object Construction
392 pages. 2021. 978-3-0343-4095-3

Vol. 278 Maria Luisa Maggioni, Amanda Murphy (eds.)
Back to the Future. English from Past to Present
250 pages. 2021. 978-3-0343-4273-5

Vol. 279 Luisa Chierichetti
Diálogos de serie. Una aproximación a la construcción discursiva de personajes basada en corpus
246 pages. 2021. 978-3-0343-4274-2

Vol. 280 Cristina Lastres-López
From subordination to insubordination. A functional-pragmatic approach to if/si-cons-tructions in English, French and Spanish spoken discourse
258 pages. 2021. 978-3-0343-4220-9

Vol. 281 Eleonora Federici, Stefania Maci (eds.)
Gender issues. Translating and mediating languages, cultures and societies
500 pages. 2021. 978-3-0343-4022-9

Vol. 282 José Mateo, Francisco Yus (eds.)
Metaphor in Economics and specialised Discourse
354 pages. 2021. 978-3-0343-4048-9

Vol. 283 Nicholas Brownlees (ed.)
The Role of Context in the Production and Reception of Historical News Discourse
376 pages. 2021. 978-3-0343-4181-3

Vol. 284 Catalina Fuentes Rodriguez, María Ester Brenes Peña, Víctor Pérez Béjar (eds.)
Sintaxis discursiva: construcciones y operadores en español
396 pages. 2021. 978-3-0343-4306-0

Vol. 285 Dominic Stewart
Frequency in the dictionary. A corpus-assisted contrastive analysis of English and Italian
178 pages. 2021. 978-3-0343-4368-8

Vol. 286 Carla Bouzada-Jabois
Nonfinite supplements in the recent history of English
386 pages. 2021. 978-3-0343-4226-1

Vol. 287 Sofía Bemposta Rivas
Verb-governed infinitival complementation in the recent history of English
340 pages. 2021. 978-3-0343-4227-8

Vol. 288 Mirella Agorni
Translating Italy for the Nineteenth Century. Translators and an Imagined Nation in the Early Romantic Period 1816–1830s
182 pages. 2021. 978-3-0343-3612-3

Vol. 289 David Hirsh (ed.)
Research Perspectives in Language and Education
276 pages. 2021. 978-3-0343-4219-3

Vol. 290 Federica Vezzani
Terminologie numérique : conception, représentation et gestion
238 pages. 2022. 978-3-0343-4394-7

Vol. 291 Stefania M. Maci
Evidential verbs in the genre of medical posters. A corpus-based analysis
498 pages. 2022. 978-3-0343-4521-7

Vol. 292 Francisco J. Álvarez-Gil
Stance devices in tourism-related research articles: A corpus-based study
170 pages. 2022. 978-3-0343-4555-2

Vol. 293 Annalisa Baicchi / Stefania Biscetti (eds.)
The Language of Fashion. Linguistic, Cognitive, and Cultural Insights
192 pages. 2022. 978-3-0343-4428-9

Vol. 294 Ana Maria Piquer-Píriz
E-learning in EMI. Academic language for university students
228 pages. 2022. 978-3-0343-4589-7

Vol. 295 Geneviève Henrot Sostero (ed.)
Alle radici della fraseologia europea
638 pages. 2023. 978-3-0343-4645-0

Vol. 296 Klara Dankova
Les fibres textiles entre synchronie et diachronie: études terminologiques
288 pages. 2023. 978-3-0343-4587-3

Vol. 297 Marta Carretero, Juana I. Marín-Arrese, Elena Domínguez Romero, Mª Victoria Martín de la Rosa (eds.)
Evidentiality and Epistemic Modality. Conceptual and Descriptive issues
414 pages. 2023. 978-3-0343-3993-3

Vol. 298 Kim Grego, Alessandra Vicentini, Virpi Ylänne (eds.)
Age-Specific Issues. Language, Spaces, Technologies
280 pages. 2023. 978-3-0343-4411-1

Vol. 299 Giovanni Garofalo (ed.) Estudios de género asistidos por corpus.
Enfoques multidisciplinarios
290 pages. 2022. 978-3-0343-4548-4

Vol. 300 Giuseppe Palumbo, Katia Peruzzo, Gianluca Pontrandolfo (eds.)
What's Special About Specialised Translation? Essays in Honour of Federica Scarpa
298 pages. 2023. 978-3-0343-4411-1

Vol. 301 Raquel P. Romasanta
Probabilistic variability in clausal verb complementation in World Englishes.
374 pages. 2023. 978-3-0343-4703-7

Vol. 302 Giulia Adriana Pennisi
A linguistic Insight into Legislative Drafting. Tradition and Change in the UK Legislation
296 pages. 2023. 978-3-0343-4700-6

Vol. 303 Javier Fernández-Cruz, Antonio Moreno-Ortiz
Economic terms in the news during the Great Recession. A diachronic sentiment and collocational analysis
192 pages. 2023. 978-3-0343-4778-5

Vol. 304 Stefania Maci, Mark McGlashan (eds.)
(Critical) Discourse Studies and the (new?) normal. Analysing discourse in times of crisis.
400 pages. 2024. 978-3-0343-4767-9

Vol. 305 Ana Elvira, Ojanguren López
Predications in competition and the rise of serial verb constructions in English. The verbal and nominal complementation of Old English aspectual and manipulative verbs.
534 pages. 2024. 978-3-0343-4644-3

Vol. 306 Stefania Maci, Giovanni Garofalo (eds.)
Investigating Discourse and Text. Corpus-Assisted Analytical Perspectives.
372 pages. 2023. 978-3-0343-4753-2

Vol. 307 Víctor Pérez Béjar
Las construcciones suspendidas en español. Un paradigma en gramática del discurso
494 pages. 2024. 978-3-0343-4799-0

Vol. 308 Javier Calle Martín / Jeús Romero Barranco (eds.):
Corpora and Language Change in Late Modern English.
408 pages. 2024. 978-3-0343-4642-9

Vol. 309 Cristina Petras /Sonia Berbinski /Daciana Vlad / Raluca Balaţchi (eds.):
Marqueurs métalinguistiques : émergence, discours, variation /Metalinguistic Markers: Emergence, Discourse, Variation.
720 pages 2024. 978-3-0343-4908-6

Vol. 310 Micaela Rossi (éd.)
Néologie, terminologie et variation - Neología, terminología yvariación – Neologia, terminologia e variazione.
418 pages. 2024. 978-3-0343-4696-2

Vol. 311 Sergio Maruenda-Bataller / Laura Mercé / Elena Castellano-Ortolà (eds.):
Discourse, gender, and violence: Insights from news and social media texts.
268 pages. 2024. 978-3-0343-4701-3

Vol. 312 Dario Del Fante
Migrating across times and cultures: Metaphorical images of migration in the U.S. and Italian newspaper discourse between the 20th and 21st centuries.
338 pages. 2024. 978-3-0343-4659-7

Vol. 313 Francisco Jesús Alonso Almeida / Begoña Bellés Fortuño (eds.)
Corpus-based Studies in Specialized Discourses.
294 pages. 2025. 978-3-0343-4261-2

Vol. 314 Elaine Millar
Multi-word verbs in English Language Teaching. Insights from research and practice
252 pages. 2025. 978-3-0343-5441-7

Vol. 315 Irene Guzmán-Alcón / Richard Nightingale (eds.)
New Directions in Instructional Pragmatics Research.
424 pages. 2025. 978-3-0343-5099-0

Vol. 316 Rosa Rabadán / Noelia Ramón (eds.)
Cross-linguistic Mediated Communication: Hybrid Text Production English-Spanish.
280 pages. 2025. 978-3-0343-5100-3

www.ingramcontent.com/pod-product-compliance
Ingram Content Group UK Ltd.
Pitfield, Milton Keynes, MK11 3LW, UK
UKHW020839290926
15470UKWH00004B/1448

9 783034 351003